Postmodernism and
social research

Understanding Social Research

Series Editor: Alan Bryman

Published titles

Postmodernism and social research

MATS ALVESSON

Open University Press
Buckingham · Philadelphia

Open University Press
Celtic Court
22 Ballmoor
Buckingham
MK18 1XW

email: enquiries@openup.co.uk
world wide web: www.openup.co.uk

and
325 Chestnut Street
Philadelphia, PA 19106, USA

First published 2002

A catalogue record of this book is available from the British Library

ISBN 0 335 20632 8 (hb)   0 335 20631 X (pb)

Library of Congress Cataloging-in-Publication Data
Alvesson, Mats, 1956–
    Postmodernism and social research/Mats Alvesson.
        p.   cm. – (Understanding social research)
    Includes bibliographical references and index.
    ISBN 0-335-20632-8 – ISBN 0-335-20631-X (pbk.)
    1. Postmodernism–Social aspects.   2. Social sciences–Research.
    I. Title.   II. Series.

HM449.A48 2002
300'.7'2–dc21   2001059109

Typeset by Type Study, Scarborough
Printed in Great Britain by Biddles Limited, Guildford and Kings Lynn

Contents

Series editor's foreword

This Understanding Social Research series is designed to help students to understand how social research is carried out and to appreciate a variety of issues in social research methodology. It is designed to address the needs of students taking degree programmes in areas such as sociology, social policy, psychology, communication studies, cultural studies, human geography, political science, criminology and organization studies and who are required to take modules in social research methods. It is also designed to meet the needs of students who need to carry out a research project as part of their degree requirements. Postgraduate research students and novice researchers will find the books equally helpful.

The series is concerned to help readers to 'understand' social research methods and issues. This means developing an appreciation of the pleasures and frustrations of social research, an understanding of how to implement certain techniques, and an awareness of key areas of debate. The relative emphasis on these different features varies from book to book, but in each one the aim is to see the method or issue from the position of a practising researcher and not simply to present a manual of 'how to' steps. In the process, the series contains coverage of the major methods of social research and addresses a variety of issues and debates. Each book in the series is written by a practising researcher who has experience of the technique or debates that he or she is addressing. Authors are encouraged to draw on their own experiences and inside knowledge.

Few intellectual currents in the social sciences have had as much impact on practitioners as postmodernism. It is viewed by some as a revolutionary position with respect to our understanding of the late modern or postmodern world and by others as a threat to the foundations of the epistemology and methodology of the social sciences. The selfconsciously critical and sceptical and sceptical stance of postmodernists on both the knowledge claims of social scientists and the possibility of providing definitive statements about the nature of social reality are well known and would seem to provide an environment that is not conducive to the possibilities of doing social research, and hence inconsistent with the goals of a series such as this.

Mats Alvesson's book is in this context yet another important contribution to the Understanding Social Research series. He writes as someone who finds many of the insights of postmodernism illuminating but who is unwilling to follow through on the negative stance on knowledge claims that is a feature of much postmodernist writing. Instead, he finds much within qualitative research that is consistent with a postmodernist sensitivity. By and large, the main way in which the postmodern approach to qualitative research has been revealed is through its critical stance on the 'findings' that ethnographers and others generate. Instead of viewing such reports as providing knowledge or understanding, postmodernists have tended to view them as written accounts whose claims and strategies need to be interrogated. Mats Alvesson examines this strand of thinking in the postmodern approach to qualitative research but goes considerably further too.

In particular, he examines the implications of postmodernism for qualitative research practice. This is an area in which most writers working within a postmodernist tradition have been fearful of treading. Thus, the humble interview comes in for scrutiny as a method of data collection that can be illuminated by and modified in the light of a postmodern understanding. His approach essentially is one of taking a selective stance in which certain key insights from postmodernism are employed within a qualitative research framework. Also, he focuses upon core themes that have concerned postmodernists, such as the notion of identity, to show how they too can be informed by the postmodernism-inspired qualitative research strategy he outlines in this book.

This is a very important contribution to the burgeoning literature in the areas of both postmodernism and qualitative research but it is also a unique book in its own right in daring to consider the implications of a position that many writers have depicted as inimical to research practice for the very activity of conducting social research.

Alan Bryman

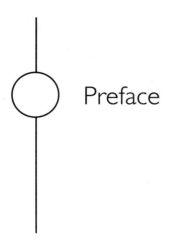

Preface

To give an introduction to postmodernism and social research is not an easy task. What is typically praised in textbook evaluations – clarity, simplicity, transparence, logic – is not what postmodernist writers celebrate.

Personally I have highly mixed feelings about postmodernism. I am not very fond of the label. I do think, however, that much of what is being said under this banner offers powerful challenges and that it may play a conscious-raising and creative role in social research.

I have on some occasions regretted that I agreed to produce this text, as it is difficult to grasp postmodernist ideas and do something with them in the sphere of social research. I am just hoping that this text accomplishes what I have intended it to do: to encourage ways of doing social research incorporating carefully selected inspirations from what is broadly defined as postmodernism. And to do so without either falling into excesses or expressing contradictory and confusing positions when navigating between the philosophical stuff and the messy empirical material offered by – or perhaps ascribed to – the settings to be investigated.

This book is in a sense part of a large research programme of mine that I have been working on for the past ten years, the writing and rewriting of qualitative method with the ambition of breaking down the division between theory and method and making issues of method less procedural and technical and more intellectual and theoretical. I think that creative powers and the sharpness of interpretations in social inquiry can be facilitated through such a project. So far, I have, with co-authors, written texts on reflexive methodology (Alvesson and Sköldberg 2000), critical research (Alvesson and Deetz 2000), discourse analysis (Alvesson and Kärreman 2000), reflexive interviewing (Alvesson 2001) and multiple interpretations (Alvesson 1996). In various empirical research projects these methodological ideas are practised and illustrated.

The book chapters draw upon a number of earlier writings. These have been thoroughly revised in this book. Chapter 2 is to some extent based on 'The meaning and meaninglessness of pomo', *Organization Studies*, vol. 15, no. 6 (1995); Chapter 3 borrows some material from 'Postmodernist and critical theory approaches to organization studies' (with S. Deetz), in S. Clegg, C. Hardy and W. Nord (eds) *Handbook of Organization Studies*, Sage (1996); Chapter 4 is a revised version of 'Taking the linguistic turn' (with D. Kärreman), *Journal of Applied Behavioural Science*, vol. 36, no. 2 (2000); Chapter 5 to a minor degree utilizes text that appeared in M. Alvesson and Y. D. Billing, *Understanding Gender and Organization*, Sage (1997); Chapter 6 to some extent uses material from 'Beyond neo-positivism and romanticism' (working paper). The first section of Chapter 8 is a summary of 'The good visions, the bad micro-management and the ugly ambiguity: contradictions of (non-)leadership in a knowledge-intensive company', paper presented at the Third Oxford Workshop on Knowledge-intensive Firms, Oxford University September 2001 (with Stefan Sveningsson). Most of the text of this book is original material.

I am very grateful to my co-authors in various projects – Yvonne Billing, Stan Deetz, Dan Kärreman and Stefan Sveningsson – for their permission to draw upon joint work in this volume and more generally for excellent collaboration relationships over the years.

I am also grateful to Alan Bryman, Robert Grafton-Small, Norman Jackson, Yvonne Billing and Stefan Sveningsson for valuable feedback on a draft of this book. Additional thanks are due to Alan Bryman and Open University Press for inviting me to write this book and being more than patient in waiting for the delivery.

Finally, I would like to thank my family, Yvonne, Miha and Mathilda, for support and patience.

Mats Alvesson
Lund, Sweden

① Introduction

'Postmodernism and social research' is a combination of words that one does not meet frequently. Actually, most people probably associate postmodernism with a lack of interest in, or even direct scepticism of, the very idea of 'social research', as conventionally understood. Social research is supposed to be about finding out how things are 'out there' in society through empirical inquiry. Postmodernism, as least as most people seem to write and talk about it, puts up a number of critical reactions. 'Finding out' is not what postmodernism is about; 'how things are' implies a truth-telling in which a preferred ordering of the world aims to discipline subjects and fix their reactions; society is not accepted as an object or empirical context but as a construction made up of professional communities (and other groups); empirical inquiry would for many postmodernists be seen as a rhetorical device giving legitimacy to the making of the mentioned truth claims, in which a particular vocabulary is arbitrarily presented as superior to others. The 'social' in social research also triggers scepticism and resistance among advocates of postmodernism, who strongly emphasize language and text as the only possible targets of concern: 'the social' doesn't really fit here.

As Rosenau (1992: 1) writes, 'The challenges post-modernism poses seem endless. It rejects epistemological assumptions, refutes methodological conventions, resists knowledge claims, obscures all versions of truths, and dismisses policy recommendations.' From the opposite angle, the average person interested in social research has little interest in or tolerance with an intellectual orientation that problematizes everything that social research tries to accomplish, without offering any obvious constructive proposals. The situation may therefore look grim for the poor author of these lines, and more than once during the hammering on the key word producing this text he (I) wondered how he could get caught in this tricky situation. 'Mission: Impossible' – with or without a question mark – could have been a subtitle to the book. Perhaps the reader is starting to worry about whether purchasing and reading this book is worth the money and time.

Leaving the reader with some unease and with the question of how to produce a text on 'Postmodernism and social research' without giving the impression that the two parts in the title are basically irrelevant or antagonistic to each other, let me address two overlapping backgrounds to contemporary ideas on how we can understand social phenomena.

The escalating critique of method and the idea of empirical work

Most versions of social science have been and are fairly strongly oriented towards empirical research. Exactly what is meant by 'empirical research' is unclear. (In a sense everything, when scrutinized, is unclear – but let us not worry about that at present.) Some time ago, 'empirical' research frequently meant that one assumed an independent reality out there, which can be perceived and measured through indications of this reality – data. Through the careful design of procedures, the collection and processing of data based on this design and analysis of these data, empirical research could say yes or no to various hypothesis about the chunk of reality targeted for study. Nowadays, it appears in many camps as old-fashioned, intolerant and theoretically and philosophically unsophisticated to favour this kind of idea in parts of social science. The label positivism – nowadays broadly defined – invites all sorts of pejorative comments. Recently, there have been more varied views on what constitutes empirical research, making the meaning of this activity quite vague. Reading texts of all kinds, for example, might be empirical research for some people.

Typically, however, 'empirical research' refers to taking a strong interest in gathering or constructing empirical material that says something of what goes on out there. Even the increasing number of people in social science sceptical about the possibility of the 'collection' and processing of data to say yes or no to various hypotheses and theories still often take an interest in empirical work. In many forms of qualitative study, e.g. in grounded theory, the assumption is that data, carefully processed, can guide the researcher to understand specific phenomena and develop theory (Glaser and Strauss 1967; Strauss and Corbin 1994).[1] In interpretive work it is assumed that we can access and study social reality from indications of the meanings and symbolic interactions that are viewed as the crucial elements in social communities.

This great faith in data and empirical inquiry as a cornerstone in knowledge development has been challenged by a multitude of intellectual streams during recent years. I will just briefly point at some of these. A powerful one is what may be referred to as 'non-objective' *interpretivist* perspectives. These put emphasis on how pre-understanding, paradigm and metaphor prestructure our basic conceptualizations of what we want to study. Our approach to, perceptions of and interpretations of what we experience are filtered by a web of assumptions, expectations and vocabularies that guide the entire project and are crucial to the results we arrive at (e.g. Brown 1977).

Somewhat more far-reaching critiques have been raised by feminists pointing to how male domination and masculine standards influence dominant epistemology and methodology in social science (Jaggar 1989). Male domination has produced a masculine social science built around ideals such as objectivity, neutrality, distance, control, rationality and abstraction. Alternative ideals, such as commitment, empathy, closeness, cooperation, intuition and specificity, have been marginalized. Scientific rationality is thus expressing male domination, rather than superior reason. If one looks at the psychology of researchers and conflicts between different groups, the idea of the cool scholar, rationally oriented towards objective truth, appears peculiar (Popper 1976; Bärmark 1984). A related point of view has been expressed by critical theorists who emphasize the political and interest- and value-laden nature of social enquiry (Kincheloe and McLaren 1994; Alvesson and Deetz 2000). It is argued that knowledge development is grounded in human interests (Habermas 1972). In social science, it is impossible to say anything of social significance without making some implications for the formation of society – social science is notoriously political. The fact that human interests and cultural, gendered and political ideals put their imprints on methodological ideals, as well as on research practices and results, makes it very difficult to see science as a pure activity, neutral and objective in relationship to the reproduction or challenging of social ideologies, institutions and interests.

Even more profound are the views from discursivists and constructivists denying science any privileged access to the objective truth about the social world outside language and language use (Potter and Wetherell 1987; Steier 1991). Language constructs rather than mirrors phenomena, making representation and thus empirical work a basically problematic enterprise, it is argued (Gergen and Gergen 1991). What (possibly) exists 'out there' (e.g. behaviours) or 'in there' (e.g. feelings or motives) is complex and ambiguous, and can never simply be captured, but given the perspective, the vocabulary and the chosen interpretation, 'reality' emerges in a particular way. Any claim of a truth thus says as much or more about the researcher's convictions and language use as about the object of study. Foucault (1980), probably the most influential social theorist (broadly defined) at present, claims that social scientific knowledge is closely associated with power (the regulation of social reality through arrangements and ordering devices), and less explores or distorts truth than creates it. It is increasingly common to claim 'that there is no clear window into the inner life of an individual. Any gaze is always filtered through the lenses of language, gender, social class, race, and ethnicity. There are no objective observations, only observations socially situated in the worlds of the observer and the observed' (Denzin and Lincoln 1994: 12).

The critique of positivism and neopositivism is massive, which does not prevent the majority of researchers from doing normal science more or less as if nothing had happened. Questionnaire researchers still assume that the Xs put in small squares by respondents make it possible to determine what goes on in the social world. Qualitative researchers still present interview statements as if they were pathways to the interiors of those being inter-viewed or mirrors of social practice, although it is broadly recognized – also among positivists – that data need to be interpreted to say anything. One problem with the critique is that it is rather categorical and provocative, is perceived as destructive and therefore is neglected. Another problem is that much of the critique addresses philosophical and epistemological issues, while the craft of doing research – for example, fieldwork – has received much less attention. These are largely viewed – at least in most textbooks and in research reports – as technical matters, separated from theoretical and philosophical ideas about knowledge production, although some change is on its way. Method – the action-related principles and ideas on how to produce and make sense of empirical material – still largely remains comparatively unaffected by all the work that has tremendous relevance for our understanding of methodological practices. The wealth of insights about problems of developing knowledge and the limitations to social science as a rational project need to be connected to research practices. Many researchers feel that all this philosophical stuff is of limited relevance (e.g. Melia 1997). I think the challenge is to try to incorporate parts of it in research practice. This rather heterogenous but rapidly expanding critique of social research and its uncertain relevance for specific methods for doing fieldwork, interpreting and writing poses a context for this book.

The limits to rationality in social research

I have read somewhere about a professor of anthropology who was once approached by a student asking what paradigm he should use and got the reply 'go out there and find out what the natives are up to'. This may sound like straightforward talk and many qualitative researchers seem to think that with a blank mind, some personal qualities (empathy, curiosity, openness), a robust methodology and a notepad, good research can be conducted. Rather than repeating the theoretical and philosophical critique briefly reviewed above, let me give some hints about the practical problems of finding out something.

Imagine a study of, say, the views of immigrants from a particular country, living in a specific municipality, on the social authorities. What are the perceptions and attitudes of these immigrants in terms of services offered, experiences of interactions with representatives of the authorities etc.? Let us assume that the researcher, on a PhD project or financed by a research grant, has two years at her disposal, spending half a year in the field and one and a half years analysing and writing up the results. Perhaps some weeks are used to gain familiarity with the municipality and the people estimated to be of greatest interest for the study. Some weeks of observation and, say, 30 interviews lasting one to two hours then form the bulk of the empirical material. Careful note-taking and detailed transcription are conducted. Some 200 pages of observation notes and 400 pages of interview transcripts are produced. If this is done competently one may assume that reliable knowledge of the subject matter is produced and that a resulting report or PhD thesis authoritatively and reliably tells us a lot about how the studied group view the social authorities in their municipality. But one may also cast doubts as to whether this is the case.

Figure 1.1 shows a simple way of illustrating the production process. Step 1 is the 'collection' of data, the researcher spending time in what she feels to be relevant parts of the local community, doing observations and interviewing people. Step 2 is production of the 600 pages of material intended to mirror what goes on. Step 3 is the structuring of this material into something manageable, getting rid of stuff that is repetitive, does not make sense, is assessed to be outside the interests of the researcher or is simply poor data, and sorting what remains into broad categories. Step 4 is the analysis and further reduction of this material into, say, 150 pages that the researcher can work with in more detail, using more nuanced categories and interpreting the meaning of what is, at first, difficult to understand. Step 5 is the arrangement of this into a particular logic and reasoning. Step 6 is the production of the final report, in which selected parts of this material appear in, say, three empirical chapters where 20 pages or so of the transcripts and notes are reproduced in revised, shortened and edited ways. These 20 pages contain data showing the validity of the investigation and making it credible that the researcher has been there and talks with authority about the subject matter.

In Figure 1.2 I have added some 'complexities' that affect, indeed govern, this process. These concern issues associated with the initial, 'data collection', phase: (a) the researcher's philosophical, theoretical and political commitments, many of which taken for granted (as is the case with paradigms,

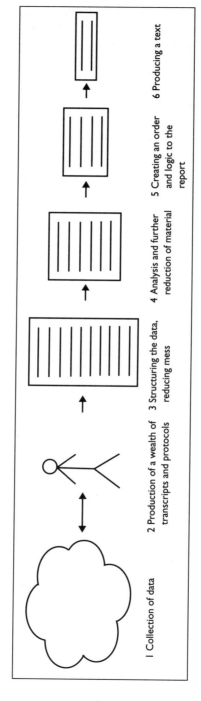

Figure 1.1 The research process: a simple version

1 Collection of data

2 Production of a wealth of transcripts and protocols

3 Structuring the data, reducing mess

4 Analysis and further reduction of material

5 Creating an order and logic to the report

6 Producing a text

by definition); (b) the expectations, interests and commitments of those being studied; (c) the complex interplay between the people being studied and the researcher; (d) various struggles to develop categories and order the material during the research process. The 'getting material together' phase includes (e) a lot of interpretative work about how to make sense of interview talk and observational notes to produce the 600 pages of text, including various moves in order to sort the material and get rid of things that do not make sense (do not fit the vocabulary and framework of the researcher). Codification involves stripping material of context and thus turning it into something different from its original form. Then follows step (f), in which all is targeted for careful analysis: here established academic wisdom, theoretical vocabularies, conventions for how to deal with the material – including the idea that there is one (or several) pattern(s) to be discovered during the process – are used. This is then followed by the writing up the results step (g). Here conventions for writing – format, language use, expectations of political correctness, the norm of being clear, rational, arriving at well grounded results presented as authoritatively and persuasively as possible – take over and the empirical material is moulded to fit.

As just one example of the highly limited rationality of the entire process, it can be mentioned that many researchers have mixed feelings and doubt about their notes from fieldwork. Even when the researchers have been ambitious, systematic and detailed in note-taking, they sometimes feel that the notes fail to capture what really went on. Some people rely more on their 'headnotes' (memory) than fieldnotes (written down impressions), as the former may appear to contain richer and less sterile material (Wolf 1992; Jackson 1995). But as memory and after-constructions are considerable sources of uncertainty and bias, one should emphasize that there is no simple way of handling the problem of how to translate fieldwork experiences into a documented form from which it is possible to work further. Even more profound sources of worry – given a rationalist belief in these kinds of projects – arise when it comes to even more 'subjective' elements of research than note-taking, such as interviewing, interpretation and writing.

All the elements involved affect the outcome. That what possibly went on 'out there' – in terms of feelings, views and experiences of those being studied – is mirrored, reflected or written about in an insightful way cannot be taken for granted. One could argue that the final result – the text – is an outcome of a multitude of processes, involving a set of complexities that cannot be handled in a rational and objective manner. The research object may have a powerful impact on the results, but it may play a limited role compared with all the other things that matters. One could argue that one, some or all of the other elements take over and make a stronger input to the final text than the reality it is supposed to inform the reader about. The interviewees, assuming that the research topic is relevant for social policies and politically sensitive, may, for example, produce certain kind of stories or

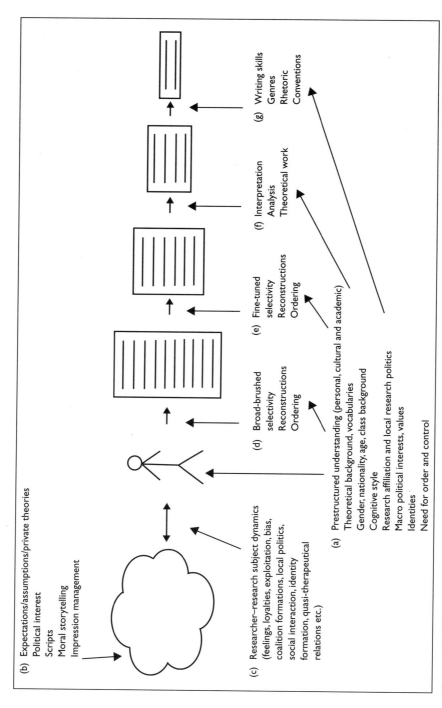

(b) Expectations/assumptions/private theories
Political interest
Scripts
Moral storytelling
Impression management

(c) Researcher–research subject dynamics
(feelings, loyalties, exploitation, bias,
coalition formations, local politics,
social interaction, identity
formation, quasi-therapeutical
relations etc.)

(a) Prestructured understanding (personal, cultural and academic)
Theoretical background, vocabularies
Gender, nationality, age, class background
Cognitive style
Research affiliation and local research politics
Macro political interests, values
Identities
Need for order and control

(d) Broad-brushed
selectivity
Reconstructions
Ordering

(e) Fine-tuned
selectivity
Reconstructions
Ordering

(f) Interpretation
Analysis
Theoretical work

(g) Writing skills
Genres
Rhetoric
Conventions

Figure 1.2   The research process: a complex version

act in certain ways in front of the gazing researcher. They may give data a particular flavour from the very beginning – interview talk may show politically guided storytelling, or behaviour in front of an observing researcher may be affected by impression management. Or the data processing activities – turning 600 pages of text into 20 that are presented to the reader – form the final results (text) more than what preceeded them in the form of interview talk or things going on before the note-taking and observing researcher. Or the conventions for writing – e.g. the norm that one should order the material and find a pattern or an order – might be a stronger determinant of the final text. Whether 'reality' is the key ingredient in the final text produced or whether any of stages (a) to (g) or some combination lead to 'reality' playing a very weak role in the final story claimed to deliver 'research results' is an open question.

One can imagine that another researcher, with another ethnic background, gender and political orientation, making some slightly different choices of people to study, presenting the project in a somewhat different way and using a different interview style, with other favoured categories and vocabularies, etc., would produce rather different research results. This could very well be the case even if the basic ingredients of the study – research topic, paradigm, methodology etc. – are similar.

One can also point at even more fundamental complexities associated with the categories employed and how they frequently steer the work and the results. One could, for example, argue that 'immigrants' – even if one focuses on people aged 20–30 who moved to the UK from Bangladesh between 1990 and 1995 and live in the south of Birmingham – are a problematic representation of 'reality'. Ascribing the quality 'immigrant' to a group of people seemingly creates order, identity and uniformity. The word 'immigrants' may conceal a heterogeneity of differences and language uses. Any study not taking seriously the ambiguity of the social reality labelled as 'immigrant' may get lost from the very start. (If you as a reader feel in a similar way, don't worry, as my point will be clearer later on.)

I can go on almost for ever with this hypothetical example or pick almost any published study – including my own – and throw a lot of doubt on it, undermining any pretence of authority. This would be in line with postmodernism: 'The core of postmodernism is the doubt that any method or theory, discourse or genre, tradition or novelty, has a universal and general claim as the right or the privileged form of authoritative knowledge' (Richardson 2000: 928).[2] My simple point here is that referring to and following methodological guidelines is totally insufficient for good research, and at least some of the complexities and uncertainties involved must be taken seriously and addressed. Some elements of self-doubt need to be built into the research process and the text. This can be done in many different ways – postmodernism can be viewed as an umbrella term for some of these.

Postmodernism: a preliminary 'description'

Postmodernism is a powerful part of this critique of conventional ideas of studying social phenomena. The scope of postmodernism is, as is elaborated below, a matter of diverse opinions. It overlaps some streams also labelled in other ways, e.g. some of the more radical constructionist versions. One can to some extent see postmodernism as a methodological critique, questioning the truth- and insight-seeking ambitions of conventional quantitative and qualitative social science. One can, however, very well produce a critique of methodology and the idea of 'doing research and finding out things' without necessarily mentioning postmodernism. And so I have done in the section above: postmodernism is only mentioned at the very end. Ideas and inspirations that may be labelled postmodernist pop up in certain versions of feminism, critical theory, constructionism etc. But there are very few, if any, specific points one needs to call upon postmodernism to make.

One can, however, also see what is expressed under the banner of postmodernism as a broad and influential intellectual stream that is not particularly concerned with methodological ideas for doing social research, but represents a 'paradigm' for novel thinking about the basic pillars of social science and how we think about, for example, language, rationality, truth, individuals, society and various cultural institutions. This clearly goes well beyond issues of method and empirical study, but does have a strong relevance for these too.

I give a broader overview of postmodernism in the next chapter and then cover some of the key themes of greatest relevance for the topic of this book (social research/methodology) in Chapter 3. In this introductory chapter, I make just a few initial points.

'Postmodernism' is a word that has attained considerable interest in the social sciences since the beginning of the 1980s, drawing upon French, and to some extent Anglo-Saxon, philosophers and social scientists. Very briefly, postmodernism can be described as 'an assault on unity' (Power 1990). For postmodernists social science is a humble and subjective enterprise, characterized by tentativeness, fragmentation and indeterminacy.

The 'fathers' of postmodernism in most cases did not use the label postmodernism; they did not see themselves as part of a specific stream and in some cases directly rejected the label. However, a number of commentators saw interesting similarities between some influential intellectuals (Baudrillard, Derrida, Foucault and Lyotard). These commentators felt motivated to

> draw attention to the presence in their respective works of a shared critical concern with a number of issues, notably: (i) the crisis of representation and associated instability of meaning; (ii) the absence of secure foundations for knowledge; (iii) the analytic centrality of

language, discourses, and texts; and (iv) the inappropriateness of the Enlightenment assumption of the rational autonomous subject and a contrasting concentration on the ways in which individuals are constituted as subjects.

(Smart 2000: 450)

These critical concerns speak strongly against the pillars of Western thinking, including mainstream versions of social theory and politics. Postmodernism is a reaction to what is labelled modernism (sometimes the term modernity is preferred – more about this in the next chapter). Modernism is a part of the Enlightenment. Through rational institutions and interventions based on objective knowledge, it is possible to get rid of rigidity, prejudice and superstitution, 'false' authorities, poverty and other forms of misery, and social life can be rationalized and a better world created. Positivism in its various forms is an expression of this attitude within society; social engineering is another, employed in organizations and politics. Certainty, control, measurement, analysis, causality, logic, order, authority and progress are key elements of modernism. Modernism is thus a general cultural orientation, penetrating thought in general and putting its imprints on social institutions such as science, politics, business and schooling. The mentioned virtues also define modernism in science and philosophy. Postmodernism is a critical reaction of the growing feelings of scepticism towards this kind of thinking.

The modern project has not so much been abandoned or forsaken by the tide of history, by the passage of events, as substantially devalued and discredited by the very development of modernity itself. The erosion of confidence, of trust and faith, in its core assumptions and objectives has been a direct consequence of modern practices and their uneven effects.

(Smart 2000: 457)

Some people expect and hope that 'the postmodern turn', leading to a stress on 'the social construction of social reality, fluid as opposite to fixed identities of the self, and the partiality of truth will simply overtake the modernist assumptions of an objective reality' (Lincoln and Guba 2000: 178). There are different opinions of the relationship between modernism and postmodernism in terms of sequentiality. At the moment, I am just mentioning the point that postmodernism is better seen as a kind of reaction to or comment on modernism, instead of a developmental phase coming after, and replacing, modernism. The terminology is a bit confusing on this point, as on so many others (sigh!).

Nevertheless, the ideas associated with postmodernism mean a strong challenge to the ambition of understanding the social world through some form of empirical enquiry. It can be seen as a large-scale and uncompromising attack on what social researchers – and other groups for that matter – normally do. The mobilization of radical questioning under the banner of postmodernism offers a strong impetus for us to rethink what we do and see if things can be done differently.

Some problems with the label 'postmodernism': initial complaints

A big problem with the term 'postmodernism', as well as its shadow 'modernism', is that it refers to a wide range of different issues. (More about these in the next chapter.) The persistent and expanding literature that includes references to these elusive concepts often clouds and distorts new ideas for ways of understanding contemporary phenomena and of doing social research. There is a risk that the words invite sweeping statements and thereby muddled thinking. The largest problem is not the terms postmodernism and modernism *per se*, but the kind of framing of issues and ways of reasoning that appears to follow from the use of this pair of concepts. This framing is, of course, not innocent, but represents a particular way of ordering how we conceive of intellectual possibilities. This ordering is not neutral to interests. It is easy to see the marketing logic guiding much talk about postmodernism. The term is fashionable. It is punchy and easy to identify and remember. People can communicate their approach by packaging it in postmodern language. It works a bit like a brand name – it is the image and surface qualities that matter. Most people writing about something labelled as postmodernism are seen as having important and sometimes distinct things to say. 'Postmodernism' facilitates the marketing of them.

The product life cycle of modernism is coming to its end, we are repeatedly told. In order to attract the academic market for new messages, a number of authors have promoted a new brand image: postmodernism. It provides knowledge products as well as scholars with an identity – although a shaky one. Postmodernism is short and punchy, and appears to be on the edge of the intellectual frontier. As Featherstone (1989: 156) notes, 'the art of naming itself is an important strategy on the part of groups engaged in struggles with other groups.' The political and commercial interests and advantages of associating oneself with and marketing one's knowledge products under the brand of postmodernism is considerable, apparently.

Apart from these somewhat shady motives for embracing the label, a more positive one relates to the capacity to excite (Burrell 1994). New labels excite, old ones do not. The possibility of gathering around a common slogan intensifies interest and puts some extra energy into current debates. This is not bad, even though the effect is only a temporary one.

One may avoid facing the bandwagon/fad critique by not using the term postmodernism frequently and by addressing a specific theme rather than covering the breadth of what postmodernism is associated with. Some time ago, a number of authors discussed themes such as the precariousness of the notion of psychological identity (Shotter and Gergen 1989), knowledge as metaphorically structured (Brown 1976), sociological analysis following a 'poetic' logic (Brown 1977), the role of rhetorics in science (Simons 1989) and the significance of reflexivity in research (Steier 1991), which many writers relate to postmodernism, without even mentioning the term. Some of these authors later associated themselves with postmodernism (e.g. Brown 1990; Gergen 1992). The use of the label 'postmodernism' does not add that much in terms of substance. Interesting and novel issues creating sensitivity to social changes or inspiring new forms of reflexivity in social science are sometimes better presented if they are not subordinated to the sweeping modernism – postmodernism contrast.

Having said this – and risking ruining my book project – I must add that there are some advantages of organizing debates a bit more broadly. It encourages more basic confrontations and mobilizes some power against traditional and often incredibly inert dominant traditions. I am thinking about not only questionnaire-based neopositivism trying to measure all sorts of stuff, but also neopositivist qualitative research obsessed with the claimed robustness of data – like grounded theorists insisting that 'the matching of theory against data must be rigorously carried out' (Strauss and Corbin 1994: 273). Postmodernism as a label, then, assembles some force by attracting broad sets of people, and thus becomes more effective in challenging the mainstream. The label postmodernism thus fulfils a valuable political function. It signals a space for a moderately coordinated assault and thus stimulates the debate. So the label is far from altogether problematic.

Where does this leave us? I am reluctant to accept some of the more common premises for writing about postmodernism and want to avoid strongly stressing the big modernism–postmodernism divide. This book avoids or at least reduces the problem with postmodernism as an all-embracing sweep, as it concentrates on a limited number of themes with specific relevance to doing social research. I deal with my ambivalence about the signifier postmodernism by sometimes shortening it to pomo. This word does not necessarily imply modernism as an Other – I do not use the expression 'mo'. The element of (self-) irony is well in line with what many authors in favour of this 'ism' preach, and sometimes also practise.

Cautiously relating postmodernism to social research

Writing about postmodernism and social research means an emphasis on a very heavy critique of neopositivist and interpretive methodologies (e.g.

Scheurich 1997) and/or ideas about new ways of experimenting with texts (e.g. Richardson 1995, 2000). Most authors seem to be more interested in ideas associated with pomo than in method or in using these ideas in field-work. The emphasis is more on doubt and uncertainty than on ideas for better ways of doing social research. My approach is different. I am mainly interested in the partial and pragmatic use of some ideas from pomo in order to produce more thoughtful, creative and interesting social research. It is here important not just to draw out general principles for social research, but to relate abstract ideas to specific research practices in ways that the researcher with empirical ambitions experiences will find helpful. It is, then, important to avoid encounters with postmodernism leading to paralysis, caution or guilt, as many say that something can be seen as 'creating the truth', 'inscribing order' or anything similar fishy.

All ideas on social research need to consider philosophy and practice. The appropriation of ideas associated with postmodernism has encouraged much more talk about philosophy than about fieldwork methods. Some-what ironically, the practices at our disposal as social researchers can be said to be: sending out questionnaires, working with (existing) statistics, placing and manipulating students in artificial and simplified settings (experiments), reading texts (document analysis), asking questions (interviewing) or hang-ing around (observation in 'natural' settings) etc. Pomo is more strongly antagonistic to the approaches which are perceived as denying or aiming to minimize 'undecidabilities', which is typical for most quantitative studies, although qualitative researchers sometimes share this – according to pomo advocates – deeply problematic habit. In this book I am mainly interested in qualitative research, especially that with an ambition to be close to specific social situations and to take issues of interpretation seriously. Pomo ideas seem to be more compatible – or at least less incompatible – with these than with quantitative approaches given the purpose of developing rather than rejecting ways of working with empirical material, with the ambition of saying something about social phenomena 'out there'. Pomo-inspired inter-viewing seems to be a more feasible idea than pomo questionnaires. I put my hope in more imaginative and bold researchers than myself to develop quan-titative pomo research.

This book thus mainly addresses qualitative studies in the social, includ-ing behavioural, sciences, although many of the themes have broad relevance, and may be inspirational for quantitative research and perhaps also fields outside the social sciences. Pomos want to get rid of disciplinary boundaries. Mainly, the idea is to investigate and contribute to the intersec-tion and cross-fertilization of interpretive and postmodernist work.

The ambition of this book is, then, to explore how themes associated with postmodernism may inspire another kind of overall thinking about social studies within a not too different use of practices such as observation of 'natural' situations or interviewing. More specifically, the intention is to:

- provide a brief and somewhat sceptical introduction to some themes of postmodernism with specific relevance for social research;
- stimulate reflection and rethinking about methodological themes such as producing empirical material (some would say collecting data), interpretation and writing.

The book is an effort to connect 'high-brow' methodology – theoretical and meta-theoretical issues – with 'low-brow' method – field practices – as well as with social theory. Such ambitions call for a somewhat relaxed attitude to rigour and holy cows. The concept of *reflexive pragmatism* is helpful here. It navigates beyond empirical ambitions and methodological rigour on the one hand and the kind of hypersceptical understandings of empirical inquiry encouraged by postmodernists on the other. This approach means working with alternative lines of interpretation and vocabularies and reinterpreting the favoured line(s) of understanding through the systematic invocation of alternative points of departure (Alvesson and Sköldberg 2000). Reflexivity here works with a meta-theoretical structure that guides an interplay between producing interpretations and challenging them, opening up the phenomena through exploring more than one set of meaning and acknowledging ambiguity in the phenomena and the line(s) of inquiry favoured. One may, for example, do social research in fairly conventional ways and then go through the entire project from a postmodernist standpoint and reinterpret part of the study. Or one may do interpretive and postmodernist readings of specific empirical materials and then assess which seem to be most interesting and 'fair'; or synthesize the readings (interpretations). Reflexivity means a bridging of the gap between epistemological concerns and method, trying to combine more philosophically informed aspects with what one is doing on the field. Pragmatism means a balancing of endless reflexivity and radical scepticism with a sense of direction and accomplishment of results. Pragmatism here means that one is not too concerned about the philosophical and methodological imperfections of doing social inquiry. All truth claims are problematic, yes. It is still worth trying to give our best shots on how to understand social issues, and empirical work can be valuable here, at least if one can avoid all the problems involved. Postmodernism may help us to steer away from a number of traps that conventional method books and common sense typically don't spot.

Overview of the book

The overall logic of this text is to start with a general view of postmodernism, then to zoom in and explore some key themes of specific relevance for social research and methodology, before discussing how ideas associated with postmodernism can be incorporated in the four overall moments or dimensions in social research, primarily qualitative studies: structuring the field, producing empirical material (some would say 'collecting data'), interpreting (or reading) the produced material and crafting a text (some may use the phrase 'writing up the results'). Finally, some overall lessons or guidelines for social research moderately incorporating pomo are formulated and some ideas for working with different degrees of pomo are launched.

Chapter 2 discusses the popularity of postmodernism in social studies and some problems associated with this. It is argued that the word conflates quite different social phenomena and lines of development, theoretical and philosophical positions. Framing issues in terms of modernism/postmodernism easily leads to insensitive conceptualizations of the varied positions within what is dumped together as 'modernism'. Ideas about contemporary society as 'postmodern' encourage an oversensitivity to novelty. It is argued that many of the themes raised under the banner of postmodernism are worth taking seriously, but there is no need to combine them in the same concept or discuss them tightly grouped.

Chapter 3 addresses five key themes in postmodernism as philosophy: the centrality of discourse; fragmented identities; the critique of the idea of representation (language as a mirror of reality); the loss of foundations and the decline of grand narratives; and the power–knowledge connection. The chapter also compares postmodernism and an interpretive approach in social research.

Chapter 4 concentrates on language and reviews some language-focused forms of social research. It is suggested that some of the major reservations about conventional social research can be counteracted with an approach that focuses strictly on language use in social settings. This is, however, easily achieved at the expense of relevance, and a 'softer' approach, labelled discursive pragmatism, is suggested as a moderate form of adoption of pomo critique.

Chapter 5 continues the exploration of language as a key element in pomo considerations about social research, but concentrates on how one can relate to key categories and their, according to postmodernism, problematic features. The motto here is 'unpacking', i.e. an effort to explore key categories critically by pointing at their tendencies to structure the world prematurily and rigidly and to lock the language user – including the researcher – through the power effects of dominant language. Related to unpacking is the defamiliarization of what is perhaps too well known. By making it strange one opens up new ways of relating to what is frozen through being familiar and taken for granted.

Chapter 6 moves further along the chain from broader philosophical issues to specific fieldwork practices, and addresses interviews. I choose this method as an example of technical research practice and explore how pomo thinking can make research projects more theoretically aware and reduce some of the weaknesses following from 'conventional' ideas about the good interview. Interviewing is used as the example because it is probably the most common qualitative method. It is also a key ingredient in most ethnographies. In the chapter I discuss implications for interview work, interpretation of interview accounts and what kind of research questions are meaningful to raise, without putting too heavy a burden on the interviewee.

In Chapter 7, I address 'post-fieldwork' themes, such as strategies for interpretations (or readings) of the textual material that are supposed to make it possible to say something about an object of inquiry. One important pomo theme here is multiple interpretations. Issues of writing – style, possible tactics for mobilizing active readings of the research texts, including resistance-oriented readings – also receive attention. The question of voice and the relationship between the researcher and the researched is also addressed.

In Chapter 8, an example of empirical research is carefully scrutinized, considering most of the postmodernist themes addressed in the previous chapters. The example, a study of 'leadership' in a professional company conducted by myself and a co-researcher, to some extent draws upon postmodernist thinking about the subject, the language and the ambiguity of social reality. Still, there is much in the empirical work and the research text that can be unpacked and problematized, through a variety of pomo thinking.

In the short final chapter, some of the key points of this text are further summarized, and some general lines for thinking and fieldworking between conventional qualitative approaches and self-constraining pomo ideas and worries are suggested. I address the question of how to evaluate research, given consideration of the pomo themes. The topic of reflexivity also gets some attention.

Notes

1 There are, however, some efforts to develop grounded theory, to move away from neopositivism and to incorporate some ideas of the constructed nature of social inquiry (Charmaz 2000).
2 In Chapter 8, I sceptically scrutinize one of my research texts.

2 Postmodernism: a sceptical overview

To provide an overview of postmodernism is not an easy task. Many of the issues covered are tricky. It is also very difficult to know what to include and what to neglect. Far from all of what is sometimes labelled as postmodernism is the exclusive property of this stream, but more or less overlaps what is frequently summarized under other labels. In this chapter I start by complaining about the problem of defining postmodernism and then address the major, not necessary very related, streams viewed as postmodernism: postmodernism as a period/the current age; postmodernism as a movement in architecture and art; postmodernism as a philosophy or intellectual style. Of greatest importance in the present book is postmodernism as a philosophy or intellectual style, but this theme receives only moderate attention in this chapter: it is focused in the remaining parts of this book. One section addresses the competing label of poststructuralism, another takes a look at one social science discipline – organization studies – and discusses claims made about contemporary social forms being postmodernist. A rather long section delivers a critique of some aspects of the postmodernism movement(s) and discourses.

Difficulties in defining pomo

To define postmodernism is hardly possible. Many of the pomo authors reject the possibility of clear meanings and definitions. As a consequence, talk about other authors' talk about pomo may not become clear. Bradbury (quoted by Featherstone 1988: 158) says that 'postmodernism has in some ways become a critic's term without ever quite becoming an artistic movement'. Within the social sciences, the same is true for commentators in relation to the major streams of social research. Here a number of people talk about the claim ascribed to social science that it is currently (or at least soon) postmodernistic, while a large majority of texts do not live up to this claim.

The phenomenon under scrutiny is that a number of academics like to use the word postmodernism, seem to use it in various ways – as many as possible – and appear to create certain messes in these operations. The various 'meanings' ascribed to pomo are coherent in a sense with many points raised under its flag, and one may even see the mess as a virtue. The more confusion and slippariness associated with the term, the better. It confirms that pomo is 'right':

> The contested use of the term remind us that words derive their meaning through a process of struggle between competing usages, and that it is ultimately futile to seek a definitive, universally agreed answer to the question of what 'postmodernism' is. Indeed, such efforts to standardise its meaning would seem to contradict what, arguably, is a distinguishing feature of the *movement/argument* of postmodernism; namely the understanding that the (modernist) project of eliminating ambivalence – typified by the establishment of seemingly well-defined rules and procedures to regulate behaviour – is not just self-defeating but fundamentally dis-abling.
>
> (Willmott 1992)

This point is well argued, but there are problems. If pomo does not have a standardized meaning, does it make sense to refer to pomo, to let the word refer to a particular style, a way of thinking, certain ideals etc? We cannot answer the question of what 'pomo' is, Willmott argues, but should one raise the question of whether pomo 'is'? If it does not have a standardized meaning (or even roughly agreed upon meaning), is 'it' then something? It 'is' of course a word, which people like to use, and perhaps an example of confusing vocabulary, but authors like Willmott also attribute it with a particular meaning, standardized or not.

As noted, pomo does not have *one* standardized meaning, but several, often quite diverse, 'relatively standardized' ones. Pomo is thus many different things, which do not necessarily have anything in common (various ideas about a philosophical style, a societal period, a view of knowledge, a post-bureaucratic organization etc.). There are two aspects buried here. One concerns standardization and stability versus the fluidity, incoherence and contradictions of meaning, i.e. a language issue; the other concerns standard in the sense of a social norm (convention), i.e. what we roughly have in mind when we utter the word pomo. It is one thing that the word pomo is ambiguous, it is another that it refers to a rather wide body of quite different ambiguous themes. (More about these below.) This double ambiguity is highly problematic. Pomo represents an effort to integrate a number of diverse, in themselves ambiguous, themes. That this point is valid for other streams and fashions does not weaken its significance in the case of pomo.

Irrespective of the particular usage of the terms, postmodernism is often understood as something that not just comes after the 'modern', but is based on a negation of the 'modern', a perceived abandonment, a break with or shift away from what characterizes the modern. Occasionally the post-modern is seen as a dimension within modernism (Calhoun 1992). Despite the confusions of the meaning of postmodernism it is common to distinguish between postmodernism as a periodizing concept and as a particular cultural, intellectual style or orientation. As a periodizing concept – normally referred to as *postmodernity* – it is used by different authors to point at different epochs. Postmodernism is also used as a label for certain orientations in the arts and in architecture. Let us begin with a brief section on the latter theme.

Pomo in the arts

Often people refer to some features associated with pomo in the arts, including theatre and literature, but also architecture. I will not go into this in depth as it falls outside the scope of this book, but a few sentences are in order. A considerable source of confusion is that the terms modernism and postmodernism in these spheres do not directly parallel the use of the same pair of concepts in philosophy and social science. Modernism in the arts, with its rejection of the idea of representation and the emphasis on challenge and the unfamilar (e.g. Picasso), is actually in some affinity with postmodern philosophy. Nevertheless, the pomo idea of 'dedifferentiation' between different spheres – such as high culture and low (mass) culture – and the break with elite ideas of a specific space and function of art make it possible to point at some overall features of postmodernism as an overall label which seem to work broadly, in a diversity of fields:

> the affacement of the boundary between art and everyday life; the collapse of the hierarchical distinction between high and mass/popular culture; a stylistic promiscuity favouring eclecticism and the mixing of codes; parody, pastiche, irony, playfulness and the celebration of the surface 'depthlessnes' of culture; the decline of the originality/genius of the artistic producer and the assumption that art can only be repetitious.
>
> (Featherstone 1988: 203)

Postmodernism began to be used in the 1970s as a term for a traditionally and locally inspired approach in architecture, in contrast to the ahistoric and super-rational functionalism. The break with rationalism and functionalism is shared with pomo in some other areas, but it is not possibly to copy standard definitions of postmodernism in any other field where the term is used, and apply them to make sense of pomo architecture.

My impression is that the use of postmodernism in all kinds of fields easily leads to exaggerations of similarities and broad trends. It can here be noted that George Marcus, one of most influential advocates of what is generally ascribed as the postmodernist turn in anthropology, does not use the pomo label as he sees no parallels between the revisions within anthropology and postmodern movements in the arts (Marcus 1992).

The pomo period: postmodernity

Debates about postmodernism as a period or epoch in societal development have created a large industry. Here, most authors talk about postmodernity instead of postmodernism, something for which we should be grateful. There are various opinions about the meaning of this epoch. Some say that postmodernity signals postindustrialism as well as postcapitalism, while others (e.g. Jameson 1983, 1984) suggest that postmodernity refers to cultural changes *within* capitalism (Jameson, however, uses the word post-modernism). The periodization idea typically indicates some notion of sequentiality – postmodernism (-ity) comes after modernism (-ty), but what this means is a matter of different opinions and debates. Whether this means replacement – postmodernity drives out modernity – or the emergence of a stream existing parallel with and in opposition to is thus subject to various opinions.

People talking about pomo as a period share the conviction that something radically new has occurred during recent decades. Jameson (1983: 124–5) writes about

> a general feeling that at some point following World War II a new kind of society began to emerge (variously described as postindustrial society, multinational capitalism, consumer society, media society and so forth). New types of consumption, planned obsolescence; an ever more rapid rhythm of fashion and styling changes; the penetration of advertising, television and the media generally to a hitherto unparalleled degree throughout society; the replacement of the old tension between city and country, center and province, by the suburb and by universal standardization; the growth of the great networks of superhighways and the arrival of automobile culture – these are some of the features which would seem to mark a radical break with that older prewar society.

There are all sorts of opinions about the scope of this change, which perhaps includes quite diverse trends, some of which have been on their way for a very long time, rather than a single or tightly coupled transformation best summarized under one term.

Postmodernity presupposes modernity, which is typically closely connected to the Enlightenment. The most common point of departure in describing modernity – and thus postmodernity – is to focus on the rationality seen as a guiding principle, as well as an attainable objective, for the modern project. Rationality is embodied especially in the certainty and precision of science and knowledge and the far-reaching control and manipulation of nature that this knowledge makes possible. Postmodernity often refers to the idea of a society characterized by widely dispersed cultural orientations that doubt the possibilities and blessings of this rationalizing project. 'Postmodern society' thus goes against the certainty, objectivity and progress orientation of modernity.

Many authors portray the entire society as completely different from an earlier, modernist one, while others emphasize more modest changes. Lash and Urry (1987) write about a 'postmodernist sensibility' and believe that 'the contemporary cultural substrate bears certain features that can best be understood under the headline of "postmodernism"' (p. 286). Contemporary culture operating 'through a combination of often figural, anti-auratic, electronic and spectacular symbols has had the effect of disintegrating older modes of individual and collective identity' (p. 312). Quite varied suggestions for what characterizes the pomo period exist, however. Some say, similarly to Lash and Urry, that information technology and mass media (particular television) have created a 'hyperreality' in the form of simulations that are more 'real' or significant than 'reality' itself – the latter term having dubious meaning (Baudrillard 1983a, b, 1984). Others claim that it is a matter of new opinions about (large-scale) scientific knowledge or political programmes (Lyotard 1984), that consumption is now more central than production (Jameson 1983), that political changes around 1990 in Eastern Europe are best seen as 'postmodern revolutions' (Madison 1991), that bureaucracies are replaced by 'postmodern organizations' (Clegg 1990) or that contemporary postmodern identities are fragmented and fluid (Shotter and Gergen 1994; Gubrium and Holstein 2001). Even though there are some connections between some of these versions – information technology, for example, may affect the view on knowledge and make simulations more significant – the suggestions for what is new are certainly rather different.

What is common in these claims is primarily the use of the word 'postmodernism' (or 'postmodernity'). If we remove that label, then the various themes are probably best discussed separately and not, as currently, in the same debates and texts. The reason for the widespread talk about a postmodern society or a radical change in that direction is that authors making highly diverse claims, many of them speculative and contestable, use the same label. The result is a misleading unity and coherence. The frequency of claims of radical change gives credibility to the thesis, but the claims do not necessarily support each other. The interest in promoting the pomo idea – by publishers, editors of journals and anthologies, and academic authors who want to market their approach – means that everyone can express his or her favourite version of pomo, thereby reinforcing the idea that 'pomo is here'. Of course, in producing this book I am not innocent in this respect either.

Bauman (1988) suggests that the virtue of the concept is in its potential to illuminate a novel experience of one, according to him, crucial category: the intellectuals. Such a modest view of the pomo period (or experience) is not held by other authors, even some of those who, in opposition to, for example, Jameson (1983, 1984), focus on more limited terrain. Daudi (1990) confronts 'modernity' as a vision of knowledge 'in which reason has a sovereign role', which was the developed in the Western world during the sixteenth and seventeenth centuries, with pomo, which is characterized as follows:

> New and challenging changes confront us, as a process of heterogeniz-ation also accelerates. The marks of this process can be seen in the bursting of the modes of life, in the plurality of philosophical thought, in religious exoticism and in galloping polyculturalism. The transition between modernity and postmodernity is taking place before our eyes with us as subjects producing it and objects experiencing it.
>
> (Daudi 1990: 286)

There are very different views on the scope of modernism, even if one restricts the area to ideas about modernism as a position with regard to knowledge (and excludes everything else that is ascribed to modernism or modernity). Daudi (1990) equates modernism with rationalism, empiricism and positivism, and says that it dominated knowledge until recently. Lyotard (1984: xxiii) includes any science that legitimizes itself with references to 'grand narratives', such as 'the dialectics of Spirit, the hermeneutics of mean-ing, the emancipation of the rational or working subject or the creation of wealth'. One is tempted to add that Lyotard's thesis in itself is broad-brushed and also legitimizes itself with a reference to a 'grand narrative' of a postmodernist age or condition.

Statements about the pomo period vary in terms of the extent to which they can be 'checked' – discussed in empirical terms – or not. Typically pomos seem to be uninterested in carefully supporting their claims. The pre-sented empirical illustrations are often weak. Jameson (1983) writes that specialization in academic work was common: for example, in philosophy with the great systems of Sartre or the phenomenologists, the work of Wittgenstein or analytical philosophy. Today we have a kind of writing that transgresses academic divisions. 'Is the work of Michel Foucault, for

example, to be called philosophy, history, social theory or political science?'
(Jameson 1983: 112). But the same could be said about the Frankfurt School
(Adorno, Horkheimer, Marcuse) 60–70 years ago or even earlier for Marx
or Weber. On a broader scale, my impression of the present state of science
and knowledge is that the overall majority of academics stick to their disciplines and subdisciplines – and that the division of academic labour is being
driven further, with very few exceptions. Blurring of genres and cross-
fertilization of disciplines happen, but in far from all fields, and the opposite
trend may be much stronger. A common complaint is that this development
has produced 'intellectual specialization to the point of fragmentation'
(Collins 1992: 187). One may even argue that contemporary social science
is, on the whole, more 'modern' than ever. There is not much pluralism or
support for relativistic ideas in, for example, academic psychology or economics, and the overwhelming majority of published journal articles in social
science proceed from a traditional epistemology. Even in the more pluralis-
tic disciplines of social science a large majority of work proceeds from a
functionalist paradigm and from a neopositivist epistemology.

More far-reaching claims of pomos, such as the degree of earlier homogeneity versus contemporary heterogeneity and fragmentation, are difficult
to explore. Unsystematic experiences and perceptions leading to such
impressions must be met by suspicion. It is not impossible that industrial-
ization, urbanization and the expansion of capitalism and the market during
the second half of the nineteenth century led to even more far-reaching social
and cultural changes, including certain forms of heterogenization and fragmentation, than people think they are witnessing at present. The slightest
sensitivity to the difficulties of language functioning in a referential way or
of 'totalizing statements' would discourage authors from such bold and
sweeping statements about the postmodern society. They are incompatible
with some of the most influential streams marketed under the brand of
pomo, although as style rather than as a period, which argue against 'totalizing frameworks' and the 'mirror' view of language (language as the
representation of reality).

A special case of the claims about drastic changes is the idea of hyperreality – simulacra – replacing the 'real world', so that simulations take
precedence in the contemporary social order (Baudrillard 1983b). This concept is not intended to point at a particular period and the reasoning is based
on a mix of philosophical and sociological ideas. But clearly the idea of
hyperreality calls for the expansion of mass media to make any sense whatsoever, and can thus be seen as an attempt to say something about contemporary society as distinct from earlier periods. The idea of hyperreality
means that any existing linguistic or representational systems are shown to
be self-referential. Such systems neither are anchored in a socially produced
as objective world nor respect the excess of an outside. They produce the
very same world that they appear to represent accurately. For example,

contemporary media and information systems have the capacity to construct images rapidly which replace, more than represent, an outside world (Boorstin 1960). Such systems can dominate the scene with an array of reproduced imaginary worlds. The referent disappears as anything more than another sign: thus signs only reference other signs; images are images of images. Such systems can become purely self-referential, or what Baudrillard calls *simulations*. In such a world, in Baudrillard's analysis, signs are disconnected from opening a relation to the world and the 'model' response to a 'model' world replaces responsive action in an actual changing one. Signs reach the structural limit of representation by referencing only themselves, with little relation to any exterior or interior. Baudrillard (1975: 127–8) expresses this relation as follows:

> The form-sign [present in a monopolistic code] describes an entirely different organization: the signified and the referent are now abolished to the sole profit of the play of signifiers, of a generalized formalization in which the code no longer refers back to any subjective or objective 'reality', but to its own logic . . . The sign no longer designates anything at all. It approaches its true structural limit which is to refer back only to other signs. All reality then becomes the place of semi-urgical manipulation, of a structural simulation.

The world as understood is not really a fiction in this situation since there is no 'real' outside which it portrays falsely or which can be used to correct it. It is properly imaginary; it has no opposite, no outside. Baudrillard used the example of the difference between feigning and simulating an illness to show the character of this postmodern representation: 'feigning or dissimulation leaves the reality principle intact; the different is always clear, it is only masked; whereas simulation threatens the difference between "true" and "false," between "real" and "imaginary". Since the simulator produces "true" symptoms, is he ill or not? He cannot be treated objectively either as ill, or not ill' (Baudrillard 1983b: 5). The only option for the researcher is to 'produce a text that reproduces these multiple versions of the real, showing how each impinges and shapes the phenomenon being studied' (Denzin 1997: 13). Inspiration from Baudrillard leads to a study of social 'unreality':

> The social world described by Baudrillard is indifferent, aleatory, indeterminate, and narcissistic; it is a world in which the real has given way to simulations, codes and hyperreality. It is a place where meaning, significance, the message, and the referent 'circulate so quickly that they are made to disappear' . . . And it is this situation, of attempting to 'live with what is left', of 'playing with the pieces', which has been described by Baudrillard as postmodern.
>
> (Smart 2000: 463)

The idea of hyperreality is clearly not easy to domesticate in a conventional empirical research programme, although one can to a degree study the hyperreal as 'real' phenomena – ads, media performances, brand names, PR activities etc. In many other respects proponents of conventional epistemologies – in which claims should be supported by data – can expect fairly clear empirical back-up for many claims about a postmodernity replacing modernity in society at large or in various sectors: politics, organizational forms etc. One may even call for careful studies of specific social and cultural sectors to be conducted before more general statements can be made. It is certainly possible that such studies would not come up with uniform patterns of development, but show quite diverse tendencies in terms of inertia versus change regarding, for example, positions among academics and broader cultural patterns, thus making it difficult to link various sectors together and permit all-embracing statements such as those preferred by advocates of the 'pomo age'. Of course, the results of such studies would be contingent upon those that do the job and what they are inclined to see or intuitively feel to be correct. I have doubts about relativism – giving privilege to the eye of the beholder – and believe that empirical results may kick back against frameworks and preferences, but when it comes to pomo, it is far too easy to perceive support for one's expectations. Given broad claims, one can find as many examples as one wants in order to support any thesis about radical change in a postmodern direction – or the continuing domination of modernity in science, politics and the management of public and private organizations. Still, empirical investigations may encourage more nuanced ideas about, for example, fragmentation, ambiguity and pluralism versus unity, coherence and order in contemporary social and personal life.

The work of Foucault is often invoked as support for various claims about pomo (e.g. by Jameson, cited above), and Foucault is often even labelled a postmodernist. That he rejected this label is hardly surprising. His suspicion of all the contemporary talk about far-reaching changes and the inclination to overreact to what one perceives as a new era should provide a warning for contemporary enthusiasts. In an interview, when asked about pomo he said:

> Here, I think, we are touching upon one of the forms – perhaps we should call them habits – one of the most harmful habits in contemporary thought, in modern thought even; at any rate, in post-Hegelian thought: the analysis of the present as being precisely, in history, a present of rupture, or of high point, or of completion or of a returning dawn, etc. . . . I think we should have the modesty to say to ourselves that . . . the time we live in is *not* the unique or fundamental or irruptive point in history where everything is completed and begun again.
>
> (Foucault 1983: 206)

Perhaps the best way to summarize the claims about a pomo age is to point to the paradox involved. A large number of quite diverse and weakly supported opinions about rapid and large-scale social change join forces and make the case for the death or expected departure – or at least widespread doubts about the basic ideals – of 'modernity'. The consensus about this tremendous change is not accompanied by any agreement about the nature of the change, making this consensus very shallow. It reinforces the suspicion that the idea of pomo society is more anchored in various commentators' preferences for labelling than any 'real' changes 'out there'. Such changes in how we use words without any direct connection to something going on 'out there' is actually fully in line with pomo as philosophy, but is at odds with the 'pomo as period' idea. This is, of course, not to deny that changes are taking place within what more appropriately can be called 'late modernity' (Giddens 1991). As Calhoun (1992: 276) remarks, 'the "postmodern" critique grasps something of contemporary life because it grasps something of a modernity that continues, not because it calls attention to something new.' The increasing doubt about the rationality of politics and other social institutions, the destabilization of certain cultural values, such as increased questioning of people's ability and right to control nature and other species, the increased significance of mass media and other 'hyperreality' promoting institutions and technologies etc., indicate important trends that call for attention and possibly new ways of understanding.

Pomo as a philosophy

Pomo as a philosophy or – less pretentiously – as an intellectual style rejects traditional ideals such as rationality, order and certainty. It is sceptical about categories and any idea of a stable meaning. Instead, ambivalence, variation, fragmentation, intuition and emotion are celebrated as guidelines for how we should understand the social world.

> Fragmentation takes the place of totality and completeness. Ambiguity reigns where once there was clarity. The old certainties vanish, leaving us with the tentative, the provisional, the temporary, the contingent. Even our cherished antinomies are denied to us, those hierarchical oppositions between thought and language, nature and culture, reason and emotion, theory and practice, white and black, men and women. In the place of clear-cut distinctions and earnest logic, there is widespread irony, parody, pastiche, playfulness.
>
> (Crotty 1998: 194)

Reason plays no important role in social life, it is assumed – except as an ideological belief. Individuals are caught within and constituted by 'discourses'. Sometimes pomos stress instincts and the drive for pleasure as central to how individuals function. Some psychoanalytic ideas are seen as delivering ammunition to the attack on 'the tyranny of reason', although psychoanalytic theory in its dominant versions is itself far from post-modernism. It is a systematic theoretical framework with aspirations to capture the true nature of human beings.

Many pomos, like some other authors, also *reject a representational view of language*. Language cannot mirror the reality 'out there', or people's mental states (Shotter and Gergen 1989; Gergen and Gergen 1991). Given the belief in the centrality of language and its active, constructing role, many advocates of pomo also question or even deny the idea of a 'reality out there' or 'mental states'. Language is figural, metaphorical, undecidable, full of contradictions and inconsistencies (Cooper and Burrell 1988; Brown 1990). Meaning is not universal and fixed, but precarious, fragmented and local. Instead of language being used to illuminate 'something', language in itself should be illuminated and 'deconstructed'. Rhetorical tricks should be exposed, not in order to reach a 'truth', but in order to understand that there is no truth – with the possible exception of the statement just made. As Brown (1990: 189) expresses it, 'postmodernism shifts the agenda of social theory and research from explanation and verification to guide and persuade themselves and each other'. Science is seen as rhetorical construction and the task of pomo is to explore this. But of course such enterprises are also carried out with language. That means that these too should be deconstructed/studied in terms of rhetoric, and so on. This launching of an alternative view on language is perhaps the most significant aspect of postmodernism and is treated at some length in subsequent chapters, especially in Chapter 4.

From this view on language it partly follows that far-reaching theories – grand or master narratives as they are called – are problematic. We cannot talk about society, family, unemployment, child-rearing, love or values in any general sense. A more sociological version of this – moving over to the pomo as period camp – stresses that these narratives are unpopular at present or, to take a more evaluative stance, that they – with pomo as an exception – are not sensitive to the *Zeitgeist*. But the philosophical version of postmodernism would emphasize the theoretical case against efforts to offer broad theoretical explanations. Master narratives are part of the tyranny of modernist ideology and they build upon a deeply problematic understanding of language. The multiplication of shaky language elements – upon which the master narratives are built – means that we arrive at a colossus on clay feet.

Pomo as a philosophy 'would abandon its generalizing social science ambitions and instead parasitically play off the ironies, incoherencies, inconsistencies and inter-textuality of social science writings' (Featherstone 1988: 205). It has little or nothing to say on its own, but relies on others to say something which the pomo then can get his or her teeth into. It tries to resist (rather than oppose) the view of others, who try to put forward a 'dominant view' (Calás and Smircich 1987). Statements establishing 'truths' should be avoided. They have the virtue, however, of keeping the pomos preoccupied.

The entire enterprise is dependent on there being something 'dominant' to counteract. Other critical theories suffer from the critique of being parasitic – as does the present text – but it is more problematic for text-focusing deconstructionists, as they concentrate on text segments, rather than larger and perhaps more significant parts of culture.

The text-focusing position is, as Parker (1992) remarks, philosophically waterproof, but would, if it became widespread, give social science a very restricted space. To only comment upon others' texts appears a bit esoteric. If all people become converted then all would be involved in the deconstruction of others' deconstructions. It starts and ends with 'writers writ[ing] about writers for other writers' (Castoriadis 1992: 16). The tax payer might start to wonder what he or she is paying academics for. Soon we must leave academia and start working in advertising agencies or engage in US politics or religious fundamentalism, where we can avoid 'the tyranny of reason'.

To be fair, many advocates of pomo are well aware of the problem of having little of political and social relevance to say (e.g. Baker 1990). Many examples of deconstruction provide valuable insights for the reflexivity of social research (e.g. Calás and Smircich 1988): they inspire the thinking through of the relationship between the researcher/author and what is being researched, as well as the text. Postmodernist ideas include quite a lot of inspiration for new ways of writing – and I hope that the present text carries at least some traces of these. They may also encourage the use of deconstructive ideas in a rather pragmatic way, thus avoiding the problem of postmodern impotency (Baker 1990). All moves to mobilize pomo ideas in a less reactive and parasitic manner than responding to others' texts through looking at loopholes risk the expression of inconsistent philosophical and theoretical positions.

There are many versions of the philosophy/style field of postmodernism. It is difficult to structure the field further. Sometimes a distinction is made between sceptical and affirmative postmodernism (Rosenau 1992). The sceptical version promotes a 'negative' agenda, based on the idea of the impossibility of establishing any truth. Representation becomes a matter of imposing an arbitrary meaning on something. Research becomes a matter of deconstruction, the tearing apart of texts by showing the contradictions, repressed meanings and, thus, the fragility behind a superficial level of robustness and validity. This approach strongly discourages empirical work.

Affirmative postmodernism also questions the idea of truth and validity but has a more positive view of social research. Playfulness, irony, humour, eclecticism and methodological pluralism are celebrated. So is local knowledge (including a preference for situated knowledge and a rejection of the search for abstract, universal truths). One example of this approach is Kilduff and Mehra (1997). Here, the problem of representation is briefly mentioned but generally taken lightly. Instead, a free attitude, 'breaking down disciplinary boundaries, challenging conventional wisdom, and giving voice to viewpoints and perspectives hitherto silenced' (Kilduff and Mehra 1997: 476), is advocated. The distinction between sceptical and affirmative postmodernism is far from unproblematic, but nevertheless indicates some of the differences of the field.

Pomo and poststructuralism

Before moving on, I feel that this is the right – or at least a not too wrong – place for a short section on the relationship between postmodernism (in this section PM) and poststructuralism (PS).

The term poststructuralism originates from structuralism. Structuralism draws attention away from the centrality of subjects and centres on 'the search for constraining patterns, or structures, [and] claims that individual phenomena have meaning only by virtue of their relation to other phenomena as elements within a systematic structure' (Milner, cited by Crotty 1998: 198). Poststructuralism, however, challenges the very idea of structure, including the idea of a centre, a fixed principle, a hierarchy of meaning and a solid foundation (Sarup 1988: 49).

Poststructuralism and postmodernism are designations that are used in diverse ways. It is thus not possible to establish any definite relationship between the two, and different authors relate them to each other in different ways. Mumby and Putnam (1992: 467) see PS as one of many schools within PM, which focuses on the discursive and linguistic patterns that are central to the production of subjectivity and identity. Derrida and his idea of deconstruction is placed in this category by almost all those concerned, apart from authors who simply 'jump over' poststructuralism as a particular variant within the broad orientation which could be called 'PM/PS', and who thus speak only of postmodernism. Foucault is generally ascribed to PS, but Margolis (1989), for instance, distinguishes him sharply from Derrida and others, and regards him instead as the 'typical example of a postmodernist'. His justification is that Foucault is not content with deconstruction, i.e. 'a reactive and parasitical' attitude *vis-à-vis* texts, but launches more 'holistic' attempts to rethink history and dominating ideas with the help of alternative ways of understanding. This argument does not cut any ice with other scholars, who describe Foucault as a poststructuralist on the grounds that he tries to rethink our conception of the subject and of the power and disciplining which produce it. Foucault himself, like most of the other central figures in the schools concerned, distanced himself from labels altogether, and particularly disliked the designation 'postmodernism' (Foucault 1983). Perhaps Rosenau best describes the difference between what most people have in mind when referring to the two 'posts' when she writes that 'Postmodernists are more oriented toward cultural critique while the post-structuralists emphasize method and epistemological matters. For example, post-structuralists concentrate on deconstruction, language, discourse, meaning and symbols while post-modernists cast a broader net' (Rosenau 1992: 3). This is, however, more a matter of emphasis than substantive differences, so efforts to divide the intellectual world once and for all into PS and PM will be of limited value.

A major reason for people's preference for the term postmodernism – also in contexts where it would have made more sense to talk about poststructuralism – is that the broader spectrum it covers makes it more well known. A problem is that once people regularly use a particular label, it is difficult not to follow it when reviewing and discussing them. Scheurich (1997), for example, defends his use of the label postmodernism – instead of the more appropriate poststructuralism – by saying that the former is more familiar among his audience (academics in the discipline of education in the USA). This familiarity is an effect of the term's use in the most varied of contexts. As said, I don't think this is necessarily a good reason for following fashion, but I also follow the stream. My frequent use of the signifier pomo as a synonym for postmodernism signals my own ambivalence.

Pomo in a specific field: organization studies

Following these complaints about the broad-brushed character of pomo talk, it makes sense to take a closer look at pomo in a specific field. This will make it possible to illustrate and assess what we are taking about. Organization studies is a suitable field for exploring postmodernist ideas. There are plenty of pomo writings in the field. As a middle-level area – between 'micro' aspects such as individuals and macro aspects such as societies and cultures – it is fairly representative. Organizations are also relatively accessible for social research interested in tracing changes and trends. The 'interiors' of individuals are not easy to study, pomo assumptions about fragmentation etc. do not lend themselves very well to empirical inquiry and the complex and large-scaled character of societies as a whole makes them difficult to study with much precision and interpretive depth.

In organization studies, as in other social sciences, postmodernism philosophy has had quite a lot of influence in its arguments for new ways of understanding organizations and organizing processes (e.g. Cooper and Burrell 1988; Deetz 1992; Kilduff and Mehra 1997; Calás and Smircich 1999). However, here I will discuss efforts to identify new features of organizations which are seen as pomo, some of which also incorporate pomo theorizing. These new ideas on novel organizational forms or modes of organizing all focus on 'post-bureaucratic' features. Large, integrated, machine-like organizations mainly emphasizing productivity have faded away to be replaced by more mixed, flexible organizational virtues, it is claimed. 'Modernist' organizational principles – division of labour, hierarchy, mass production, large size – lose terrain. As summarized by Lee and Hassard (1999: 394), 'the coherent bulk of the large organization, once a source of pride, now appears one of strategic, operational and frequently financial embarrassment. This is the era of organizational networks, strategic alliances, "factories within factories", outsourcing and business process re-engineering.'

A salient proponent here is Clegg (1990). He draws upon the concept of dedifferentiation. This is a term sometimes used in pomo writings, especially those pointing at social trends, and there refers to an erosion of boundaries between various branches of the arts or between science and culture (Lash 1988). Clegg, however, gives it a different meaning from what is common (i.e. the blurring of genres in art and science), and instead refers to an all-purpose reversal of the division of labour. Pomo organizations can be defined by their oppositions to bureaucracy and Fordism. They are typical of Japanese companies. The organizational dimensions of modernity/pomo are described as follows: specialization versus diffusion, bureaucracy versus democracy, hierarchy versus market, disempowerment versus empowerment, inflexible versus flexible, individualized versus collectivized and mistrust versus trust (Clegg 1990: 203). As Thompson (1993) remarks, this sounds entirely consistent with current thinking in pop-management – a field known for broad-brushed, positive-sounding and uncritical claims. Pomo is good. Clegg is, however, worried about divisions between the new postmodern organizations and traditional organizations, and the accompanying social differentiations. He is thus not painting the rosy picture that pop-management writers habitually do.

Kincheloe and McLaren (1994) also talk about postmodernism in relationship to what they see as new organizational forms. The 'postmodern' here refers to consumer-driven production, the language of democracy, total quality management and outsourcing. 'Whereas the managerial appeal to efficiency is a guise in the modernist workplace to hide worker control strategies . . . in the postmodern workplace *cooperation* becomes the word du jour' (Kincheloe and McLaren 1994: 148).

According to Thompson (1993), there is no evidence that points to more far-reaching changes in how organizations function. Perhaps he is under-estimating the current changes, but it is unlikely that they are clearly due to a change from modernist to postmodernist organizations. Such a choice of terminology would just add another meaning to an already overloaded term.[1]

Another version of postmodern organization theory talks less of post-bureaucracy and more about undecidability, non-rationality and images. Berg (1989: 207) emphasizes chaos and ambiguity bringing about 'the final rejection of the grand narrative of organizations as tightly coupled rational machines run by conscious and mature men in full control of operations and proactive strategic choices'. The argument here is a mix of philosophical and periodization. Berg also stresses the role of images and hyperreality. I agree that images – as an area of special attention – matter more than they did some decades ago. I do believe that certain economic and sociocultural changes have made 'images' – loosely coupled to (other, more materially anchored parts of) organizational 'reality' – a particular theme open for salient influence and control, especially in certain type of organizations, which through size, changes, intangible products and other sources of ambiguity are difficult to grasp and understand (Alvesson 1990). It is easy to overstress the point when couching the change in terms of postmodernism. Again I do not think that the elements that Berg addresses are tightly connected or that the term pomo illuminates the changes very well. Whether or not people are rational, conscious or mature is not necessarily related to chaos and ambiguity. In addition, the question is how far the rational machine criticism should be pushed. Many organizations seem to reach a relatively high level of rationality in terms of the production and distribution of goods, at least in the Western world (which is what this book is mainly concerned with). I don't think we need or benefit from the word pomo when describing this change. A nuanced appreciation of changes should imply that we don't paint with the broadest brushes.

A third version of pomo organization theory addresses management principles in relationship to some types of normative control associated with corporate cultures. Willmott (1992) talks about pomo thinking in relationship to a critical discussion of the ideas of excellence and corporate culture in the pop-management literature during the 1980s (e.g. Peters and Waterman 1982). Like Clegg (1990), Willmott views pomo as antithetical to bureaucracies, but unlike Clegg, who claims to move on a robust ontological ground with a traditional epistemology, Willmott draws upon key themes of pomo as philosophy, such as indeterminacy, play and chance. He sees parallels to the corporate culture literature, which prescribes 'large doses of hoopla and celebration', and concludes that 'advocates of strong corporate cultures focus attention upon the productive value of the postmodern virtues of play, indeterminacy and even anarchy'. There are possible parallels between some pomo ideas and certain popular proposals for management, and Willmott makes interesting points. But it is not unproblematic to transfer pomo ideas focusing on the indeterminacy of language to an understanding of normative principles for management, or to use an abstract definition of pomo thinking that equally well fits texts in general and some contemporary corporate practice. The same words may refer to quite different things – which are glossed over by references to general pomo thinking. A problem with the notion of pomo is that it seems to encourage such glosses. If we take the idea of indeterminacy seriously, we cannot properly describe corporate practice, but only look at the indeterminacies of claims of indeterminacies (characterizing pomo organization rhetoric), comparing such claims with the indeterminacies of claims of standards and predictability (characterizing bureaucracy rhetoric).

Another debatable point concerns the relationship between the pomo principles and bureaucracy. It is hard to compare the significance of different principles for organizational control, but I think that play, indeterminancy and even anarchy as virtues in corporate cultures of 'excellence' are complementary ideals in essentially bureaucratic organizations, rather than principles that radically transform the latter. After all, it is a matter of profit-oriented capitalist companies, with division of labour, rules, career and promotion patterns, management control systems and so on.

I am thus rather sceptical about what use pomo – as a new label or vehicle for novel theorizing of phenomena existing 'out there' – has been to organization theory. Parker (1993: 206) makes a similar evaluation of the claims of a more general change in terms of organizational forms from modernism to postmodernism:

> The modern/postmodern couplet echoes many of the other dichotomies of control versus commitment, Taylor versus Mayo, formal versus informal, mechanistic versus organic and so on. There seems no reason then, apart from academic fashion, to introduce a term which appears to have little empirical foundation and provides no convincing theoretical reasons for adapting a periodization of organizational forms.

The field is probably already sensitive enough to new trends without needing the overall story of general change signalled by the pomo (as a period) concept. The possibility of much stronger signs of the continuing domination of 'modernism' is lost in the one-sided receptiveness to 'post-bureaucracy'. Anthony (1994: 66) has a point when remarking that organizations are still like machines: 'the evidence lies all around us from burger bars to the manufacture of our televisions and word processors'. Today's typical businesses are McDonalds and call centres, and these are not easy to marry with pomo vocabulary. Empirical studies of changes often come up with the impression of relatively modest changes in structural terms (Thompson and Warhurst 1998; Ruigrok et al. 1999). Research along conventional lines may well have a conservative bias and be insensitive to some changes that are perhaps better illuminated through some of the interpretive or reading ideas expressed by pomo philosophy, e.g. the idea of hyperreality and the imaginary. The idea of emphasizing fragmentation and ambiguity rather than systems and totalities in organizations is promising, and may lead to the productive rethinking of notions such as corporate cultures (Martin 1992) and leadership (Alvesson and Sveningsson 2001). However, any credible backing up of ideas on more dramatic changes motivating a shift of attention from modernism to postmodernism is still lacking and pomo ideas on the subject seem speculative and exaggerated. There is a value in pomo's provocations and radical challenge and one may argue that it is more important to look at the marginal and novel rather than the typical and established, but one should then be clear and modest about such an enterprise. Seldom are such virtues visible in pomo texts addressing social and organizational changes.

More modest attempts to use postmodernist ideas about institutional changes and new forms are definitively possible. There are some phenomena – such as the significance of image and brand name in business life – that lend themselves nicely to pomo language. One could also argue that even if 90 or 98 per cent of everything does not fit well with pomo talk, there are sufficient examples of novel changes and phenomena that can keep a pomo researcher occupied, and there is a case for taking an interest in new phenomena, as we know less about them.

Organizations are of course only one area of many, and studies of other fields may well come up with other indications on postmodernist changes. The present book has no ambition to say anything about whether we live in a postmodern world or not. My point is to emphasize the value of not just assuming or claiming postmodernity but of considering sceptically these claims and marshalling empirical work. There seem to be sound reasons for doubting the bolder claims about 'postmodernity' being a good way of universally making sense of the current state of the social.

The choice between pomo period 'out there' and pomo philosophy

Do postmodern period and postmodern philosophy walk hand in hand or can – indeed should – they be uncoupled and treated independently of each other?

Many authors have stressed the importance of making a choice between seeing pomo as a philosophy (style, perspective) and a period as a matter of conducting pomo social science or doing social science about pomo (Featherstone 1988; Kellner 1988). As Parker (1992: 10) writes, writers must 'be clear when they are trying to find postmodernity and when they are being postmodern'.

A number of researchers have taken firm and coherent positions in this respect. Some focus only on pomo phenomena, typically of a rather large-scale nature ('postmodern age', new social forms), and proceed from a more or less traditional ontology and epistemology. They can then investigate and assess whether there are, for example, new organizational structures, new forms of politics, an impact of mass media and digitilization on people's experiences that are in line with a postmodernization thesis. Others go for the philosophical line and concentrate on the rather narrow task of deconstructing texts, or go for new ways of experimenting with how to produce challenging, unorthodox narratives trying to exhibit contemporary experiences of a fluid social reality. The two positions are in different ways vulnerable, however. The often rather far-reaching and speculative statements of changes which have references to something existing 'out there' run the risk of being met by demands for empirical support:

> theories of the postmodern often talk of an ideal-type channel-hopping MTV (music television) viewer who flips through different images at such speed that she/he is unable to chain the signifiers together into a meaningful narrative, she/he merely enjoys the multiphrenic intensities and sensations of the surface of images. Evidence of the extent of such practices, and how they are integrated into, or influence, the day-to-day encounters between embodied persons is markedly lacking.
>
> (Featherstone 1988: 20)

The pomo as philosophy approach runs the risk of being accused of wanting to turn all social science into literary criticism or to do social research that is highly subjective, intuitive and preoccupied with the researcher/author and her or his worries about text production. Thompson (1993) suggests that pomo should restrict itself to the fields of art and literature. Parker (1992: 11) formulates the problem as follows, in the field of sociology of work and organizations:

> If the real world does not exist in anything other than discourse, then is the act of writing one interpretation of a discourse a worthwhile pursuit? The problems of (fictional) individuals in (mythical) organizations are safely placed behind philosophical double-glazing and their cries are treated as interesting examples of discourse.

It can be tempting to separate postmodernism as saying something about the present society or culture or transformations of specific social institutions from postmodernism as a philosophy and intellectual style. Alternatively, one can emphasize the connections and the creative potential of a combined approach where the framework and the social phenomenon go hand in hand and mutually define each other: one could argue that 'a postmodern age calls for a postmodern philosophy'. One could also turn this around and say that social studies based on a postmodern philosophy tend to produce a postmodernist social reality: everything is turned into hyperreality or rhetoric or is in a state of flux and indeterminancy. Given a preference for a framework emphasizing ambiguity, fragmentation and the separation of language from any underlying reality 'out there', and focusing on social texts, social phenomena can only be approached in certain ways. This would typically not work that well in the study of conveyor belts, apartheid, the Holocaust, extreme poverty, the high mortality of bus drivers caused by heart problems or other phenomena where there is a substantive, material core. I am not saying that these areas cannot be approached as 'texts' to be deconstructed, but I do believe that there are more urgent projects.

If pressed to choose between either a combined pomo period and philosophy package of locked intellectual systems with certain 'truth-like' claims or separating the period and the philosophy ideas, I would choose the second, separation option. But such strict choices are seldom necessary. It makes sense to allow for a soft interchange between the period and the philosophy. The latter inspires new questions and new lines of interpretations which may encourage a sensitivity to dimensions and aspects of social reality that conventional approaches easily miss or pick up in somewhat square ways. From the other angle, some social phenomena – such as the possible destabilization of categories like nations, gender, organizations, family, career – may inspire the use of new vocabularies and new modes of writing. Studies of hyperreality – to the extent that such projects are possible – may also call for a combined pomo period and philosophy approach.

Critique of postmodernism

Pomo leaves few people untouched. Its advocates are often highly provocative, and a lot of the critique is profound and fierce. The countercritique follows the same route. Although I have not succeeded in holding back a number of complaints about postmodernism in previous sections, the more heavy artillery is put into action in the following part. I express critique in four sections focusing on: (a) attributions to modernism – how the construction of modernism and postmodernism typically sets up a particular version of the former which makes the latter look good; (b) pomo as a catch-all term – the categorical character of much pomo writing; (c) pomo as destruction – the unconstructive and, at times, hypocritical orientation of pomo; and (d) self-defeating elements – the frequent deviations from espoused ideals in much pomo that tries to be socially relevant (mixed discourses).

Attributions to modernism

The first issue is to scrutinize how postmodernists construct the term that opens the space for pomo, i.e. modernism or modernity. The popularity of pomo presupposes that something that is not pomo, i.e. modernism or modernity, is not popular. A few authors (e.g. Featherstone 1988; Kellner 1988) are neutral or critical when writing about pomo, viewing changes summarized by this label as a mixed blessing, but in general pomo stands for something good. Quite often, the word modernism is used in strongly value-laded ways. Thou should not be 'modern', meaning outdated and tyrannic, if not dead!

Let us see which tactics are used when modernism is constructed.[2] Daudi suggests that 'the philosophy and epistemology of modernity has "a dictating role". Modernism is contaminated and must be avoided. If we stick to it . . . we end up telling various truths about ourselves and producing a world of conformity and mental totalitarianism. Ultimately, the only way for us to avoid this sort of subjugation is by disavowing modernity' (Daudi 1990: 285–7).[3] Cooper and Burrell (1988: 92) describe two epistemological positions: 'modernism with its belief in the essential capacity of humanity to perfect itself through the power of rational thought and postmodernism with its critical questioning, and often outright rejection, of the ethnocentric rationalism championed by modernism.' Calás and Smircich (1987) also say that modernism is about domination, while pomo is viewed as resistance (see also Foster 1983). Pomo is, then, the brave fighter. (There is, however, also an unpleasant form of pomo – reactionary pomo – which fails to do its duty.) Other portraits of modernism stress its stiff, lifeless and boring features. Willmott (1992), for example, talks about 'modernism's dry, bloodless discourses and practices'.

Modernism, then, is easily constructed in ways that make postmodernism the option for anyone but bad and boring people: who wants to be 'dictating', 'conforming', 'ethnocentric' or 'dry'. My interest is not in saving (aspects of) modernism or 'modernist social forms' from critique. I am not a great fan of dictats, mental totalitarianism, ethnocentric rationalism, omnipotency fantasies, domination, tyranny, extensive division of labour or boring discourses. Postmodernism has a point in the sense that quite a lot of social science deserves critique. Think of most questionnaire-based studies, for example: seldom fun to read. This does not, of course, mean that 'postmodernists' score better in avoiding many of the critiques they generously launch against their favourite target. But I believe that modernism is too broad, slippery and confusing a word to be of any help in the enterprise of delivering well argued critique against forms of unpleasantness. As a target it is too broad and, at the same time, too easy and too difficult to criticize. It actually often includes all major versions of social theorizing. Attacks on modernism for embracing 'totalizing' discourses can (rightfully) be counteracted by arguing instead that many forms of modern thought are rather narrow and fragmented (Reed 1993). A look at almost any contemporary scientific journal confirms this view. Pomo may be more 'totalizing' (Featherstone 1989). Pomo authors would benefit from avoiding painting with the broad brush when commenting on 'modernism', cultural change, individuals (subjects) etc.

Pomo overviews of the intellectual terrain normally reduce everything to either modernism or pomo. Diversity and pluralism give way to the standardization and homogenization ideals of advocates of pomo, projected on to modernism. Many (most, all?) pomo writers thus, despite espousing the celebration of diversity, really advocate uniform categories for the grasping of a rich variety of different kinds of intellectual traditions and/or sociocultural phenomena.

The colonialistic aspirations of many pomo authors are illustrated by the fact that much of what is said in the name of pomo is far from being the exclusive possession of that 'stream', but is 'a standard feature of much contemporary, if not modernist, thought' (Margolis 1989: 22). Neopositivism, excessive belief in rationality etc. were thoroughly critiqued by a large number of authors before postmodernism (Rosenau 1992; Crotty 1998).

Categorical statements: pomo as a grand narrative

From the broadbrushed characterizations of modernism (or modernity for that matter) follows a strong inclination to use correspondingly sweeping statements about pomo.

One of the most interesting features of some of the texts about modernism and pomo is the attack on general frameworks (grand narratives, totalizing discourse etc.), combined with a preference for categorical statements, especially on the nature of 'modernism', but also on subjects such as language or the individual. Of course, this position is rather paradoxical, as a number of authors have pointed out (Featherstone 1988, 1989; Kellner 1988). Pomo criticizes modernism for a kind of intellectual imperialism, but many advocates of pomo are even more vulnerable to this type of critique.

The paradox can perhaps be avoided if one says that the grand narratives of pomo about the nature of language, the individual, scientific knowledge, rationality, formal organizations and so on are exceptions to the generally untrustworthy nature of the grand narratives. The message then becomes: avoid master narratives other than those advocated by the pomos! And that is, I think, what many pomos are saying. The only narratives to be trusted are those marketed under the brand of pomo: language is a game of distinctions, rationality is a myth, the subject is discursively constituted etc.

A profound difficulty in many debates on postmodernism is the contradiction between taking pomo seriously as a philosophy (style), on the one hand, and understanding a 'new' social reality (e.g. pomo organizations or pomo society), on the other. These topics are treated in the same text mainly because the same signifier is used to signify two quite different phenomena. From the position of pomo as a style of critical analysis which opens up ironies, inter-textuality and paradoxes, and takes the ambiguity of language seriously, attempts to devise a theory of pomo society (postmodernity) are essentially flawed efforts to totalize or systemize (Featherstone 1988). The rejection of master narratives or language as representation means that it becomes impossible to illuminate great chunks of social reality (Kellner 1988). A possible defence for postmodernists would be to emphasize that they are less troubled by the possibility of contradiction and incoherence than their opponents: coherence may be an overvalued quality in social studies.

To understand the popularity of the term postmodernism and the tendency for a large number of authors and orientations to present themselves under this banner, one needs to consider the social logic involved in how academic communities work. Pomo writers are embraced by and organized in special issues of journals, conferences, communications etc. and in books such as the present one. Thus they (we) are promoting and marketing their (our) careers around a use of the key concept which too often avoids not only stuffy ideals such as definitions and clarity, which are perhaps not necessary, but, worse, sometimes lacks common preoccupations broadly pointing in the same direction.

That the appeal of 'postmodernism' as a label is related to its marketing qualities is sometimes confirmed by its advocates. Scheurich (1997), for example, uses the term postmodernism instead of poststructuralism even though the latter, he says, is more appropriate for his work. His reason is that the former is more familiar for the audience. As one of his major critiques of 'modernism' is that it only recognizes the familiar and denies the unfamiliar, the ambiguous, the Other, his choice of label for his work is not without its ironies. It also undermines his critique: why should others be bothered about a critique of work that only acknowledges the familiar if the critic himself goes for this? Unfortunately, I cannot say that I resist the marketing logic either. I am unhappy with the term postmodernism and to some extent distance myself from it, but I still reluctantly use it, partly because the people and texts discussed in this book use it, and partly because the publisher and I think it will attract a larger audience. A defence is that I use it in a sceptical and ironic way and partly follow others' use of this term. It is, of course, up to the reader to judge whether this is acceptable or not.

There is, however, a better reason for people to want to associate themselves with postmodernism, and this is its usefulness for the mobilization of power. Given the broad terrain the postmodernism label covers, it offers some protection against the tendency for people who are pursuing 'odd' agendas to run into difficulties. Deviating from established traditions and ideas about science may lead to the fate of not being published or read, or even to unemployment. The frequent use of the term postmodernism means that it cannot that easily be neglected or marginalized. This point is to a considerable extent in line with the marketing aspect just mentioned – the more effectively one can spread the word, the better protected one is against the powerful mainstream. 'Postmodernism' thus works as a protective shield.

Pomo as parasitical and destructive

Postmodernism emphasizes negativity. It opposes 'positive' knowledge, positive in the sense of telling the truth, suggesting insights or offering vocabularies seen as capable of bringing thinking and understanding further. Pomo is committed to showing the futility of and cracks in such projects. Postmodernism 'seems to condemn everything, propose nothing . . . demolition is the only job that the postmodern mind seems to be good at' (Baumann, quoted by Billig and Simons 1994: 6). Parker (1993: 205) also complains that 'Postmodernists may be correct about the dangers of assuming that I write the truth but they do not give me a clear reason for wanting to write at all.' Pomo thus encourages a retreat from saying something of relevance and interest to audiences other than (some of those in) academia, audiences presumably interested in knowledge of value to aid their understanding and possible problem-solving. Castoriadis (1992: 16) notes a 'contemporary tendency of writers toward self-containment: writers write about writers for other writers'.

The negativity of pomo writings is pointed out by Rorty (1992) and Calhoun (1992), for example, who argue that Lyotard, like postmodernists more generally, in a passion for pluralism that argues against general rules and criteria for science, overemphasizes the problem of relating different positions to each other. 'In most postmodernist accounts, the coming together of people from different traditions, or those abiding by different rules from within the same tradition, seems primarily an occasion for communication to break down, not for . . . mutual learning and growth' (Calhoun 1992: 266–7). The fact that the languages of different theories are not perfectly translatable and commensurable does not prevent a person from learning more than one language. Lyotard makes too much of his insights into the problems of translation and the diversity of criteria in science. Rorty argues that the failure to find a grand narrative that may serve as a universal translation manual does not need to obstruct the possibility of making peaceful social progress, within and outside science.

'Anything goes' is a slogan invented by Feyerabend (1975), and sometimes taken up by pomos. This sounds liberal and tolerant, but as Latour (cited in Rosenau 1992: 123) writes, this implies a positive, affirmative view. The postmodernist ultra-scepticism about claims of contributing something 'positive', i.e. claims about what exists or how we can understand matters, can instead be summarized as 'nothing goes'.

Again, as with virtually all statements about pomo, it must be recognized that those placing themselves, or being placed by others, in the postmodernist camp are in no way uniform. There are softer, more affirmative versions of postmodernism which do not readily fall victim to the attacks launched here. However, the more distinct and, perhaps, typical examples of pomo writing can hardly be called constructive as we typically understand this term in the context of knowledge creation.

Self-defeating elements in pomo

A major argument against taking pomo too seriously is that you can easily paint yourself into a corner. It is easy to run into self-contradictory situations if one is not extremely cautious, moving within a highly confined terrain.

The idea so cherished by pomo writers, that language is not transparent or expressive and cannot reflect a real world, is almost impossible to live up to in handling one's own texts in the social sciences, at least if these aim to say something about 'social reality', and are not just pure texts. An example of this is the feminist appropriation of postmodernism. Postmodernism is sometimes celebrated, as it questions dominant truths and challenges categories that are seen as oppressive to women. On the other hand, post-modernism prevents the expression of claims about the current state of affairs and the formulation of political interests. Sometimes this leads to a peculiar mix of, and even contradictory, positions, so that postmodernism is brought forward when disliked things are targeted, while it is pulled back when one's own progressive position is put forward.

Weedon (1987: 22) emphasizes the fact that language cannot reflect or express either the social or the 'natural' world's inner meanings, but also writes that 'We need to understand why women tolerate social relations which subordinate their interests to men and the mechanisms whereby women and men adopt particular discursive positions as representative of their interests' (Weedon 1987: 12). The statement seems to refer to 'actual' phenomena, such as women's tolerance, their interests, social gender positions, mechanisms and discursive positions which represent the said interests. According to the pomo creed, language cannot make such reflec-tions possible, at least not in the unequivocal way that Weedon's statement implies. From a postmodernist perspective the entire statement may appear as a suitable text to be deconstructed, where the categories 'women', 'inter-ests', 'social relations' etc. would be seen as questionable elements in an effort to inscribe order in a messy and fluid world.[4]

Another example is Scheurich (1997: 67), who argues against con-ventional views on interviews, emphasizing that the 'reality' of these is 'ambiguous, relative, and unknowable'. This does not prevent him from claiming that interviewees are active resistors of the dominance of the inter-viewer or from stating that 'I have found this to be true in my own inter-viewing as a researcher.' He also claims that 'I find that interviewees carve out space of their own, that they can often control some or part of the inter-view, that they may push against or resist my goals, my intentions, my ques-tions, my meanings' (Scheurich 1997: 71). Not much is 'ambiguous, relative, and unknowable' in these 'findings', which are presented as robust facts.

Parker (1992: 3), recognizing that there are many versions of modernism, with divergent politics and methodologies, describes the core of modernism as 'a rationalism that is unchallengeable and a faith that it is ultimately possible to communicate the results of enquiry to other rational beings'. In contrast, pomo suggests that this is a form of intellectual imperialism that ignores 'the fundamental uncontrollability of meaning'. Such a description captures essential aspects of what some people talk about in terms of modernism and pomo. Given this formulation, most individuals writing about pomo – even many of those who say they advocate it – really are 'modernists'. If you take the fundamental uncontrollability of meaning seriously or doubt that it is possible to communicate the results of enquiry to other rational beings, then there is no point in writing papers and books for an audience of academics – which normally pass reviewing and editorial processes before appearing. As Habermas (1984) notes, if you don't anticipate at least some potential for rationality in communication, there is no point in saying or writing anything, at least not in academic settings. This point is underscored by Bernstein (1983), who emphasizes the common ground between authors stressing conflicting viewpoints – even if they leave mutually shared assumptions unespoused – and the possibility of enlarging or changing intellectual horizons through dialogue, conversation, the learning of new language games etc. (see also Calhoun 1992; Rorty 1992). Of course, people may be more or less prepared to accept the rationality of actors or the uncontrollability of meanings, and one may define a pomo as someone who is relatively suspicious of the former and who like non-fixed meanings (the free play of signifiers). We can say, if for some odd reason (e.g. market value, confirmation of identity, sentimentality) we want to stick to the labels, that there are persons who are modernists who flirt with pomo, or sometimes visit the postmodern world, 'a fine place to stay cool' (Berman 1992: 46). Without some minimal anticipation of rationality – possibly a very soft and uncertain one – there seems little point in debating the meaning and virtues of postmodernism.

This does not, of course, imply any great faith in human rationality. Most enlightened modern citizens are sceptical about the rationality of human actors – after all, who hasn't heard about psychoanalysis, world starvation, ecological crises, wars, religious fundamentalism, Nazism, gulags and McCarthyism? – and frequently feel misunderstood. We could also say that we are all pomos, but adapt to modernist rules in order to get anywhere in work and life – and especially to get published and gain academic credentials.

My text here drifts a little bit away from my main point in this section. My complaint about postmodernism is not only that at least a hard or strong version of it severely constrains what it is possible to say (write), but also that the pomo advocate too easily contradicts himself or herself. Claims that language is unable to say anything about the world out there, that reality is indeterminate and unknowable or that there is no possibility of rationality and communication of meaning, call for highly cautious navigation and severe self-constraints when one moves on and tries to explore a theme.

Conclusions

Postmodernism is a popular label for a rather broad spectrum of artistic and intellectual orientations, as well as claims about a range of novel social trends and forms. Of interest in the present context is postmodernism as a way of grasping the unique features of contemporary (postmodern) society and/or specific social institutions, but of greater interest is postmodernism as a philosophical/theoretical perspective. There are good reasons not to mix these two projects prematurely, although occasionally postmodern theorizing may facilitate sensitive inquiry into what are referred to as postmodern social phenomena, such as fragmented contemporary identities or a social world 'made up' of freely floating images.

Thompson (1993: 201) follows a similar path, arguing that when concepts move away from their original fields and are widely dispersed, 'modernism and postmodernism become conceptual catch-alls, conflating quite distinct social processes'. Quite often pomo represents intellectual imperialism, despite the claims to the contrary. The frequency with which the word is used creates the impression that it stands for something 'real' and significant. The persistence with which this message is hammered home means that it may, in the end, create its own 'truth effects'. 'We talk about pomo, therefore it is' seems to be the motto, but most researchers and journal editors are still not convinced, as any look at the journal shelves in university libraries teaches us.

Postmodernism is a successfully marketed label. I wonder if Lyotard's book *The Postmodern Condition* (1984) would have been as successful without the use of this rhetorically effective label. Of course, pomo is not the only word that is overconsumed and used to refer to a wide range of diverse phenomena or positions. Recognition of this does not shield the use of the word pomo from accusations that it is extraordinarily problematic. The problem is, of course, not the word in itself, but how it has been institutionalized to encourage problematic intellectual moves. As Parker (1993: 209) points out 'the problem is really that postmodernists have themselves totalized at least four centuries of post-enlightenment thought under one pejorative label'. This can partly be seen as an outcome of political moves to marginalize various streams in order to celebrate the originality and novelty of one's own. Sangren (1992) suggests, with reference to anthropology, that pomo ideas are used as means of power for defining out earlier work and creating a space for new careers. If there are problems with 'modernism' and (almost) all earlier work can be labelled modernist, then you have a perfect position for your career without having to be bothered with the possibility that most things have been said before. On the other hand, people with a postmodern inclination may have considerable career problems in fields strongly dominated by conventional epistemologies, so the other side of this imperialist political move is the counteraction of marginalization as part of a defensive project. As with all phenomena, as advocates of postmodernism will have it, there is no single, self-evident or best interpretation. The gathering of a variety of streams under the pomo label may be seen as a matter of marketing, as self-contradiction (as pomos disfavour grand narratives), as a political move to assemble strength against the dominant forces of the dark (modernism) or as something one should not – as I have done – make a big fuss about. After all, signifiers cannot be controlled and a playful orientation is to be preferred. Perhaps I complain too much about the postmodernism label. But I still feel that the points made are worth making. The rest of the book balances issues in a more pro-pomo direction. I am here in the first chapters trying to implant a sceptical attitude to postmodernism, facilitating some resistance to its seductive powers.

The reader may feel some discouragement in reading about an approach that the author does not seem to be entirely optimistic about, to say the least. However, at the core of postmodernism is, as noted by Richardson (2000), a doubt that any theory, method or novelty can offer a privileged form of knowledge. Not all postmodernists seem to bear this in mind when addressing their preferred form of knowledge. But expressing doubt about postmodernist ideas is not necessarily anti-postmodernism, and can be seen as well in line with a postmodernist ethos. Being pro-pomo – and taking this seriously – also implies being a pomo-sceptic. My own position is 'pro-pomo-sceptical', positively ambivalent about the use of pomo ideas in social research.

From what is written above, the reader will understand that I will not join forces with the pomos in a full-scale attack on 'modernist' versions of social research. I am unsympathetic to the very idea of catching it all under this sweeping and misleading term. I don't think it is necessary or productive to accept and work within a full-scale pomo framework. It is far too self-constraining and unconstructive for work seriously interested in 'what the natives think they are up to', as qualitative research often is.

With the exception of the more extreme versions of postmodernism many of the ideas are less novel than they appear. Within what many pomos describe as modernism there is a long tradition of scepticism and questioning (Rosenau 1992). Nevertheless, some important ideas launched or reproduced in intensified forms under the label postmodernism are worth taking seriously – although there is a need for careful consideration of how seriously – in social research. These may include more modest, self-critical and innovative ideas about how to deal with the problem of representation – how to re-present something 'out there' in texts – as well as questioning and rethinking established categories. Forthcoming chapters develop this.

Notes

1 Dedifferentiation means totally different things if it refers to the transgression of cultural boundaries or to the reduction of labour in bureaucracies. The former means primarily a change in mental patterns or artistic practices, while the latter signifies a change in social and behavioural structures. A loosening of boundaries between various forms of art and the reduction of division of labour in organizations refer to quite different phenomena.

2 It would be very naive, and certainly inconsistent with many forms of pomo thought, to say that 'modernism' is just mirrored in descriptions. Whatever social, cultural and intellectual reality exists 'out there', what is referred to as modernism is so complex that it can be portrayed in an endless number of ways – as actually is the case.

3 Lincoln and Guba (2000: 184) also refer to the 'dangers' of conventional texts and 'the forms of tyranny embedded in representational practices'. These bad things are thus parts of modernist research (even though they don't explicitly use the label) and avoided by postmodernists.

4 To be precise, Weedon (1987) uses the term poststructuralism.

3 Key themes in postmodernism

Having in Chapter 2 got some of my frustration with a lot of pomo stuff out of my system, I will now attend to the stream in a more positive way. Despite the multiple uses of the term postmodern and the notorious confusions contingent thereupon, it is possible to produce common themes in which variation in key authors' agendas are downplayed and commonalities highlighted. I will now concentrate on these. In postmodernism as a philosophically based research perspective, which is the major concern in this chapter as well as the rest of the book, the following, on the whole interrelated, ideas are often emphasized:

1 The centrality of discourse – textuality – where the constitutive powers of language is emphasized and 'natural' objects are viewed as discursively produced.
2 Fragmented identities – emphasizing subjectivity as a process and the death of the individual, autonomous, meaning-creating subject. The discursive production of the individual replaces the conventional 'essentialistic' understanding of people.
3 The critique of the idea of representation, where the undecidabilities of language takes precedence over language as a mirror of reality and a means for the transport of meaning.
4 The loss of foundations and the power of grand narratives, where an emphasis on multiple voices and local politics is favoured over theoretical frameworks and large-scale political projects.

5 The power–knowledge connection where the impossibility of separating power from knowledge is assumed and knowledge loses a sense of innocence and neutrality.

Where does all this lead us? One possible answer is to the idea that research aims at resistance and indeterminacy, where irony and play are preferred to rationality, predictability and order. Let us consider each of the five key characteristics of a postmodernist framework for knowledge development briefly.

The centrality of discourse

Postmodernism grew out of French structuralism by taking seriously the linguistic turn in philosophy. This meant a two front war, with the objectivists ('positivists') on the one hand, with their science aimed at predicting/controlling nature and people, and with the humanists (e.g. phenomenologists) on the other, privileging the individual's reported experience and advancing a naive version of human freedom. The focus on language allowed a constructionism that denied the objectivist claim of certainty and objective truth and the humanists' reliance on essential claims on meaning, which led them to miss the social/linguistic politics of experience. The linguistic turn enabled a postmodern rejection of humanism through a critique of autonomy and unitary identities, and a rejection of objectivism through a critique of the idea of representation. The emphasis on discourse means a third line of argumentation: it is not objective reality out there, or human experience and meaning, but discourse that is the crucial issue and The Thing to investigate. Discourse is a tricky concept, used in a variety of ways without authors necessarily being very helpful in indicating what they are up to (Alvesson and Kärreman 2000). In this section, it refers to language use anchored in an institutional context, expressing a fairly structured understanding or a line of reasoning with active, productive effects on the phenomenon it claims to understand 'neutrally'.[1]

From a postmodernist point of view (here represented by Derrida), 'language is a structure of material marks or sounds which are in themselves "undecidable" and *upon which meaning has to be imposed*' (Cooper 1989: 480, emphasis in original). Symbolic systems such as language do not contain fixed meaning. Instead,

> Meaning is scattered or dispersed along the whole chain of signifiers; it cannot be easily nailed down, it is never fully present in any one sign alone, but is rather a kind of constant flickering of presence and absence together. Reading a text is more like tracing this process of constant flickering than like counting the beads on a necklace.
>
> (Sarup 1988: 35–6)

The distinction between language and external realities is, from this point of view, a red herring. Language is external and real. It – and potential meanings – precedes any experience of what is external to it, since experience gains its shape and intelligibility through language. This implies that: (a) experience is always mediated through a layer of meaning – a 'text'– which cannot be eliminated; (b) meaning is fundamentally uncontrollable since there is no inherent quality in language that regulates it; and (c) language is not primarily a system of reference (instead, it is a system of differences – of distinctions – that are always to some extent arbitrary).

To note the primacy of discourse is to suggest that each person is born into ongoing discourses that have a material and continuing presence. The experience of the world is structured through the ways discourses lead one to attend to the world and provide particular unities and divisions. As a person learns to speak these discourses, they more properly speak him or her, in that available discourses position the person in the world in a particular way prior to the individual having any sense of choice. As discourses structure the world they at the same time structure the person's subjectivity, providing him or her with a particular social identity and way of being in the world. The person, *contra* humanism, is always social and language-driven first, and only mistakenly claims the personal self as the origin of experience. Everything – gender, family life, how we relate to employment, career, consumption, sickness etc. – is constituted within discourse. There is, for example, no essential or universal meaning attached to motherhood or unemployment, no 'objective' condition or innate experience outside discourses on women, parenthood, paid labour and being employed, according to postmodernism.

There are two major versions of this theme. One emphasizes discourses in a special linguistic sense, where language in use is intrinsically related to meaning and perception. All perception and meaning entails a 'seeing as' and this 'seeing as' is described as a fundamental 'signifying' or 'language' relation. We see the world through language, which acts as a lens and sense-making apparatus. Being exposed to and learning new vocabularies means the construction of a new world. The distinctions historically carried in language enable a reproduction of specific 'seeing as' relations. Different discourses are always possible – although they may be more or less powerful or marginal. As a linguistic phenomenon, discourse is weakly coupled to material practices in this version (e.g. Weedon 1987). Another, Foucauldian, version views discourses as systems of thought that are contingent upon as well as informing material practices, and that not only linguistically, but also practically, through particular power techniques (clearly visible in prisons, psychiatric hospitals, schools, factories and so forth), produce particular forms of subjectivity (Foucault 1977, 1980). In both versions, human subjectivity can be relatively open or closed. Discursive closure, according to the first version, is temporary, though often continually reproduced, while

Foucault tends to emphasize a more systematic fixation of subjectivity as a result of the network of power relations in operation. There is more about this in the section on power and knowledge.

Fragmented identities

The position on the 'person' follows directly from the conception of discourse. Postmodernism rejects the notion of the autonomous, self-determining individual with a secure unitary identity as the centre of the social universe. Even though many other traditions have done this (for example, behaviourists, structuralists and to some extent psychoanalysts), postmodernists have pushed the point strongly and in a sophisticated manner. There is, of course considerable variation in how far pomos take their positions (Rosenau 1992). Generally, the human subject is viewed as an effect of, or at least strongly constrained by and constituted within, discourse. Discourses produce subject positions – not that different from roles (but determined by language rather than norms and expectations) – that individuals are located in (locate themselves in). These subject positions then drive individual's perceptions, intentions and acts. The point can easily be illustrated by indicating the various credible ways of interpellating a particular human subject: you, as an academic, as a European, as a woman, as a young person, as a Muslim, as a person living in a free, democratic country, as being overweight . . . etc. If one was to shadow an individual during a day, observe all his or her encounters with different people and see how the individual is very different in all these situations, and how contingencies seem to define the subject, then the fluidity and fragmentation of human life would become visible. The assumption that there is a core or essence behind all this surface behaviour would be seen by postmodernists as an illustration of the kind of thinking that they want to question: the inclination to impose order and unity.

There are two versions of this critique of a secure, unitary identity: one historical and one emphasizing a point beyond historical variation, a kind of anti-essential essentialism. The first suggests that the Western conception of *man* has always been a myth. This myth represents a rather ethnocentric idea. Freud's work on tensions and conflicts as central to the human psyche is used to show the growing awareness in Western thought of the fundamental inner fragmentation and inconsistency, but postmodernists go further in their deconstruction of the Western self-image. The conception of a unitary self is considered to be a fiction used to suppress those tensions and privilege masculinity, rationality, vision and control. To the extent that dominant discourses produced the person (including the idea that the individual is the source of thought), the person gained a secure identity but participated in the reproduction of domination, thus marginalizing the other parts of the self. The sense of autonomy served to cover this subservience and give conflict a negative connotation. The assumption is thus that there has never been a core or an essence of human nature or a stable, fixed sense of subjectivity. Place a subject outside the setting and present him or her to a new discourse and he or she will respond and be re-created. The strong thesis that there has never been an essence of human nature can thus be seen as an 'essentialist position' against essentialism. The 'essence' (or essence-lessness) of human nature is its exposure to and adaptiveness to discourse and its potential or actualized fluidity and flexibility.

The other version suggests that the view of the individual as coherent, integrated and (potentially) autonomous has become false in the contemporary historical and cultural situation. If identity is a social product, identity will be relatively stable in homogeneous and stable societies with few dominant discourses. One may also ascribe some stabilizing powers to kinship relations, geographical stability and a material situation that defines subjectivity, although it is hardly good pomo to ascribe any relevance to 'non-discursive' dimensions. In contemporary, heterogeneous, global, tele-connected societies the available discourses expand greatly. They also change rapidly. The variety and dynamics of discourses mean that fragmentation is virtually inevitable. As society becomes more fragmented and hyperreal or virtual (discourse is disconnected from any world reference, images reference images), the identity-stabilizing forces are lost. Gubrium and Holstein (2001: 2), for example, write about 'the almost dizzying array of institutions comprising the postmodern environment, a world where selves are regularly decentered from their inner recesses and recentered in institutional life.'

The differences between two versions – emphasizing human nature *per se* or the contemporary, Western variant as discursively produced and fragmentary – are often a matter of emphasis. Of course, the more there is an interest in contemporary forms of subjectivity viewed as related to social change and actual social conditions, the more inclined are authors to talk about a postmodern society or age, opening up the idea that human subjects some decades or centuries ago were 'different', or calling for understanding through a different logic or vocabulary from that expressed by the pomo period camp.

Irrespective of which specific version one favours, this view of the human subject creates possibilities as well as difficulties for the development of political action. It suggests the possibility of tremendous freedom and opportunities for marginalized groups and aspects of each person to resist a dominant discourse and enter another, but also insecurities that lead to normalization strategies in which people 'voluntarily' cling to consumer identities offered by commercial forces, or organizational and occupational selves orchestrated by corporate cultures and professional standards (Willmott 1994; Deetz 1995).

The critique of the idea of representation

Most versions of social science, as well as most of us in everyday life, treat the presence of objects as unproblematic and believe that the primary function of language is to re-present them. We assume that groups, individuals, race, attitudes, intentions, the state, societies and symbols exist and that we can create accurate or valid representations of these in our research practices and reports. When asked what something is we try to define it and list its essential attributes. Postmodernists find such a position to be illusionary in the same way as the conception of identity. The *stuff* of the world only becomes an *object* in a specific relation to a being for whom it can be such an object. This does not imply the standpoint that there is no objective reality, although for social scientists it is a socially constructed reality, in which consciousness, social definitions and language use are central elements, and of particular interest to study. But irrespective of how one conceives 'objective reality', we don't have a direct access to it. Linguistic practices are thus central to object production. This position has been familiar for some time in the works of philosophers as varied as Mead, Wittgenstein and Heidegger, but it continues to lead to misunderstanding: the most common is the claim of relativism. Postmodernists vary in the extent to which they espouse a relativistic position, i.e. saying that all claims depend on the point of departure, theoretical perspective or language used, and claiming that one cannot establish that one claim of truth or insight is superior to another. Most would agree that the vocabularies and perspective used create a specific version of the world, and that any statement or claim is valid, at best, within a particular frame or discourse. Many postmodernists do not go into the debate(s) about relativism. The pomo position is, however, typically not relativistic in any loose or subjective way. As Bernstein (1983) emphasizes, relativism is often better understood in relationship to scientific paradigms and communities of researchers than as connected to the subjectivity of individuals. Those making the charge about relativism misunderstand the conception of objects or the strength of the conception of discourse. Most postmodernists are not concerned with the chance of being called relativistic, they are more concerned with the apparent stability of objects and the difficulty of unpacking the full range of activities that produce particular objects and sustain them.

Postmodernists argue for a decoupling of the signifier (the uttered word) and the signified (the phenomenon the signifier is supposed to refer to). Normally we think of the sign as a tight integration of the signifier and the signified – the word and the object it refers to trigger a concept or an image (the sign). But, argue postmodernists (such as Derrida), there is no one-to-one relationship or harmony between language use and objects in the world. Sarup (1988: 35) explains the argument as follows:

Suppose you want to know the meaning of a signifier, you can look it up in the dictionary; but all you will find will be yet more signifiers, whose signifieds you can in turn look up, and so on . . . The process is not only infinite but somehow circular: signifiers keep transforming into signifieds, and vice versa, and you will never arrive at a final signified which is not a signifier in itself.

As mentioned in the section on fragmented identities, postmodernists differ in the extent to which they describe discourse in textual or more extended forms. On the whole, however, they start with Saussure's demonstration that the point of view creates the object. He meant this to apply to the importance of the value-laden nature of the system of distinctions in language, but the linguistic and non-linguistic practices quickly interrelate. Let us use a brief example. A 'worker' is an object (as well as a subject) in the world, but neither God nor nature made a 'worker'. Two things are required for a 'worker' to exist: a language and a set of practices which makes possible unities and divisions among people, and something to which such unities and divisions can be applied. The questions 'What is a worker really? What is the essence of a worker? What makes one a worker?' are not answerable by looking at the something that can be described as a worker, but is a product of the linguistic and non-linguistic practices that make this something into an object. In this sense, a worker is not an isolated thing. A worker already implies a division of labour, the presence of management ('non-workers') and people not engaged in paid labour ('unemployed', 'students', 'retired', 'housewives'). The 'essence' of worker is not the properties the 'object' contains but sets of relational systems, including the division of labour. The focus on the object and object properties is the mistake. Attention should be paid to the relational systems which are not simply in the world but are a human understanding of the world – they are discursive or textual. The meaning of 'worker' is not evident and present (contained there) but deferred to the sets of oppositions and junctures, the relations that make it like and unlike other things.

Since any something in the world may be constructed/expressed as many different objects, limited only by human creativity and readings of traces of past understandings, meaning can never be final: it is always incomplete and indeterminant. The appearance of completeness and closure leads us to overlook both the politics, social conventions and norms in and of construction, and the possibilities for understanding that are hidden behind the obvious. Language is thus central to the production of objects, in that it provides the social and historical distinctions that provide unity and difference. Language tells us that there are 'managers', 'executives', 'professionals', 'workers', 'unemployed' and 'retired'.

The thesis that language cannot mirror the reality 'out there', or people's mental states (Shotter and Gergen 1989, 1994), can be pursued more or less strictly. One extreme is to emphasize that we must refrain from addressing extra-textual reality and, in a sense, give up the idea of empirically grounded social research. Another is to give up the idea of a close fit or photograph-like relationship between language use to describe something and this something *per se*; more softly, we may talk about perspective, illumination, producing credible and informed narratives about social reality out there. The originality of postmodernism lies in the emphasis on the first extreme, while any ambition to study social phenomena – and avoid social science being turned into literature critique – must avoid this extreme. A major challenge for a postmodernist social science is how to handle this dilemma. I try to address this constructively in Chapter 4.

The loss of foundations and master narratives

The power of any position has been traditionally gathered from its grounding. This grounding could be to either a metaphysical foundation – such as an external world in empiricism, mental structures in rationalism or human nature in humanism – or a narrative, a story of history – such as Marxism's class struggle, social Darwinism's survival of the fittest or market economics' invisible hand. With such groundings, positions are made to seem secure and inevitable, and not opportunistic or driven by advantage.

Again, as in the case of identity, postmodernists take two different but not incompatible stances, one categorical (valid throughout history and social context) and one interested in recent historical trends (thus overlapping the philosophy/periodization distinctions). Following the first position, foundations and legitimating narratives have always been a hoax. They have been used (usually unknowingly) to support a dominant view of the world and its order. Feminists, for example, have argued that the historical narrative has always been *his*tory. Empiricists' appeal to the nature of the external world covered the force of their own concepts (and those borrowed from elite groups), methods, instruments, activities and reports in constructing that world. The significance of discourse and the inability of language to represent contribute to a general scepticism towards the legitimizing (meta)narratives underpinning Western scientific thought (Lyotard 1984), since no privileged access to external realities can be granted. The influential idea that different vocabularies cannot be strictly compared or evaluated in terms of empirical support (see Kuhn 1970) is mobilized as a support for this scepticism.

Following the second position, other postmodernists note the growing social incredulity towards narratives and foundational moves. Lyotard (1984) showed the decline of the grand narratives of 'spirit' and 'emancipation'. The proliferation of options and the growing political cynicism (or astuteness) of the public leads to a suspicion of legitimating moves (Giddens 1991). In Lyotard's sense, perhaps all that is left is local narratives, i.e.

accounts focusing on a particular setting and with limited generalizability over space and time. Research on gender would, for example, be clear about having studied gender relations in a particular social group at a particular time, and be modest about what this might say about gender relations generally, in other settings or at another point in time.

Not all postmodernists see the retreat of grand narratives and a strong emphasis on the local as necessarily positive. Certainly, the decline of foundations and grand narratives takes away a primary prop of the dominant group's offer of security and certainty as a trade for subordination. But the replacement is not necessarily freedom and political possibility on the part of marginalized groups. Lyotard demonstrated the rise of 'performativity', where measures of means towards social ends become ends in themselves. Access to computers and information – contingent less upon knowledge integrated in the person ('scholarship') than upon financial resources – has become a significant source of knowledge and power. Along with this come new forms of control directed not by a vision of society and social good but simply by more production and consumption.

As several critics have noted, Lyotard and Baudrillard come close to being caught in a contradiction between rather general statements about general cultural conditions existing 'out there', and problematization of the ideas of representing the whole (master narrative) notions of the 'real' and representation (hyperreality) (Kellner 1988). Critics have been quick to respond to Lyotard's thesis about the end of metanarratives:

> that not only does the thesis itself betray the traces of master narrative, a criticism which Lyotard acknowledges when he asks 'Are "we" not telling, whether bitterly or gladly, the great narrative of the end of great narratives?', but also that it might be necessary to distinguish between different orders of grand narrative.
>
> (Smart 2000: 456)

The difficulty for postmodernism with the claimed fall of grand narratives, as in the concept of fragmented identities, is how to generate a political stance with regard to these developments. One victim of the increased doubt of grand narratives is the idea of knowledge as a source of emancipation. If one rejects an essentialist foundation and believes that more than local resistance is needed, some kind of combination between postmodernism and critical theory may well provide the best remaining option. The great interest in debates between Habermasian and Foucauldian perspectives (e.g. Kelly 1995) and the frequency with which contemporary critical researchers draw upon Frankfurt School ideas, as well as Foucault, is promising (Alvesson and Deetz 2000). Although there are clearly tensions between the positions, the sceptical emancipatory project of the Frankfurt School, with its uncompromising cultural critique, and the Foucauldian interest in how power and knowledge are intertwined, and the insistence that seemingly progressive knowledge is dangerous, encourage an interesting blend of shared interests and productive dissensus.

The knowledge–power connection

Within postmodern writings power is treated far differently from in most writings on this topic. Many pomos address political issues in such a fragmentation- and micro-oriented way that issues of domination and force become neglected: every representation and all textual moves become political. Foucault is here different, and he is also the most explicit scholar among the pomos in his treatment of power – and I must remind myself and the reader that only a widely stretched use of the term postmodernism makes it possible to include Foucault. He is far more oriented towards incorporating a material referent in his treatment of various issues. For Foucault (1977, 1980; see also Clegg 1994) the power that is of interest is not the power that one possesses or acquires. Such appearances of power are the outcome of more fundamental power relations. Power resides in the discursive formation itself – the combination of a set of linguistic distinctions, ways of reasoning and material practices that together organize social institutions and produce particular forms of subjects. Power is intimately linked to knowledge. Whereas we normally think of knowledge as a resource for accomplishing something, knowledge for Foucault is 'a power over others, the power to define others' (Sarup 1988: 73). Knowledge orders and structures the world; the world is formed by the knowledge institutionalized within it. As mentioned, language in the Foucauldian position is less strictly focused than in many other variants of postmodernism.

The form of the subject and its way of relating to itself and its world is discursively constituted. Thus phenomena such as 'reason', 'madness', 'criminality', 'morality', 'sexuality', 'needs' and 'motives' appear not as natural objects that are part of man's way of being, but as artificial objects which have been constituted so that they appear at one and the same time as the object for certain forms of knowing and as the target of historically specific reform and regulation projects (Beronius 1991). 'Madness' is thus not something that exists 'out there' in the minds of particular individuals; it is something that has been brought to the fore during a particular period and with the help of various techniques and procedures as a special object of knowledge and attention (incarceration, treatment). The 'raw material' is there, in the shape of behaviour, gestures, biochemical processes and so on, but what is perceived as possession by evil spiris, the wrath of God or mental illness is the result of a process of differentiation, classification and positioning on material and epistemological dimensions.

Knowledge and knowing are thus central concepts in Foucault's thinking. He argues that 'power and knowledge directly imply one another, that there is no power relation without the correlative constitution of a field of knowledge, nor any knowledge that does not presuppose and constitute at the same time power relations' (Foucault 1980: 27). Various forms of knowledge are in the service of power and function as instruments of discipline, among other things by indicating what is normal and what is deviant. Accepted ideas in science and other societal institutions about what is natural, normal and reasonable thus help to regulate the individual's self-perception and behaviour. As Foucault sees it, knowledge and knowing cannot be separated from power and cannot indicate neutral insights. Power and knowing are parallel concepts, but not of course identical. His interest is in how 'games of truth' (a game is an ensemble of rules for the production of the truth) 'can put themselves in place and be linked to relationships of power' (Foucault 1984: 16). However, sometimes one gets the impression from Foucault's writing that the exercise of power and the advancement or application of knowledge are very intimately related. By creating normal curves, by classifying, codifying, calibrating and subdividing phenomena, it is possible both to handle these phenomena and to acquire (additional) knowledge about them. There is, as Habermas (1987: 53) summarizes Foucault's position, a 'constitutive connection between the human sciences and the practices of supervisory isolation' – at school, in psychiatry, correctional treatment, sex therapy, childcare, working life etc. Power refers to a certain coherence in social relations contingent upon, as well as making possible, the construction of a grid of intelligibility.

One of the most useful terms to arise from this has been Foucault's (1977) concept of discipline. The demarcations prescribe norms for behaviour supported by claims of knowledge. Training, work routines, self-surveillance and experts are discipline in that they provide resources for normalization. Normative experts in particular and the knowledge they create provide a cover for the arbitrary and advantaging discursive practices and facilitate normalization (Hollway 1984, 1991).

Foucault's project does not aim to separate truth (science, knowledge) from ideology (which is then roughly equated with something false or misleading, e.g. prejudice, distortions), but to reveal the mechanisms whereby the 'politics of truth' are constituted in a power–knowledge relation. 'Truth' to Foucault is always a social construction, which constitutes and is constituted by discursive practices in a particular historical period. Foucault is inspired by Nietzsche, who claimed that the will to know is intimately connected with the will to power. Knowledge lies at the root of the exercise of power, while the exercise of power also produces knowledge. To put it another way, power becomes a central dimension not only of knowledge supported by institutional practices, but also of institutional practices based on knowledge. Not only repressive knowledge but also 'supportive' and 'progressive' forms of knowledge are associated with power, and operate in discipline-imposing manner. Discipline in the sense of a branch of knowledge makes discipline in the sense of a system of correction and control possible, and vice versa. Walzer (1986) remarks that Foucault sometimes appears to be committed to nothing more than an elaborate pun on the word 'discipline'.

It is perhaps more easy to see the knowledge–power connection in those human sciences explicitly addressing or forming a basis for institutional practices: psychiatry, pedagogy, psychology, criminology etc. In all social science, the claim of knowledge implies the will to power. In the seemingly detached and neutral as well as – and in particular – 'progressive' forms of knowledge, social science includes an element of domination. All knowledge is, for Foucault, dangerous.

The same can be said about Foucault's and postmodernist knowledge. Its emphasis on the 'negative' – abstaining from claims of what exists and insisting on disordering and problematization without implying a better route to follow – makes pomo knowledge less fearsome than the seemingly harmless knowledge of more conventional researchers. However, for the latter group and for the (other) representatives of various institutions exercising disciplinary power, Foucault's knowledge is exceptionally dangerous. It challenges their claims and threatens to undermine their status.

Implications: research as resistance and indeterminacy

In later chapters I go more specifically into possible implications of taking the five themes reviewed more or less seriously in social studies. On a more general level, a few comments can be made here. The themes raised mean that the role of postmodern research is very different from the more traditional roles assigned to social science. It primarily serves to attempt to open up the indeterminacy that modern social science, everyday conceptions, routines and practices have closed off. The result is a kind of anti-positive knowledge (Knights 1992), i.e. it does not say how things are or how they should be best understood as much as it points at problematic understandings. It does not contribute to or accept Big theory – theoretical frameworks useful for structuring and explaining reality – or the delivery of robust empirical results about 'how things are' or 'the views of people', but points at the problems with these ambitions and with specific examples of realizing them.

Not all pomo sets of ideas encourage 'anti-positive' studies wholeheartedly. One can try to study discourse and say something about its operations. One can try to explore human subjects in terms of decentring and fragmentation – one can, for example, show how they are constituted by discourse, how subjects in specific settings shift subject positions and express different identities. Even if one accepts pomo authors' harsh critique of the idea of representation, one can find research tasks that are not that problematic in terms of representation. (I explain this in the next chapter.) A lot of qualitative work is not necessarily that vulnerable to the grand-narrative-is-not-any-longer-fashionable critique, as it focuses on local reality. The power/knowledge dilemma can perhaps partly be coped with by focusing on the knowledge claims of others – as Foucault does – but this means that social researchers set for themselves a fairly narrow agenda. The sceptical study of knowledge claims rather than phenomena about which we develop knowledge does not escape the power/knowledge issue, as this knowledge also builds upon a will to power. The effect of encouraging scepticism to and the decreased authority and legitimacy of scientific knowledge about psychic and social problems, gender inequality, racism etc. is not necessarily harmless.

Postmodernist ideas thus do not necessarily imply a negative or destructive position, but the major thrust of pomo work and the most apparent and possibly also novel and interesting implications go in the direction of radical doubt and questioning.

The primary 'anti-positive' methods following from postmodernism as here sketched are deconstruction, resistance readings and genealogy. These terms have been used in many different ways and I will here only give a brief presentation. *Deconstruction*, in Derrida's work, works primarily to critique the ideal of representation by recalling the suppressed term (the deferred term) that provides the system and thus allows the positive term to appear to stand for an existing object. When the suppressed term is given value the dependency of the positive term on the negative is shown and a third term is recovered, which shows a way of world making that is not dependent on the opposition of the first two (see Cooper 1989). Deconstruction stands for an analysis that shows how a discourse undermines the philosophy it asserts or the hierarchical oppositions on which it relies, by identifying the rhetorical operations behind the argument or key concept. The term 'deconstruction', of course, is used in a variety of ways. Morrow (1994: 246) notes that it is increasingly employed rather loosely to refer to any kind of rhetorical analysis critically illuminating naive, realistic and unreflexive conceptions of representation.

Resistance reading is less narrowly focused on terms. It both demonstrates the construction activity and provides indeterminacy based in the excess of the outside. The positive and the polar construction are both displayed as acts of domination, with subjectivity doing violence to the world and limiting itself in the process. In this move, conflicts that were suppressed by the positive are brought back to light and the conflictual field out of which objects are formed is recovered for creative redetermination – constant dedifferentiation and redifferentiation. Given the power of closure and the way it enters common sense and routines, especially in simulations, such rereadings require a particular form of rigour and imagination. The rereadings are formed out of a keen sense of irony, a serious playfulness. A good example of such readings is Calás and Smircich's (1988) account of a mainstream positivist journal article, where they start with the question 'why should we believe in this author?' and then point out the rhetorical tricks used to persuade the reader. Another interesting example is Sangren's (1992) critical review of *Writing Culture* (Clifford and Marcus 1986). Sangren, drawing upon Bourdieu (1979), uses their points about the politics of representation – intended to indicate the problems of ethnographies in mirroring cultures, as exemplified through important anthropological works – against themselves, showing how representations by Clifford, Marcus and their co-authors of earlier work in the discipline can be seen in terms of politics. Particular kinds of representations are used to create the impression that earlier works are flawed and that there is a large and open space for novel contributions from (and the career options of) the new heterodoxi (Clifford, Marcus *et al.*) and their claims to a more informed view on the politics of representation. Sangren's approach partly takes the opposite position from the texts it is discussing, meaning that it becomes more a 'conventional' opposition than a resistance reading, which avoids trying to take the opposite stance and convincing the reader about its position.

Genealogy is an approach closely associated with Foucault's ideas on power/knowledge. It takes an interest in historical study as a way of understanding the present. It is about locating traces of the present in the past. By tracing historical ruptures and changes we can understand how the present has been produced. The intersection of power, knowledge and the body is here central. Geneology denies that there are any fixed essences, underlying laws or logic: the world and its institutions and subjects are temporary products of power/knowledge practices characterized by discontinuity and arbitrariness (Burrell 1988).

The point of social science is not to get it right but to challenge guiding assumptions, fixed meanings and relations, and to reopen the formative capacity of human beings in relation to others and the world, qualities that Gergen (1978) and Astley (1985) displayed as essential to any important theory. As Sangren (1992) illustrates, challenges to dogma, fixed ideas and reopenings imply new dogmas, fixations and closures. Postmodernism is in no way immune to such implications (Alvesson and Sköldberg 2000: Chapter 5).

One outcome of the themes reviewed above – in particular the critique of the philosophy of presence and the loss of master narratives, but also hyperreality and the focus on resistance – is a strong current interest in experimenting with different styles. At the end of the day the research text is what matters, and it is here that a number of the tricky elements in research and knowledge development can be coped with. This idea is prominent in anthropology (Clifford and Marcus 1986; Marcus and Fisher 1986; Geertz 1988; Rose 1990) but also turns up in many other fields. Typically, 'realist' ways of writing are superseded or complemented by other styles: for example, ironic, self-ironic or impressionistic ones. In an investigation of texts in organizational culture, Jeffcutt (1993: 32) shows how they are 'distinguished by heroic quests for closure; being dominated by authors adopting representational styles that privilege epic and romantic narratives over tragic and ironic forms. These representational strategies expose an overriding search for unity and harmony that suppresses division and conflict.' Perhaps the inspiration to develop new ways of writing will turn out to be one of the most powerful and interesting contributions of postmodernism (see Chapter 7).

Summary

In this chapter important ideas associated with postmodernism and of the greatest relevance to method have been reviewed. These ideas concern:

1 The centrality of discourse – textuality – where the constitutive powers of language are emphasized and 'natural' objects are viewed as discursively produced.
2 Fragmented identities – emphasizing subjectivity as a process and the death of the individual, autonomous, meaning-creating subject, where the discursive production of the individual replaces the conventional 'essentialistic' understanding of people.
3 The critique of the idea of representation, where the undecidabilities of language take precedence over language as a mirror of reality and a means for the transport of meaning.
4 The loss of foundations and the power of grand narratives, where an emphasis on multiple voices and local politics is favoured over theoretical frameworks and large-scale political projects.
5 The power/knowledge connection, where the impossibility of separating power from knowledge is assumed and knowledge loses a sense of innocence and neutrality.

The ideas to various degree intersect with and/or are coupled to each other. The centrality of discourse is typically seen as the key explanation for the fragmentation of subjects. Foucault's ideas on knowledge/power are also connected. But the idea of loss of foundations and the lack of credibility of grand narratives can be accepted or rejected without any specific consequences for how one idea relates to the others. We are not necessarily talking about something that you either take or leave as a package. Postmodernism is not a tightly integrated field. The key figures of postmodernism do not see themselves as belonging to a specific camp, and most have distanced themselves from the label postmodernism.

Acceptance of (any, some or all of) these sets of ideas encourages a mainly 'anti-positive' stance. 'Going out to the natives and finding out what they are up to' is viewed with suspicion, and the alert pomo is typically ready to show the futility and danger of this kind of project. Deconstruction and resistance readings are the means by which the danger can be counteracted. These projects differ from critique by pointing at loopholes, contradictions and ambiguities in texts (claims), rather than arguing against a basic flaw in what is addressed and for a superior position following from the critique (e.g. classless society, gender equality, a more theoretically robust idea).

The reviewed ideas make radical challenges to social research. They seriously question not only neopositivism but also interpretive approaches. They give an important input to rethinking and thus may inspire novel ways of working. There is considerable potential for creativity, as the basic assumptions and lines of thinking encouraged differ radically from what is common in social studies, including qualitative work.

It is not, however, necessary to buy the sets of ideas fully or uncritically. The centrality of discourse may be addressed through the ascription of more or less muscle to discursive powers – we can assume that language and language use are the key elements of inquiry because it is difficult or impossible to get outside, without necessarily assuming that subjects are fully constituted by discourse. The fragmentation of identities may be viewed as an open question rather than accepted as a 'truth' or treated as a methodological doctrine. And so on. My point is that we can be inspired by careful consideration of these ideas without necessarily drawing upon them exclusively and heading towards a full-scale postmodernism. This is addressed in the remaining chapters.

It is, of course, important to meet pomo ideas with the same kind of questioning attitude that these ideas express against other fields, which was done in Chapter 2. For example, knowledge claiming fragmented identities and process subjectivity is neither more true nor less innocent than knowledge claiming the opposite. And this knowledge, although at odds with positivism-dominated social institutions, may well go hand-in-hand with the practices of advertising specialists and managers, favouring and producing flexible subjects, sensitive to new fashions and subtle forms of social control.

The forthcoming chapters connect to the five themes addressed in this chapter to various degrees. Chapter 5 treats the need to unpack categories and signs normally treated as having specific and general meanings. This relates to the centrality of discourse, the critique of representation and the critique of grand narratives. Chapter 6 deals with research practices, and these are related to fragmented identities and to some extent the power/knowledge connection, as well as the centrality of discourse and the critique of representation.

Note

1 Later I address a particular branch of study, discourse analysis, which uses the term discourse in a slightly different way.

4 Taking language seriously

Introduction

As elaborated in the previous chapter, postmodernists make language a key problematic for social research. There are certainly writers other than those labelled postmodernists that take this road, but typically not in an equally radical manner. Postmodernism has been salient in the linguistic turn of philosophy and social science, viewing language and text – rather than meaning, experience and social structure – as central. The linguistic turn has brought a 'double crisis' of representation and legitimation: the problem of how to describe, portray or measure objects of study and the problem of creating valid and trustworthy knowledge in an authoritative way (Denzin and Lincoln 1994: 11).

More and more people share the conviction that language is poorly understood if viewed as a simple medium for the mirroring of objective reality through the passive transport of data. Language use, in any social context, is active, processual and outcome-oriented. Language is used to persuade, enjoy, engage, discipline, criticize, express feelings, clarify, unite, do identity work and so on. Language is also context-dependent. The same statement may have different meanings. For instance, the statement 'it is 9 o'clock' might be a rebuke ('you are late'), a signal to start a meeting, a response to a question or preparation for the coordination of action by the synchronization of time, depending on the situation.

In a sense the problem of using language to map an external world is obvious and ought to be broadly recognized. It is even possible that 'everyone' in academia knows that language is not a simple medium for the transport of meaning. At least 'everyone' knows that language is complicated. But working and writing *as if* language is a medium for the transport of meaning seems to be common in social science. Some researchers insist on the use of literal language. They wish to avoid metaphors or other modes of expression that seem to deviate from the ideal of making possible correspondence between research language and empirical reality. Or, less extremely, they want to limit the use of metaphors and other tropes to the initial, generative phase of research (Pinder and Bourgeois 1982; Tsoukas 1991). In almost all empirical research, the research design and the research text are developed and written as if language is strictly controlled by the researcher, a simple tool through which he or she mirrors the world. This is most obvious in questionnaire studies, as they presuppose that the respondent understands the formulated questions exactly as intended.

The great majority of qualitative work, however, follows a similar logic. The difference is typically that qualitative research takes a greater interest in the level of meaning and seeks to provide a space for research subjects to express their opinions through their own words. By being able to choose the words themselves, the research subjects are presumed to communicate their feelings, thoughts, values, experiences and observations in a way that renders their 'inner worlds' accessible to the researcher. Interview statements, for example, are seen as reflections of these 'inner worlds'. Language and language use represent something other than themselves.

The researcher, following this mirror logic, collects data and builds a case on these data, with the potential exclusion of material that is considered irrelevant or of low quality. In qualitative research the researcher presents selected portions in order to prove the case. In quantitative studies statistical data and correlations are presented as if they offered a window to conditions outside the questionnaire filling situation. Given methodologically competent research practice, the language use of informants (questionnaire respondents) is viewed as a reliable indicator of the issues in which the researcher is interested.

There are relatively few examples of studies that do not follow this logic, apart from specific streams such as discourse analysis (developed below), although in qualitative work researchers sometimes make more interpretations around the language used by interviewees. The most obvious examples are studies focusing explicitly on language and language use in social contexts – these are addressed below. In a questionnaire-based study of work satisfaction and social commitment among US and Japanese workers, Lincoln and Kalleberg (1985) found that the former scored higher. This is obviously not in line with conventional wisdom, so the authors speculate as to whether the responses to these issues reflect cultural conventions of expression rather than the true level of satisfaction and commitment. For once, language use triggers some doubts on the mirror view. In the rest of the article, such doubts do not surface. This is normal practice in research work, at least as it appears in empirical papers in leading journals. This practice is, as is elaborated below, deeply problematic. There is, for example, reason to believe that norms for expression and language use do affect responses to questionnaires and interviews, even when the results live up to expectations.

The present chapter should be read against the background of the continuing domination of the language-as-mirror practice and the challenge of postmodernism. In pragmatic contexts, such as the composition and use of train timetables and the counting of people, the view of language as a mirror of reality has practical advantages and functions. Here it makes little sense to emphasize a critique of representation. In social sciences that study complex phenomena constituted within a specific vocabulary, the situation is difficult.

As mentioned in previous chapters, pomo may lead down many routes. One extreme is 'pessimistic' or 'anti-positive' and leads to deconstructions or resistance readings. The other extreme is more joyful and 'free' and encourages experimentation with style and the use of literary means of expression (Rosenau 1992 writes about 'sceptical' and 'affirmative' postmodernism). These diverse and rather extreme implications of postmodernism do not exhaust all the responses to the problems of language. Most current versions of postmodernist methodology – to the extent that one can use such an expression – do not really consider the possibility of a careful study of language use as a comparatively rigorous interpretive approach. Instead of the negative (although sometimes healthy) deconstructive search for the failures of texts to make the points they are claiming to make ('nothing goes') or the positive, affirmative, happy and free-spirited pluralism ('anything goes'), one may study discourses, e.g. language use in social contexts, in ways that are empirically oriented in not too unconventional ways but that also avoid or at least reduce the problems of representation emphasized by pomos.

In this chapter I treat some versions of a language-sensitive approach to social research, taken relatively seriously pomo critiques of conventional views and exploring the methodological implications. One important input beside postmodernism is discourse analysis. While postmodernism can be said to represent a philosophical–theoretical version of the linguistic turn, discourse analysis can be seen as a behavioural–observational version of this turn.

The linguistic turn in the social sciences

Texts and language have come to the forefront in social research in several ways. We will point at three significant areas: *the language itself*, *language in use* and *the production of research texts*.

One focus is on *language itself*, its very nature and the possibilities and impossibilities that it brings with it in terms of the representation and power effects. Against a conventional view of language as a transparent medium for the transport of meaning, critics have emphasized its ambiguous, metaphorical, context-dependent and active nature. Language is a system of distinction, building upon the repression of hidden meanings, postmodernists (poststructuralists) argue (Cooper 1989; Deetz 1992). Efforts to say something definite, to establish how things 'are', rely on shaky foundations, postmodernists claim, and ought to be deconstructed. This includes showing the false robustness of, the contradictions in and the repressed meanings of statements. Other authors emphasize how language and understanding are fused with, and indeed rely on, metaphors. Language, as a vital part not only of our cognitions, but also of our basic way of relating to the world, is metaphorical (Brown 1977; Morgan 1980, 1983b). We understand and relate to our workplace by using metaphors such as iron cage, family, jungle, an internal labour market, a career platform etc.

A second focus is on *language in use*, e.g. how it works in the real world, as studied by discourse analysis and similar orientations. Language is viewed as an empirical phenomenon that we can study, e.g. in the accounts and conversations produced by people in various contexts. Empirical work calls for accessible phenomena. If the representational capacity in language is in doubt or denied, language use is what is left as a robust and reliably replicated empirical phenomenon. The productive, functional, interactive and context-dependent nature of all language use – including research interviews – is believed to be central. While this focus to some extent draws upon the general critique of a mirror view of language, the interest is not in producing philosophical investigations of the nature of language, but in studying social practices – language use – in social contexts.

A third important focus is on the research process, and in particular the *production of texts*. Instead of a research report being viewed as just the writing up of research results, the construction of a credible text is viewed as an extremely complex enterprise. As such, it stands in an ambiguous relationship to any observations or experiences of the social reality perceived by the researcher. This focus has been most pronounced among anthropologists and other ethnographers (Clifford and Marcus 1986), but has achieved a wider impact and affected many other areas of social studies (e.g. Jeffcutt 1993; van Maanen 1995). While fieldwork has traditionally been viewed as the crucial aspect of ethnographic research, the focus has changed, so that textwork is now seen as being critical and as deserving the focus of attention (Geertz 1988). Genre, rhetoric and style have been brought to the fore. Reflection upon how a persuasive, authoritative account is put together is a vital part of ethnographic studies, in particular, and also of research, in general (Clifford and Marcus 1986; Geertz 1988; van Maanen 1988; Watson 1994). There are obvious parallels between the researcher's and the informant's/interviewee's situation: the production of an account is a complex accomplishment and needs to be understood as such. Accounts are, as stated above, more than just simple mirrors of experiences, observations and insights relating to the world out there, or even personal, subjective reality (feelings, meanings).

Postmodernist texts frequently draw attention to the first and third of these foci, and so, then, does this book as well. The second focus is often neglected. Although it may fall outside the core of pomo ideas it is nevertheless worth taking seriously as a response to some of the problems it raises.

Postmodernism and discourse analysis

Conventional conceptions of social reality and its relation to language, which is precisely what is at stake, are challenged not only by ideas stemming from the domain of 'speculative' thought, such as pomo philosophy. Based on observations in 'natural settings', students of linguistic behaviour conclude that:

1 People do not use language primarily to make accurate representations of perceived objects but rather to *accomplish* things.
2 The variety of means employed to achieve these accomplishments are vastly underestimated in conventional research (Potter and Wetherell 1987).

Both postmodernists and discourse analysts point out a central weakness in the conventional understanding of the relation between language and social reality: that it privileges the idea that language *represents* reality. The postmodern argument highlights the theoretical problems with this view: for example, how can one know that the word A truthfully represents the thing T or that an account of one's attitude to 'foreigners' or 'sex equality', or motives for purchasing a particular car, say something valid about true attitudes on a specific topic? Discourse analysts show that the emphasis on language's representational capacities conceals and obfuscates the more productive question of its creative and functional capacities, i.e. what language use actually accomplishes. The word A may or may not represent the thing T, but why is the word A invoked in the first place, and what does it accomplish?

However, few, if any, have considered the thrust of the combined argument of postmodernism and discourse analysis (DA), and its full consequences for methodology, empirical research and fieldwork practices. In particular, the profound problems with a traditional view of language – that words represent and correspond to objects, whether people's inner life (intentions, cognitions, values, feelings) or external life (social practices, interactions, relations) – have far-reaching implications for methodology and research. This chapter explores and elaborates these consequences. It also suggests principles for research practices, consistent with and informed by significant versions of the 'linguistic turn' in social analysis.

Before we move on some words of clarification of the word discourse are needed. Discourse in discourse analysis means something partly different from discourse as the term is used by Foucault, and many other popular uses of 'discourse' mean something different again (Alvesson and Kärreman 2000). Discourse is a highly fashionable word that is used in a variety of ways. In DA the task is to study discourse as texts and talk in social practices. The focus is not on language as an abstract entity, such as a lexicon and set of grammatical rules (in linguistics), a system of differences (in structuralism) or a set of rules for transforming statements (in Foucauldian genealogies). Instead it is on the medium for interaction: analysis of discourse becomes analysis of what people do with language in specific social settings (Potter 1997: 146). Discourse is used 'to cover all spoken interaction, formal and informal, and written text of all kinds. So when we talk of "discourse analysis" we mean analysis of any of these forms of discourse' (Potter and Wetherell 1987: 6). In order to distinguish discourse in this sense from what Foucault means by the term, I will talk about Discourse or Big Discourse. Foucault is, in opposition to DA, less exclusively focused on language use in micro settings, and refers to broader, institutionalized ideas or reasoning patterns with a material practice referent and with power to define and structure part of social reality. In the present chapter, Foucault's ideas are *not* in focus.

Discourse analysis, as described by Potter and Wetherell (1987), proposes a distinct research programme focusing on language use in specific contexts (a related approach, such as conversational analysis, is even more specific; see Silverman 1993). This approach is empirical in the sense that it works with material that lends itself to representation, aims for rigour and pays attention to detail. One may even refer to this research orientation as 'hyper-empirical'. Interviews, for example, are viewed as occasions for the study of interview behaviour, and not as tools for the advancement of the Truth about something else. Accounts are recorded in detail, presented carefully to the reader and studied as accounts. We can here talk about a strict *discursivist* research orientation. This language-in-use focused approach does not place validity and reliability burdens that the material cannot carry. The ideal is that empirical material will be treated for what it is, nothing else. Statements in an interview are, for example, empirical material that say something about talk in a particular social situation. They are not indicators of what may or may not be applicable in other situations (e.g. how the interviewee expresses feelings about marriage or how she 'leads' her 'subordinates' at work).

Are DA and postmodernism similar or competing intellectual orientations? Postmodernism is, of course, a much broader and more mixed stream, and addresses a whole set of issues from philosophical points of view. DA is a specialized research orientation and draws only to a limited extent explicitly and strongly on philosophical thought – although postmodernism, including Foucault, and Wittgenstein are sources of inspiration. DA researchers emphasize more empirical observation in social settings. The interest in the details of the text and the claim of accurate representation means that postmodernists can accuse DA, together with other streams, of masking 'the unstable ambiguities of linguistically communicated meaning' and hiding 'the overwhelming absent presence of the researcher and her/his modernist assumptions' (Scheurich 1997: 63). Nevertheless, DA is less seriously guilty of these vices than most other methods. DA and pomo share a sceptical stance towards the idea that language mirrors the world. Thus, in this context it is proper to call it a behavioural–observational version of the linguistic turn. This perspective also requires that we rethink dominant and widespread assumptions of how language and social phenomena interact, not only in our professional vocabularies, but also in our ordinary lives. Other versions of this behavioural-observational linguistic turn are ethnomethodology and conversational analysis (Silverman 1993).

Having thus briefly situated DA in relation to postmodernism, we can now go into DA in somewhat more depth.

Discourse analysis, language use and meaning

A focus on language in use

Although discourse analysts may differ in focus and approach, most are critical of and reject what Potter and Wetherell (1987) call the 'realist' model of language. Indeed, discourse analysts claim that the realist model of language is harmful to our understanding of what is going on in the social world:

> people's language use is much more variable than indicated by the widely held 'realistic' descriptive model of language – which treats discourse as a relatively unambiguous pathway to actions, beliefs, or actual events. Researchers who presuppose the realistic mode assume that when people describe the same event, action, and belief their accounts will, broadly speaking, be consistent. And, for methodological purposes, they will take consistent accounts to mean that events did happen as described . . . There are two basic problems with this. First, consistency in accounts is often overstated by the various techniques commonly used by psychologists . . . Second, there is no reason to suppose that consistency in accounts is a sure indicator of descriptive validity. This consistency may be a product of accounts sharing the same function; that is, two people may put their discourse together in the same way because they are doing the same thing with it.
>
> (Potter and Wetherell 1987: 34)

Potter and Wetherell (1987) claim that the failure of scholars to pay serious attention to variations in people's accounts is a result of particular analytical strategies. These strategies have favoured the restriction, categorization and selective interpretation of utterances. *Restriction* means that scientists 'lock up' subjects by applying various techniques which force them into certain reaction patterns, by choosing one of a few alternative prestructured options as a response to a fixed question or statement. This is the case in most experiments, questionnaires and to some extent structured interviews. The subject is obliged to adapt to the set-up of the situation. Variation is prevented and ambiguity avoided – at least at the point of the response of the studied subjects (which become objects for the researcher).

Gross categorization means that all accounts are referred to various broader categories, which are then treated as the primary empirical material. The fact that different evaluators may refer a particular utterance to the same category – a criterion of validity in conventional analysis – does not stop important distinctions and variations within a certain category from being missed. Similar evaluations may also arise because researchers share certain preconceived ideas or linguistic conventions (contingent upon paradigms, school education or cultural background), and may reflect shared biases rather than do justice to the empirical material.

Selective interpretation means that on the basis of predetermined ideas the scientist structures an account in such a way that a potential multiplicity of meanings is neglected in favour of what is regarded as a 'primary' meaning. It may also mean that such a meaning is found 'behind' the variety, ambiguity and inconsistency of the statements in the accounts: the researcher believes that the subject probably means 'this'.

The case of cross-categorization as a technique for attaining consistency is instructive on how vital aspects of the workings of language in its context are repressed. Using content analysis (focusing on the frequency of words in texts) as an example, Potter and Wetherell claim that the procedure inherent in content analysis *produces* consistency within informants' accounts, rather than discovers it, since it cannot deal with the functional and constructive aspects of language use:

> Function is a problem in content analysis because of the difficulty of dealing with the sheer subtlety of a situation where participants may be constructively using their language to produce different sorts of effects. As ethnomethodologists have emphasized, when a person is trying to persuade, for example, part of their effectiveness may well depend on producing their talk in a way that conceals that it is an attempt to persuade; what could be more persuasive than the 'mere description of the facts'? Context is a problem because, if the meaning of a section of discourse depends on the contexts in which it appears, the criteria for what counts as an instance in a particular coding category may be impossibly complicated.
> (Potter and Wetherell 1987: 41)

The model of language advocated by Potter and Wetherell (and others) stresses that language is in itself active and constructive. It is stressed that language is used for a variety of functions, with a variety of consequences. The positivist dream of a pure observational language is not only pointless and misguided but also contradicts everyday use of language. Discourse analysts propose that language is constructed in a manner that allows the same phenomena to be described in a number of different ways. Consequently, considerable variations in accounts should be expected.

Discourse analysts emphasize that the point is not to distinguish between 'accurate' or 'literal' accounts and 'misguided' or 'rhetorical' accounts, since there are no foolproof means of distinguishing between 'fact' and 'fiction'. The point is to take an interest in the various ways people use language, not only in the accounts they describe, but also in the realities their accounts attempt to produce (or reproduce), and in the realities to which their accounts respond.

The study of discourse and the absence of meaning

The challenge is to treat language and the use of language seriously, but without necessarily constraining oneself to the strict focus of discursivism. The level of talk constitutes an important area of research, but any study remains incomplete without the incorporation and consideration of the level of meaning, although the interpretive and pomo views on meaning clearly differ. In one sense, the level of meaning is always present in any attempt to make sense of what people are doing or saying, since we cannot see something without seeing it *as* something (Asplund 1970; Geertz 1973). Seeing people engaged in verbal exchange as talking to each other is in itself an interpretation – and this remains true if one chooses to see them as carrying out a particular practice. In this sense, the level of meaning is not absent in discursivistic research. It is only under-investigated.

The meanings produced by the researcher to make sense of the phenomena under investigation are but one aspect of the level of meaning. In the context of empirical research, the meanings produced by the people belonging to the field are perhaps of even greater significance. To consider the level of meaning implies – apart from being aware that all observations are to some extent also interpretations (Geertz 1973) – an interest in what people mean by the expressions they use and how they understand the communication of others. It also implies an interest in what meaning they ascribe to the practices they, and others, deploy.

Taking the level of meaning seriously includes efforts to figure out what yardstick the 'natives' are using in deciding what stands for consistent and inconsistent vocabulary use. And, in terms of the practices employed by the 'natives', any serious interest in the level of meaning includes an attempt to figure out how they make sense of what they are doing – or at least an effort to establish to what extent accounts make sense to 'natives', and what sense there is.

Discourse analysis and related orientations demonstrate a certain 'thinness', because they do not seriously consider cultural meanings. Studies on the discourses deployed by 'natives' in social settings may reveal the ways in which people use language to produce certain effects. But, as long as one restricts oneself to the level of talk, those who are actually talking become curiously fugitive. It is as if an utterance produces other utterances through people, thus inverting the conventional understanding of things: language becomes the agent and people become the medium. This is not necessarily a bad understanding of the relation between people and language – as poststructuralist writers argue (Weedon 1987). It still is a relatively fresh one. However, it is a 'thinner' way of looking at twitches and winks, for example, since it cannot account for the difference between a twitch and a wink, other than as words that produce different kinds of discourse. The practical meaning and, thus, the effects become lost. On all other kinds of possible effects, those dedicated to the level of talk must remain silent.

A strict focus on language use as a methodological approach thus has some problems. In particular, such research seems to have a limited research agenda. It also seems to avoid questions of meaning that make the understanding of discourses and conversations problematic. At the same time, the critique of the overreliance on accounts and what subjects can communicate in, for example, interviews or the 'naturally occurring settings' of traditional approaches indicates great difficulties in the study of meanings. Problems in accessing these meanings contributed to Silverman's movement from social phenomenology (Silverman 1970) to conversational analysis (Silverman 1993, 1997). How can we cope with this dilemma, so crucial to present and forthcoming social research? In other words, how can we seriously consider meaning and pursue a broader research agenda, and at the same time avoid naive romanticism and ensure that a sophisticated methodological awareness of language guides research? The sections that follow deal with how the trade-off can be accomplished in a productive way.

A reconstruction of research options in social studies

The various linguistic turns discussed in the previous section proceed from different points of departures and research interests. Consequently, they arrive at different implications for social research. They all offer powerful arguments against a naive view of language as a mirror of an external social reality or as clues to someone's inner world – in terms of either shared meanings or personally held beliefs, ideas and world views. Postmodernists and others argue, from a philosophical–speculative point of view, against the assumption that language is a simple medium for the context-free mirroring of reality, under the control of the analytical powers of the researcher. Discourse analysis, as an observational–behavioural project, shows that in specific uses of language, accounts do not operate as vehicles of transformation of information. Each of the critiques motivates a revision of the conventional understandings of social research. Taken together, they provide strong reasons for changes to points of departure, methodologies and research practices. The reviewed directions diverge, however, in their preferences. Here, I explore three potentially fruitful paths for language-conscious social studies: two of these I label *grounded fictionalism* and *data constructionism*, which are present in all current research efforts to one degree or another. The third is a modest attempt at synthesis, particularly tuned to the specific demands of social research, of the strict view on *discursivism* proposed by DA and similar orientations and a somewhat broader consideration of wider social terrains. I label this version *discursive pragmatism*.

As previously stated, I discuss the approaches from an 'empirical' point of view.[1] This means a focus on other people's realities (including linguistic behaviour) used as input in research efforts, and the extent to which the approaches accept the distinctions between different realities as valid. Put another way, the approaches are analysed with consideration of whether they accept the distinction between *first-order concepts* (a research vocabulary which consists of the vocabulary of a particular group) and *second-order concepts* (which consist of the researchers' vocabulary on the vocabulary of the group under study; see Geertz 1973), and what they make of it.

Grounded fictionalism

While discursivistic research such as discourse analysis responds to the complexities of language with a rigorous empirical research agenda aiming to explore phenomena in detail, others see the implications leading in the opposite direction. This is generally the case among people within the postmodernist camp. Researchers within this orientation often have not much to say on the subject matter and produce only general and somewhat vague ideas about method and empirical work (Rosenau 1992). As noted above, they are often 'against' – they favour deconstruction rather than construction etc. The deconstructionists, like discourse analyst, look at the details of a text. But, unlike discourse analysts, they tend to bracket its social effects. They favour playfulness and imagination over rigour and empirical detail (e.g. Martin 1990). They sometimes view statements on the emergence of texts as another text, with no particular privilege or trustworthiness in terms of revealing the truth of how the original text emerged.

Other researchers, even less interested in the details and fragility of the text, see language as a medium so different from other phenomena – out there in the form of institutions and practices or 'in there' in the form of psychological or cultural phenomena (meanings) – that the 'empirical' (social reality 'out there') cannot really be accessed by research. From this point of view, it is pointless and meaningless to claim that language can communicate and reveal empirical realities. All texts are literary accomplishments. To the extent that empirical studies exist, they exist as a literary genre. 'Empirical studies' are, thus, structured and put together after the canons of the genre, and not after (mythical) empirical findings, which are – and must be – textual artefacts anyway.

To uncouple the text from 'social reality' may be labelled *grounded fictionalism*. A move away from empirical concerns – as traditionally understood – may be unavoidable if one emphasizes the inability of language to say something definite about something else (Gergen and Gergen 1991). Traditional empirical work becomes solely a matter of receiving inspiration, not of anchoring theoretical ideas, concepts and interpretations in empirical material. The researcher may offer ideas, images and vocabularies, for example, that are useful for practitioners in understanding and taking pragmatic action in their worlds. Empirical work – interviewing, observing – aiming to say something 'beyond language use' and/or deconstruction may, then, be undertaken, but will not lead to valid representations of reality. Instead, free and creative ideas, indicating multiple realities, and a plurality of possible ways of relating to these realities, becomes central.

One version of this is 'ethnographic fiction', which means that all the elements of a narrative providing the empirical material are based on the experiences and perceptions of the ethnographer, but their arrangement into a particular story is an effect of his or her literary arrangements. Rhetoric and invention are crucial aspects of text production and thus of the research process and result as a whole. The study is empirically based, but not in any strict way, and the researcher applies few restrictions in writing up the text (Watson 2000). This kind of approach is a mix of 'truthful' and 'invented'. The first element concerns the empirical details – 'the events, emotions and insights are all ones derived from observations and experiences gained by the writer as an ethnographic researcher' (Watson 2000: 490). The fiction part relates to how they are combined, and the entire writing project and the rhetorics involved refer to the fiction part. The difference between this and conventional efforts to follow the data strictly can be debated. For a postmodernist, the idea that the ingredients of the story flow from observations and experiences is not easy to swallow, and Watson also rejects the pomo idea of the collapse of all meaning, and views the purpose of ethnography as being to 'advance our understanding of human signifying practices' (Watson 2000: 500).

The ideas of grounded fictionalism in various ways partially respond to postmodernist concerns – in recognizing the gap between language and extralinguistic reality or the impossibility of writing ethnographies that reflect the object of study in a non-fictional way – but still insist that the idea of doing social research says something 'positive' and grounded about the area addressed.

Data-constructionist research

The complexities of the construction of data and the profound fictional elements in research text production remain, even if one tries to adopt a more ambitious attitude to 'data' than that represented by grounded fictionalism. From a moderate postmodernist position, there is, despite the best of intentions, a rather loose relationship between what goes on 'out there' and the 'data' produced by the researcher. There is also a loose relationship between these 'data' and the final research text. In this approach, empirical material is considered important but not as important as what is done with it. Interview accounts, observations and texts, being part of the social phenomenon studied, do provide strong inputs to the research process and the results, but all these empirical materials are shaped and formed in a rich variety of production processes, where frameworks, the researcher, vocabularies etc. mould the empirical material in complex ways. Qualities other than the robustness of data and the research design are important for judging the value of the research. This approach to research may be referred to as data-constructionist research. The idea is to take the problems of representation, and also social reality outside language, into consideration. The nature of language and the dynamics and politics of language as used in social settings, such as interviews and (observable) 'naturally' occurring situations, mean that the empirical stuff is downplayed, but also that space is made for relatively bold interpretations of social phenomena.

One illustration of this is the idea that root metaphors are basic starting points and interpretive lenses that guide research (Morgan 1980, 1997). In order to relate to the world, structure our perceptions and make sense of them we need to form gestalts. We do so in a metaphorical way. We think of society and social institutions as organisms, theatres etc., and these metaphors give empirical material a particular meaning, determined as much by the metaphor as anything 'out there' offering input for the metaphor-driven structuring and interpretation process. Data constructivism means that data are partly, not totally, projections of the metaphors consciously or unconsciously used. If one switches metaphor – say, that schools are seen primarily not as mechanisms for learning and development but as sites for social control or as strange arrangements built around exotic rituals – this leads to attention to different themes in research, but the same data get new meanings. The different metaphors create very different views of the object of study.

Data constructivism thus emphasizes the two ingredients – empirical material and the messy, often half-conscious and imagination-dependent use of metaphors that give the theory and research question a particular under-tone – in different, sometimes hard to define, ways interfering with (helping but also constraining) the research process.

Discursive pragmatism

Research may, however, also be conducted in a way that does not ask that much of language as a medium for the transport of knowledge about social phenomena. One implication might be that the area of analysis is limited to issues relatively close to the specific, empirical 'core situation', e.g. the inter-view or questionnaire-filling behaviour. Much observation also has talk as core empirical material.

The study of these situations may be carried out through 'discursivistic' orientations such as discourse and conversation analysis. These are method-ologically robust, strict and constrained at the expense of capacity to address broader themes. One may consider a somewhat extended and less myopic version that allows for the communicative capacities in language and not only for the study of its constructive and functional aspects. This approach can be labelled *discursive pragmatism*. The major interest is in discursively produced outcomes, such as texts and conversations. However, such an approach also allows interpretations beyond this specific level. The study of discourses (i.e. specific verbal or written accounts) provides a means of illuminating issues 'close' to discourses, e.g. espoused values, attitudes taken or taboos (indicated, for example, by people being reluctant to make state-ments on certain issues), or certain practices in which language use is cen-tral, e.g. teaching, counselling, managing, childrearing or quarrelling.

Discursive pragmatism acknowledges, given the plasticities of language, the multiplicities of meaning and complexities of social practices, but still aims to say something about broader patterns in the interface between lan-guage use and discourse-constituted patterns of meaning. It is not so much the details in a micro-context as the broader orientation of language use in a somewhat broader context that is studied. Compared to discursivism, this means that social relevance and applicability are bought at the expense of methodological rigour. A case study illustrates this approach later in this chapter.

Comments and comparison

Of the three sketched positions on how to relate to empirical material as conventionally understood, i.e. what people are up to outside 'texts', the first is more in line with pomo thinking and the third is somewhat at odds with it. The data-constructivist approach may be what softliners among pomos favour or at least accept, without feeling inclined to use the anti-modernist, pejorative vocabularies. Discursive pragmatism is not strongly related to postmodernism but is a possible response, in that it recognizes the centrality of language and is careful about speculation about social reality or meanings beyond language use. It also has a somewhat freer attitude to research and writing than DA, which is more in line with pomo thinking. As this chapter partly aims to add to the pomo–method interface the study of language use as a productive way forward – both for pomos caught in a text interest and obsession that prevents them from relating to a world outside texts (or a textual understanding) and for social researchers taking the pomo problematics seriously – the next section continues exploring DA and discursive pragmatism.

Implications for research practices in social studies

Most qualitative studies in social science are studies of talk in various situations. This is most evident in interviews. However, most observations in ethnographic and participant observation studies also focus on various types of talk between social inhabitants – studies of psychotherapy, education and leadership mean, for example, studying interactions between subjects (therapist and client, leader and subordinates etc.) in which talk is central. One may observe the therapist (teacher, leader) or the client (student, subordinate) in non-interactive situations, but arguably interactive situations exhibit more and richer aspects of the phenomenon targeted.

There are few occasions and events accessible to the social researcher that are not infused, ingrained and embedded in talk. There are even fewer occasions where research results are not converted into textual artefacts, which brings us to the level of analysis construction. From Potter and Wetherell's (1987) point of view, the production of scientific discourse – such as texts on social behaviour – is as functional and constructive in its character as other, and less sacrosanct, types of discourse. To repeat, one of the key points of postmodernism and related streams is that, contrary to popular opinion, research texts are not – and cannot be – objective and clinical reports of 'how the facts are'. Instead, they engage in the persuasive construction of 'facts' through powerful modes of construction, where the use of the voice of the clinically objective researcher is one powerful – although not necessarily defendable – mode (Watson 1994; van Maanen 1995). The impression sought after, and created, is that competent mastery of the rules of science – in combination with the use of a disciplined talent for innovative and analytical thinking – produces the result. This is made possible through the skillful denial of any relevance of the pre-structured understanding of the researcher, his or her class, gender, nationality, his or her paradigmatic, theoretical and political preferences and biases, the vocabularies employed, the dynamics of the research process, the expectations and more or less politically skilled operations of the informants, the more or less arbitrary decisions about informants, the selective presentation of evidence and rhetorical tricks and conventions of writing (Alvesson and Sköldberg 2000; see also Figure 1.2).

At the level of fieldwork, approaches informed by the linguistic turn demonstrate the importance of *not* understanding the conversations the researcher engages in and overhears in empirical situations to be unproblematic providers of 'facts' and 'truths'. They refer neither to 'objective' phenomena nor to people's beliefs and attitudes. Potter and Wetherell (1987) show, for example, the potential in remaining sensitive to the productive, constructive and contextual character of language use, and provide some clues as to how to deal with this in a systematic fashion and how to explore empirical variation and vital aspects of micro-reality. They encourage an interest not just in how language in various ways inscribes order under a pretence to represent, but also in what language use *does* in specific social situations. On the level of analysis, DA presents a framework that might be considered instructive for the study of viable 'truth-effects' through the tracking of statements and responses in verbal interaction. It also, for sure, presents an argument that adds more fuel to unresolved debates concerning the discipline's epistemological status.

DA and other forms of critique of the realistic approach call for more caution in drawing conclusions from accounts and acts of speech about other social phenomena – when such inferences are not simply rejected. On the other hand, we see no reason for distancing ourselves altogether from the possibility of interpreting meanings in utterances – meanings that go beyond the utterances themselves and their micro-context. (We have in mind cultural and personal meanings as distinct from the meaning in accounts, i.e. fairly stable meanings rather than temporary meanings in specific statements.) DA tends to emphasize excessively the importance of the inconsistency, variation and context dependency of acts of speech. Meaning is fluid and varies with language use. One might even say that Potter and Wetherell (1987) are guilty of the 'sins' they ascribe to other approaches, namely selective interpretation, since they tend to prefer interpretations that show the inconsistent, variant and contextual qualities of language use. It is indeed difficult not to privilege a particular line of interpretation.

As a counterweight to the comparatively naive, 'realistic' approaches, which are common in much natural science-imitating social research and also in much interpretive research, this is justified. At the same time, inconsistency and variation are an expression of the yardstick used. A detailed study of utterances or word usage immediately reveals the overwhelming multiplicity of meanings. But it is also worthwhile to draw attention to the *relative* capacity of language to (equivocally) convey insights, experiences and factual information, as well as the *pragmatic* value of emphasizing its capacity to clarify phenomena. Criticism of a naive view of representation does not motivate a categorical rejection of the communicative powers of language, a move that easily is read as destructive. As Rorty, in a critique of Lyotard (1984), puts it: 'For language no more has a nature than humanity does; both have only a history. There is as much unity or transparency of language as there is willingness to converse rather than fight' (Rorty 1992: 66).

I would like to emphasize the *partial* ability of language to convey something beyond itself, in contrast to the view held by discourse analysts and postmodernists, as well as in contrast to the 'realists'. I would also like to stress the *variation* in the relative consistency and value of different utterances as clues to phenomena other than repertoires of language usage. Variations in accounts, in research interviews, for example, do not necessarily mean that they do not point at something 'outside' the contexts of the acts of speech. They may indicate an ambiguous and inconsistent social reality or a varied, even contradictory, set of beliefs or values actually 'held' by interview persons or actors expressing themselves in 'natural' settings. They may indicate nuances by pointing at different aspects of complex issues rather than serving to illustrate the unreliable nature of accounts.

This means recognizing the potential – however imperfect, mediated and partial – capacity in accounts to indicate realities beyond the situational and functional aspects of language use. It also means remaining reflective and sceptical, but not categorical, about the discursive level in research. It is, thus, essential to consider the extent to which various utterances can appropriately be treated simply as utterances, and how far they can be used as the starting point for more extensive, speculative interpretations of other conditions. When such interpretations are made, it is important to:

1 Think carefully about the extent to which an account may be treated as an indication of something else, corresponding to, or telling us something reliable about, social phenomena such as behaviours, relations, events, ideas, values, emotions and intentions.
2 Indicate why there are good reasons to treat the account in this way.
3 Be explicit about the speculative element involved.

The reason for going beyond the discursive level might, for example, be that a specific account points at other phenomena in a logical and coherent way. It might be that it refers to phenomena that are not 'too complex' or open to an endless variety of representations. It might also be that observations provide some support for the account, and that the account appears to be perceptive and insightful, thus adding depth to the understanding of a phenomenon 'out there'. In the absence of these or other good reasons for viewing accounts as valid indicators of 'something else', what remains is to take the accounts seriously, as such. As discourse analysts have shown, this may not be as bad as it sounds.

Focusing on language or using language as an indicator

The problem of representation as relative

Instead of treating the problem of representation as an absolute, categorically assuming that we cannot represent anything whatsoever (except, perhaps, texts), *we can see the problem of representation as relative and contingent*. There are many situations and phenomena where representation does not seem to be very problematic and where researchers might be wise to treat the relationship between a signifier or a combination of signifiers as saying something about social reality. The statement that this text was originally written with some sort of writing device (in my case, a Macintosh word processor) is probably acceptable by most people irrespective of cultural or theoretical background, and the value of emphasizing the undecidabilities of the signifier 'Macintosh word processor' seems to be limited in most situations where people use it. This is probably also acceptable for those rejecting a correspondence view of language. The same goes for statements such as: 'the use of condoms may protect people against AIDS or sex diseases', 'the Nazis murdered millions of Jews, Romanies and other people', 'penicillin is more effective than prayers for a number of diseases' and 'the Old Testament is not an instruction manual for how to play bridge'. The representational capacity in language may always be a problematic issue, but the significance of this problem will vary, depending on the issues at hand. Language may not be capable of representing reality *in toto*, but it indeed seems capable of sometimes providing the means to communicate instructively in and on various realities. This does not imply that we basically adopt a view of language as capable of representing reality as if words can mirror nature. A problematization orientation to language and representation can be adopted, but not necessarily in a strong and categorical manner. It is unsatisfying to say that we can represent certain phenomena while the idea of language as a medium for the representations of others does not work, but we can position ourselves on the issue in careful terms and try to exercise judgement when picking the phenomena or discourses that become objects for anti-representational discussions (deconstructions, resistance readings or more general problematizations).

A move towards a focus on micro-events and actions can reduce the burdens put on language to carry meanings that say something 'empirically relevant' about what may go on in a specific setting 'out there'. To try to measure how the degree of 'charisma' of 'managers' correlates with degrees of 'satisfaction', 'motivation' or 'performance' of 'subordinates' may well be to expect far too much in terms of what language can do. It might also overstate what the 'knowing subjects' can actually accomplish when asked to summarize their presumed knowledge (about themselves or something around them, e.g. their managers or the characteristics of their companies) by putting an X in a small box on a piece of paper labelled questionnaire, or even in a 'depth interview' (Alvesson and Deetz 2000). To describe the language use in a specific interaction between two persons in some detail is certainly not unproblematic, as a written text may poorly reflect the nuances, punctuations, pronunciations, body language, physical setting and other elements that make the verbal interaction immensely richer and more complicated than what comes through in a protocol. The latter, even if typed in detail and with technical notes indicating breaks, changes of tone etc. in the talk, is typically an impoverished and quite different version of the actual verbal interchange. Nevertheless, the typed protocol based on recorded material may still be a more rigorous enterprise than any attempt to study people's beliefs about the world or their actions. A relatively high degree of 'empirical accuracy' can be said to characterize this sort of research.

Beyond language? Studying talk versus using talk as indicator

Apart from the level of talk, I claim – as hinted in previous sections – that the study of social activities also generally includes *the level of practice* and *the level of meaning*. Empirically speaking, the three basic levels of research focus – practice, meaning and talk – intersect, interact and intermesh with each other in various degrees and fashions. Utterances, for example, carry various meanings and may have practical implications, i.e. convert into action on the level of practice. Talk may even be the cornerstone of practice, e.g. teaching, managing, selling, childrearing, policing or counselling. However, there are very good reasons, from a methodological point of view, to keep the levels analytically distinct and to regard any actual relationship between the levels as an open question. This does not mean the utterances made have no meaning, or that meanings have no practical significance. It means that we, as researchers, have no foolproof way of knowing what meaning certain forms of talk take on. We cannot know for sure what relevance utterances on practices have in relation to actually performed practices. And we cannot exhaustively grasp the various meanings ascribed to practices – the meaning ascribed to practices by those who perform them, those who design them and those who order their execution, to mention but a few possible subjects.

For example, utterances made in an interview regarding social practices might reflect some aspects of actual practices. But they might instead reflect morally binding conventions for how social members speak on these matters – how you as a competent member ought to describe actual practices (Silverman 1993; Baker 1997). They might reflect some of the interpretive repertoires that are available to social members on the matter and/or in the situation – the way they speak on specific practices and in specific circumstances (in interviews, for example) – instead of describing the practice *per se* or expressing a privileged meaning (Potter and Wetherell 1987). Or, for that matter, they might provide all of this: their utterances might reflect actual practices, cultural information and the discursive strategies available.

The hard thing, of course, is to distinguish the extent to which utterances made in interviews do all or any of these things. Treating *utterances as indicators of how people speak* on specific matters, at least in certain social situations, seems to be least problematic. In this case one does not have to leave the level of talk and speculate as to whether what is said is significant beyond revealing discursive moves deployed on the matter. Still, there are problems in deciding on the interpretation of statements. Since meaning is rarely self-evident, what informants mean and how they interpret specific statements might need clarification. Talk in interviews may differ from language use in other settings. As Boje (1991) points out, when people talk in 'real life' they do so in specific settings, assuming a lot of pre-understanding and shared frameworks which mean that stories are told in a particular way. The meaning and effects cannot be fully understood outside these situations. When people in interview situations report about this talk or these stories, the performative aspect of the talk that is so central in everyday settings is lost, and there is a strong discrepancy between interview talk and the social interactions and language use this talk is intended to mirror. Another issue concerns the ways in which people talk in front of the researcher compared to in other settings. In interviews, but also when someone is performing before the researcher observer, certain themes are mentioned that might be more or less rare in the other situations the research is supposed to cover. When one is studying discourse or the use of specific vocabularies, it sometimes makes sense to make inquiries about the salience or frequency of these. It might be economical (although not unproblematic) to get informants' evaluation instead of tape-recording several hundreds of hours of talk. Some interviewing may, therefore, be used to supplement observational studies of language use. Studying talk is thus far from simple, but still much less problematic than studying behaviour, meaning, feelings, cognitions, structure or other phenomena which call for going beyond language and using language to get information about something else.

Viewing *utterances as providers of cultural information* is a more daring endeavour, except for information about cultural rules for language use. This includes involving the level of meaning and, thus, some guesswork as to how meaning is produced, how interpretations are made and what counts as significant among those under study. As previously stated, the idea that utterances stand in any definitive relationship to ideas, values, beliefs, motives or other cultural-level phenomena is, on the whole, questionable. If accounts reflect moral standards for expressing oneself in a cultural context, the accounts say something about culture, but more so on the level of the espoused than the meanings and symbolism non-consciously believed in and acted upon. Of course, one option is to view accounts as very local cultural material: they may thus be treated as indications of situation-specific meanings, ideas and values. Whether these are congruent with other local cultural materials, manifested in actions, in talk in other contexts and/or in cultural artefacts, is an open question, difficult but possible to investigate.

Finally, viewing *utterances as reflecting actual practices* is even more daring, at least if we consider non-trivial phenomena, and if by 'practice' we refer to more than language practice. Practice includes cognitive, linguistic, behavioural, cultural, material and relational elements, but with some emphasis on regularized behaviour/actions. To see interview accounts as reflecting social phenomenon 'out there', e.g. the behaviours of criminals or discrimination against a minority group, implies that: (a) the accounts reflect people's 'genuine' beliefs and knowledge about a specific phenomena; and (b) these beliefs and knowledge are not basically cultural, and do not reflect personal meanings and consciousness (including prejudices and cognitive errors), but stand in an accurate relationship to 'facts' about the practices (actions, events, situations, processes, structures, and relations) 'out there'. This includes guesswork and assumptions on all three levels. What does an account say, i.e. what is the meaning of a seldom crystal clear statement? Does what the speaker seems to say reflect what he or she thinks or believes? Does what he or she thinks or believes reflect how 'it is'? One cannot simply assume a high degree of 'robustness' of all the elements involved. It must be shown or at least made plausible. This is difficult to accomplish on most issues studied by social scholars. Many pomos would say impossible. They claim that language simply cannot live up to what is demanded of it. But, as said, one's attitude does not need to be that strict.

Caution in making firm statements on or ambitious interpretations of culture (and other aspects on the meaning level) and practices can, however, be recommended. Discursive pragmatism – a fairly strong rather than an exclusive focus on language use in social settings – should be considered more seriously. Arguably, there is work available that demonstrates the fruitfulness of being sensitive to the framing power of context and language and the possibility of focusing on the level of language use in 'empirical settings', showing the meaning and/or effects of language and language use. Such work includes the study of leadership in social, interactive situations rather than as an abstract behavioural style (Knights and Willmott 1992), of power as it is expressed in action, in which linguistic behaviour is central, rather than as general resistance-crushing capacity (Alvesson 1996), of the vocabulary of motives rather than motivation (Mills 1940), of talk as an administrative device rather than as a carrier of abstract principles of administration (Gronn 1983) and so on.

A case: identity work among advertising people

To illustrate a discursive pragmatism approach I will draw upon a study of the advertising profession in Sweden that I have conducted. The study is an ethnography of an advertising agency, combined with interviews with professionals from other agencies and studies of documents, such as professional journals. During the course of the study the emphasis to some extent changed from cultural in-depth meanings to discourse. (For a fuller account of the study, see Alvesson 1994.)

Self-presentations

When the advertising workers described themselves, in interviews and in everyday situations, with reference to their workplace and advertising work, the following themes were salient: friendship and 'personal chemistry' are vital; it is important that people are having fun and laugh in agencies; advertising workers are emotionally involved in their tasks; they are free, independent, even a bit lawless; they know better than the customer what is good for him or her; they are, in contrast to some of the other advertising agencies, 'serious' (Alvesson and Köping 1993). For space reasons I refrain from illustrating all these discourses and concentrate on emotions in advertising work and the importance of having and being fun in advertising agencies.

Advertising workers emphasize that their product is very emotional and difficult to evaluate or measure.

> Good advertisement speaks for itself. But sometimes it can be difficult to explain why something is good. You are yourself convinced that this is RIGHT. But there are no rational, logical explanations for it. Finally it becomes a matter of gut feelings – you think with your stomach rather than with the brain. It is nothing rational, but emotional.

Not only the way people relate to ads, but also advertising professionals, are described as strongly emotional:

> Advertising people are normally very outgoing and they are emotionally loaded. Because feelings and things like that are the basis of creativity, so to speak. They are often very rich in ideas and associative, they can quickly associate to various phenomena. They are normally rather difficult to steer and jump to the ceiling when they become happy and when they become mad. The amplitude of their reactions is much higher than, for example, in people on companies' accounting departments. Advertising people are seldom very systematic or structured.

Related to the emotional nature of the workers, the work and their product is the significance of having a positive work climate. It is very important, according to those we talked to, that advertising people should be fun and be able to laugh. As one interviewee emphasized, serious and boring people seldom fit into advertising agencies.

The functions of these discourses

How can we understand these accounts? A possibility is, of course, that statements reflect reality, either outer 'objective' conditions or ideational ones such as beliefs and values. One could emphasize, for example, the vital importance of friendship because social relations among the studied people 'objectively' have this quality or because the values, beliefs and understandings of organizational members circle around the notion of friendship. Perhaps this is the case, but even after an ethnographic study, including months of observation, it is not easy to say.

Because it is hard – and for the present purposes not very interesting – to determine the 'actual' degree of emotional content in the creation of an advert or the irrationality of clients, I will not deal with the issues *per se*, but will elaborate on the diversity of functions of discourses in the context of advertising agencies. The idea is that talk not only reflects what is, but produces effects. What are the possible effects of the accounts of these people?

Some statements may function as *conjurations* (Alvesson and Köping 1993: Chapter 9). Conjurations chase away threats by verbal means. Talking about friendship can counteract labour turnover rates or at any rate reduce anxiety regarding them. A large problem for agencies in Sweden is that people – individually and in work groups – defect from them and start competing businesses. Through talk about friendship, good relations and a positive climate, one draws attention to the positive aspects of work and can: (a) counteract people's inclinations to consider alternative employment or self-employment; and (b) reduce the feelings of worry about human capital returning to the workplace after the weekend.

Statements are an important element of the production and reproduction of the somewhat idealized picture of (one's own) agency, occupation and branch that one will wish to emphasize. By means of the statements mentioned, new members of the profession and organization learn how they should relate to and express themselves. The statements contribute to *socialization and reproduction*, i.e. the newcomer learns the correct values and attitudes – or at least ways of talking about these – and the profession and organization is reproduced and continues without too many drastic changes. They give guidelines for the field's orthodoxy and ease the maintainance and continuance of a certain habitus, i.e. a certain disposition for being and appearing (Bourdieu 1979). From a discourse pragmatist position, socialization leads not as much to the internalization of a set of ideas and values as to a learned capacity to talk and act in the correct way, expressing these ideas and values with sophistication.

Discourses are also invoked in the struggle to safeguard the uniqueness and unification of advertising work, as well as to strengthen the individual and collective *identity* of advertising workers. Identity typically refers to the experience of coherence, consistency over time and distinctiveness of a person or a group (see Eriksson 1968; Albert and Whetten 1985), although postmodernists would have it differently and see identity as multiple, fluid and processal (see Chapter 3). Irrespective of how one positions oneself on this issue, broad groups tend to agree that in modern society identity is often precarious and people have to struggle for it (Lasch 1978). Many of the modern occupations, such as advertising, consultancy, personnel, counselling and psychology, are probably particularly vulnerable because of an ambiguous work content and performance and a high exposure to the arbitrary assessments and feedback of people around them (Alvesson 2001). Their identity construction projects are more difficult than for those working with material objects or on other tasks that more clearly signal an impression of competence. Astute assertions concerning the characteristics of advertising people counteract the threats against a specific competence and identity. Self-presentations facilitate 'identity work'.

Advertising people underline their strength in relation to clients by emphasizing the clients' inability and irrationality and sometimes even their complete lack of understanding of the conditions of the advertising production process. The differences between advertising professionals and the clients are stressed. This is also the case with regard to the statements about the 'lack of seriousness' of a minority of advertising agencies and professionals. The competent and moral advertising person – the person talking about seriousness and the lack thereof – then appears against the background of these two negative models, protected by the uniqueness of his or her own area of competence and special identity, which is made clearer by stories of stupid clients and inane advertising people. An internal mobilization creates and recreates the symbolic environment that safeguards one's own identity. An assured identity is crucial for success in this career (while at the same time, of course, success also influences identity).

It should perhaps be added that this does not imply a fusion between talk and identity. Discursive pragmatism emphasizes the process and practice of language use and its intended effects; it does not aim to fix an outcome. It would be speculative to say that discourses bring about a stable, coherent identity. Discourses can be flexibly invoked in temporal regulations of identity. Different discourses may be drawn upon (speaking to and through the subject) to produce different senses of self and identity, contingent upon context. At one moment one has strong social bonds with fellow workers, at another one is free and eager to break away from established patterns (Alvesson and Köping 1993: Chapter 10).

Identity work is also crucial to the ability to 'sell' one's own profession. The emphasis on advertising people's special characteristics salient in interview statements gives the impression that they have something special to contribute to clients. The meaning of the discourses discussed is that they ease the *marketing* process of the advertising person. The discourses supply the advertising people with linguistic resources for a particular portrait, an identity, a style which is controlled by a certain symbolism that enables them to convince clients of their uniqueness and competence. As Gergen (1989) maintains, it is about the ways in which people account for their own (and others') inner self and reach credibility and legitimacy. 'What we take to be the dimension of self . . . are symbolic resources for making claims in a sea of competing world construction' (Gergen 1989: 75).

This case illustrates a discursive pragmatism approach. The level of language use is in focus, but not strictly so, and a broader understanding of social reality is aimed for; in the present case, the self-presentations and identity constructions of an occupation.

Conclusions

The attack on dominant and conventional assumptions regarding the relations between language and social reality has far-reaching, but poorly acknowledged, implications for empirical research in social science. Despite the linguistic turns in social science and philosophy, the great majority of empirical studies treat language in a simplistic, uncritical and misleading way. Efforts to produce and check the measures do not involve any deeper reflections on the nature of language. Literature on method often does not address language with much care or sophistication, and implicitly treats it as a transparent medium for the transport of meaning. This chapter identifies three responses that accommodate the critique given by proponents of postmodernism, discourse analysis and other language-sensitive orientations: grounded fictionalism, data construction and discursive pragmatism.

Grounded fictionalism simply acknowledges the impossibility of language mirroring social phenomena (indeed, anything outside language itself), which means that predictions, reliability and validity become problematic. Research work may still be empirical in the sense of utilizing insights gained from talk with people or observations, and can produce ideas or theories that are relevant for practitioners, but any formal inquiry or claims of grounding leading to the research text are abandoned as an ideal, indeed as a possibility. The research text is too loosely coupled to a distinct empirical reality. Given the observation that those social theories that are viewed as most interesting have seldom received much empirical support (Astley 1985), this line can be celebrated to the extent that liberates theory development from the straitjacket of verification.

Data construction recognizes the impossibility of carrying out empirical studies according to traditional methodological ideals, such as grounded theory (for a critique, see Alvesson and Sköldberg 2000: Chapter 2). If language cannot mirror reality, grounding appears to be a rather shaky enterprise. The problems (and potentialities) of language and language use mingle with other complications – the significance of pre-structured understandings, the politics of the research process, the infinite number of possibilities, as well as rules for the production of research texts. This motivates a freer attitude. Data-constructionist research does not advocate rigour with respect to discourse in action as a solution. It stresses complications other than those associated with how those being studied use language and the inability of, for example, interviews to mirror reality. Instead it is the researcher's constructions that are emphasized, e.g. cognitive input, selectivity in interpretation and favoured vocabulary, and creativity in putting a research text together.

These two types of research involve a more or less drastic liberation from the rather sterile idea of theory and data being separable and the idea of a 'fit'. The linguistic turn might, however, imply a somewhat different direction and take texts – talk and documents – seriously as objects of study. While we recognize that there are areas of interest other than those related to discourse (language use in a social context), this level of study is all too easily overlooked in social analysis, including that by some postmodernists. There is a cultural bias for action over 'mere' talk and a misleading opposition between action and talk, counteracting a full interest in the latter (Marshak 1998). Discourse analysis – as well as related language-focused approaches – provides insights that facilitate and enrich reflective thinking on social phenomena in general. It also suggests underdeveloped domains of research (e.g. how social members speak in certain situations, what they achieve with these forms of speech), and ways and means that make it possible to conduct a study on the level of talk.

Discursive pragmatism is a broader and less strictly focused version of what I refer to as 'discursivism'. Discursivism (e.g. discourse analysis and conversation analysis) means that to take language and, in particular, language use seriously makes a detailed study of language in operation in a social context (a) justified and (b) the only real option for empirical inquiry, given high criteria for rigour and validity. Accounts provided by informants in situations set up by researchers (e.g. interviews) or in 'naturally occurring settings' are treated as empirical data and to be studied as such, not as sources of speculation on what may go on in the minds of people or in situations other than those in which the accounts have been produced.

In discursive pragmatist research, this constraint is less strict. There is more room for speculation about what discursive material might indicate in addition to informants' use of discursive repertoires, i.e. meanings and effects contingent upon language use. Observed linguistic interaction in a manager–subordinate situation might, for example, help one to make some conclusions about leadership patterns, or talk among the unemployed might give us some hints not just about the details of talk among people in this category, but also about norms of expression and the kind of positioning that (some) unemployed people are inclined to take. A wide spectrum of social phenomena can be reconstructed to narrow the gap between a specific area of interest and what it is possible to say about it, given an appreciation of the nature and dynamics of language use.

The three versions lead to rather different methodological implications:

- grounded fictionalism takes a rather liberal view on empirical material and uses it mainly as a source of inspiration;
- data constructivism pays careful attention to the perspective, vocabulary and operations leading to certain constructions of data;
- discursive pragmatism takes a rather ambitious view of empirical material and studies language use in depth.

Nevertheless, they can be seen as alternatives that are compatible with, and emerge from, the same basic premises emphasized by pomos: the nature of language as context-dependent, metaphorical, active, built upon repressed meanings and constituting/perspectivating 'other' phenomena. They are all consistent with an understanding of language users as socially situated, discursively constituted, sensitive and responsive to dominant cultural norms, social rules and available scripts for talk and oriented towards the effects of language use. They do not presuppose informants as being abstract, disengaged tellers of truths in their questionnaire responses or romantic revealers of genuine experiences in interviews.

The linguistic turn encourages greater interest in the level of language use and other themes of discourse. This means a trend away from a focus on subjective or cultural meaning and on social practice (structure, behaviour). The turn encourages great caution in addressing the latter themes. However, methodology calls for some degree of pragmatism. Different research interests and problems call for different methodological responses, even though methodological insight must govern which research questions are meaningful to address. For certain not very abstract research tasks, where the level of ambiguity is low (e.g. correlation between biological sex, height and income), one can generously give some space to treating language as a means for accessing what goes on 'out there'. Taking language seriously does, however, limit what we can accomplish in terms of making valid empirical claims, testing hypotheses, building theory on data or verifying theory with empirical findings. From the linguistic turn it follows that it is important to make *an analytical separation of the levels of text, meaning and practice.* Although these levels are generally simultaneously active in natural settings, it is a fallacy – all too often made in social analysis – unreflectively to use empirical evidence stemming from the level of language use to draw conclusions regarding aspects concerning other levels.

Note

1 The concept 'empirical' is difficult. It is used here to indicate some aspects of the reality (practices, ideas, language use) of one or a group of persons, as indicated by research practices (interviews, observations, text analysis).

5 Unpacking categories

For the pomo, the social world is basically open, ambiguous and undecidable. This is, at least for those sharing dominant views on knowledge, not acceptable and should be replaced by certainty, closure and firm knowledge. As expressed by Scheurich (1997: 74):

> The researcher then fills this indeterminate openness with her/his interpretive baggage, imposes names, categories, constructions, conceptual schemes, theories upon the unknowable, and believes that the indeterminate is now located, constructed, known. Order has been created. The restless, appropriate spirit of the researcher is (temporarily) at peace.

For postmodernists categories used by researchers and other people do not reveal the truth, they do not assist us in developing frameworks and describing phenomena so that knowledge providing insights about the world can be developed. 'Categories' here refer to concepts seen as capable of assisting the sorting and naming of the chunks of reality studied by a researcher. Categories impose order, they structure the world according to a particular logic. Categories are not only valuable tools for understanding but also mechanisms for power and control fixating our ways of seeing. They are not so much sources of misunderstandings as basic ingredients in forms of understanding that are insufficiently problematized and give too little space for uncertainty and variation.

Postmodernism means an effort to refuse using categories in a straight-forward and 'progressive' way. While most versions of social research work with categories as positive aids in their projects, postmodernism encourages a look at dominant categories as highly unreliable support in knowledge development. When encountering the attitude of closing and fixing the social world through categories – capitalism, market, organization, state, occupation, knowledge, health, values etc. – the pomo takes on the task of making the social world open, ambiguous and undecidable. Major categories in the area of study call for unpacking – problematization, deconstruction – rather than development and instrumental use. This chapter addresses how the categories forming basic elements in the formulation of research questions, structuring the field, working theoretically, analysing empirical material and arriving at conclusions call for careful scrutiny. The pomo problematics associated with the role of discourse, the power/knowledge connection and the fragmentation of identities are all relevant to this suspicious review of dominant categories and categories proposed as superior to these.

This chapter relates the ideal of unpacking of categories to the ideal of research as defamiliarization, i.e. turning the well known and self-evident into the opposite. I then go into an important area, gender, and try to show how categories such as women are problematic and freeze thinking and political and practical orientations into taken-for-granted ideas. I choose to concentrate on a core category that may be seen as self-evident and unproblematic and then address this in some depth as an example on how unpacking can be done. The idea of 'women' is also suitable, as it has attained a lot of interest from postmodernist feminists. The chapter ends with some ideas about implications of an unpacking orientation for research practices.

Defamiliarization

A particularly important element in critical research is to avoid seeing the social world as self-evident and familiar, and to conceptualize it as basically or in certain vital respects a rather strange place. Research then becomes a matter of defamiliarization, of observing and interpreting social phenomena in novel ways compared to cultural dominant categories and distinctions. Defamiliarization means that we see things not as natural or rational but as exotic and arbitrary, as an expression of action and thinking within frozen, conformist patterns (Ehn *et al.* 1982; Marcus and Fischer 1986; Alvesson and Deetz 2000).

This is a difficult enterprise. Researchers, like other members of a society, are trapped by cultural ethnocentrism and parochialism – meaning that the cultural phenomena they encounter are not recognized as such but are seen as natural, as part of the world order, and not bound to national or late capitalistic/post-industrial society and culture. Gregory (1983), an anthropologist working in the organizational culture area, remarks that the literature often says 'more about the culture of the researchers than the researched' (p. 359). This kind of research problem is more generally recognized by anthropologists (Marcus and Fischer 1986). Going even further, some proponents warn against the study of one's own society. Leach (1982: 124), for example, writes that:

> fieldwork in a cultural context of which you already have intimate first-hand experience seems to be much more difficult than fieldwork which is approached from the naive viewpoint of a total stranger. When anthropologists study facets of their own society their vision seems to become distorted by prejudices which derive from private rather than public experience.

This is bad news for anthropology and other forms of cultural research that have increasingly targeted social groups within the researcher's own society during the past few decades.

Culture – including taken-for-granted assumptions and ways of thinking – is, however, not the only element in the inclination to reproduce a well known world in research. The other, and according to most pomos even more basic, issue is language. We create and recreate familiar words through the use of language in conventional ways, where the terms we use guide our perceptions, descriptions and interpretations. Central here is the key categories that we are caught in and apply. These are from a sceptical perspective seen as devices ordering the researcher rather than fine-tuned instruments with which the researcher explores and reveals the world. Here, a dose of postmodernism may make a positive difference.

Somewhat crudely put, pomo social science can be seen as the negation of the packing industry. Its business is unpacking. One option is to try to avoid all cherished categories and antinomies, structuring the world and our knowledge in self-evident ways. Another, less difficult and probably more productive, route is to choose one or a few dominant categories in the field one is working in, investigate their problematic impact and then perhaps indicate challenging ways to approach the subject matter. If this is well done, it can in itself be a valuable research contribution. Perhaps it is most easily recognized by people sympathetic to postmodernism and (other versions of) critical research, but an elegant and convincing unpacking of a dominant notion can also impress people with more conventional tastes. To accomplish this is a challenge for the pomo-inspired researcher.

On the social construction and deconstruction of gender: beyond men and women

I will now dive into one particular area and try to illustrate how it is possible to unpack a dominant category. Gender appears to be a highly relevant and informative case. The existence of 'men' and 'women' can be seen as unproblematic and self-evident, but there are good reasons to unpack these categories.

Gender studies is an important field. Perhaps the most crucial issue for gender studies is how to conceptualize women and men. What creates gender? Is it division of labour in the household or the labour market? Are culturally formed sex roles significant? Or do early development processes – including the individuation and separation phase, the resolution of competition/identification with parental figures and socialization – play the vital role? Are women different from men? Or are they similar? These are not good questions if we take postmodernism seriously, as they all rely on the assumption that there is something homogeneous and uniform that we can label gender. The trend is to raise doubts about this, partly as an effect of the growing influence of postmodernism, but even more so as a result of the voices of wider groups of women pointing at the great variety of experiences of females, associated with ethnicity, sexual orientation, class etc. There has been a critique of earlier feminists who tried to universalize the views of middle-class, heterosexual, white women. The critique has been followed by an increasing emphasis on diversity among women. This can, of course, be addressed with no acknowledgement of postmodernism – but the problems of the seemingly homogeneous category of 'women' still play well for pomos.

The interest in gender in social research started with attention being paid to specific problems and aspects of the situation of women in comparison with men. Sex as a variable was seen as important as a corrective to theories generalizing from the study of groups of men without any consideration that the social situations, experiences or orientations of women might be different. Some research then moved on to take the experiences and interests of women seriously, and took a political standpoint, aiming to strengthen the situation of women and challenge patriarchy. Women were at first seen as a fairly homogeneous group, sharing similar experiences and interests, associated with being defined as 'the second sex', and as such regularly discriminated against. More recently, and partly related to the increasing popularity of postmodernism, but also to ethnic groups and homosexuals raising their voices, the tendency to assume a universal, homogeneous female subject has been strongly criticized and the variety of groups of women emphasized. The recognition of this variation joins forces with postmodernism in the sense that gender becomes difficult to pin down and describe in general terms: it intersects with and changes meaning with sexual orientation, age, class, ethnicity etc., making 'grand narratives' and broad truths problematic.

Many authors in gender studies say that they reject a biology-based concept of sex, refuse to use the latter term and claim that they are interested in gender as a social construction. This is potentially less alien to postmodernist thinking than comparing men and women, but it depends on what is meant by social construction. This term sometimes implies robust outcomes of social processes and a view of the woman as broadly constructed in homogeneous ways (e.g. as a sex object, a caretaker and subordinate to men), sometimes more fragile, temporary and hard to pin down constructions, where the process element is seen as ongoing and variations are emphasized. The latter is easier to accept for postmodernists.

Leaving postmodernist feminism and postmodernist ideals for a good understanding of social constructions aside for a moment, I think that as a whole many gender studies take only short and uncertain steps along a constructivist road. In a basic respect a great part of the gender literature is *not* addressing gender in any ambitious social constructivist perspective, at least not in a consistent and elaborated way.[1] Biology (body characteristics) is central to most authors' ways of dealing with gender. Men and women are routinely identified through bodily criteria, primarily sex organs.[2] That variable research/number-counting studies do so is not surprising. All statistics on gender rely on the ability to identify subjects as men and women easily, and here body and not social being is what counts. But even more sophisticated social constructionist gender studies appear to proceed from body criteria when talking about men and women; for example, male and female waiters/waitresses (Hall 1993), unemployed women or the interests of men. The social constructions of these males and females enter in the next phase, where the 'fact' that some are men and some are women leads to certain social processes in which these two sexes are turned into genders – for example, friendly waitresses and less friendly waiters – according to the views of those involved. The problem is that body criteria are easily used in a self-evident way and too strongly imprint on how one interprets what is assumed to be social constructions. The very categories of men and women are viewed as unproblematic and as basic starting points for study. Claims such as 'the reality of male privilege affects the life of every woman, whether she is conscious of it or not' (Wolf 1992: 133) are common, but as said, risk homogenizing all women – and male privilege, for that matter – and tie women to a biological defined existence. But the categories of women, male privilege etc. needed to be scrutinized and unpacked in relation to their world-confirming and ordering capacities. This is, of course, not inconsistent with a critical interest in exploring domination and repression.

Almost every time signifiers of man and woman are used they impose a taken-for-granted unity. Normally it is assumed that identifying a subject in these terms is highly informative: 'Who has written this book? A man. Aha!' 'Ninety-five per cent of all the executives in the company were men.' 'Margaret Thatcher was the first female prime minister of the UK.' The assumption that biological sex says something important about subjects is shared by the public and most students of gender.

Of course, few would argue against the view that men and women differ in terms of chromosomes, sex organs and a few other bodily aspects, although there are a large number of possible dimensions involved in identifying biological sex and these far from always go together, making biological sex far from simple in many cases (Kaplan and Rogers 1990). What is to be disputed is whether these differences are a relevant starting point or focus for social analysis. I am not denying the existence of objective differences between the two sexes, but there are also objective differences between those taller and shorter than 175 centimetres and between those who can carry 50 kilograms and those not capable of this. The interesting aspect is what criteria and what kind of distinction are used as a base for forming categories, and what the consequences of these distinctions are. The biology-based distinction may be more relevant for the gynaecologist than for the student of gender. As Coser (1989: 203) writes, without going in the same direction as me,

> there is a tendency in feminist theorizing to extoll one experience that women have in common: the experience of the female body and female sexuality. I believe that this is a variant of sociobiology, namely, the notion that women must be different because their body is different. Such an assumption, while being based on truth, is neither original nor helpful.

As the common view is that we need to take more interest in women, their interests and experiences, and as most problematizations have targeted the idea of women as a uniform and an analytically and politically helpful category, I will also to some extent concentrate on women, even though men and masculinities could receive the same attention and deserve unpacking in the same way as women.

Even the biological sex of women has different and perhaps even contradictory meanings in different situations: in the gynaecological clinic, in relation to marriage and sexuality, children, family, different employment situations, political elections etc. Because of these considerations some researchers think unitary notions such as 'woman', 'feminine gender identity' and 'mothering' are problematic, as they imply a false unity and suppress divergence and variety (Fraser and Nicholson 1988).

It can, of course, be argued that female biology is ascribed a particular set of psychological and social meanings, bringing about the social construction of women. Sex (biology) leads to gender (a specific social version of men and women) in society. But the idea of separating sex and gender implies that there is clear distance between them. Gender is not necessarily a distinct and uniform sex role imposed on the body through some form of standardized cultural mechanics. Nor is the distinction very meaningful if one assumes that there is a specific psychology being developed on the basis of biological sex differences, only marginally affected by cultural conditions. The social construction processes are complex, multifaceted, heterogeneous; they vary over time and with class, race, occupation, age etc. The social construction of gender does not prevent some women from becoming tank commanders and bank robbers, some men from becoming kindergarten teachers and strippers, and both male and female managers showing a spectrum of different kinds of leadership behaviour. Perhaps female managers are, in their work contexts, at least sometimes constructed as managers rather than women, and the relevance and value of the notion of 'female manager' is problematic, as it identifies and orders a subject in a particular way – the subject may be represented as a 'non-female professional' or in any other contestable way. There are good reasons for agreeing with postmodernists when they point at the problems with the use of universal concepts of men and women (Fraser and Nicholson 1988; Scott 1991).

The meaning of 'woman' is not universal, but varies with the language contexts – discourses – in which it is used. Other favoured concepts, such as masculinity, dominance, hierarchy and discrimination, may also indicate a misleading unity, if the use is not governed by an appreciation of the local context that gives these words some meaning in particular instances.

The ideal of gender studies could be to contribute to reducing the significance or even abolishing the identities of man and woman, at least in broad areas, e.g. the labour market. As Deetz (1992b: 30) expresses it, the aim is to make the 'gender distinction irrelevant at the place of work so that the identity of people constituted as women, as well as pay and routine treatment practices, would be based on other dimensions of distinctions and other constituted identities'. This would call for not using this kind of identification. Individuality would not be sacrificed to the definition of a person as a 'woman' – whether produced by others or by the person herself. On the other hand, the centrality and persistence of the men–women distinction is a historical fact, and effects such as sex segregation and pay discrimination have materialized in most social settings. In order to work against these effects, the woman identity is necessary for women to organize themselves and express their distinct group processes in a gendered society. The woman label contributes to separate women and men socially, marginalizes 'women's' diverse experiences and denies personal complexity, but also forms a basis for resistance and productive conflict, Deetz says. When feminists try to accomplish the latter, there are sometimes unintended effects in the direction of the former.

Defamiliarization of gender

One possibility in gender studies would be to minimize the use of the labels man and woman as part of research vocabulary, i.e. not to use the distinction and the resulting categories and to avoid accepting or claiming that man and woman signify something specific. One could, however, in line with discursive pragmatism, observe and investigate when and how 'natives' use the distinction and the categories. From a postmodernist position, the intention would not be to discover uniform patterns of sex labelling or to invoke sex categories in social life, but to explore variation and inconsistency, and possibly to show the unstability and ambiguity of the use of these signifiers.

One might therefore try other vocabularies for labelling what is conventionally, but unreflectively, ascribed to man and woman. If one is interested in identifying bodies through conventional criteria, one can talk about the bio-man and the bio-woman (or body man and body woman). One can also focus on the perhaps most salient bodily differences, different sets of chromosomes, thus referring to them as XY-persons and XX-persons. XY- and XX-persons figure in all gender statistics and in the majority of all gender research, taking some (biological) criteria as the crucial issue for addressing gender (or rather sex).

Many feminists have understood the specific female in terms of sets of 'motherly' experiences with children and nurturance that bring about a specific set of values or orientations. The interesting quality is that of having been a primary caretaker (of infants/children) (Hartsock 1987; Grant 1988; Cockburn 1991). Hartsock, for example, emphasizes the significance of a 'deep unity with another through the many-levelled and changing connections mothers experience with growing children' (p. 167). This experience of reproduction is routinely equated with 'women', but the point here is that we in research work should be very careful in using this imprecise term, overburdened with unexplored meanings and ambiguously referring to biological and sociocultural aspects at the same time. We should also hesitate to talk about 'mothers' for the same reason (Fraser and Nicholson 1988). It could be argued that with regard to pregnancy, childbirth and breastfeeding the signifier 'mother' is hard to escape and fairly unproblematical, but in other situations Nature does not tell us to divide up primary caretakers into 'mothers' and 'fathers'. Through the routine labelling of subjects in this way a basic distinction is made self-evident and natural. The primary caretaker may be an XY-person (the XY-parent rather than the XX-parent). There may also be two, in such cases often one XY- and one XX-person. Any naturalization of the idea that it must be an XX-person should be avoided. That this has been the case historically, but that does not mean that one should reproduce it. The present vocabulary – used not only by people being studied but also by researchers – works in this way. Sometimes psychoanalytic writers addressing the early mothering of the child realize that it may not necessarily be the biological mother, and then use the mother label irrespective of the sex of the primary caretaker, but the distinction between 'mother' and something else is still reproduced and normalized.

One should also be careful about not equating primary caretaking with XX-persons and seeing this as the source of women's (XX-persons') specific orientations. Far from all XX-persons have had these experiences. Some XX-persons never give birth to a child, many have not yet done so at a particular time (e.g. at the time when they are studied). *If* these experiences were central to the formation of a woman's 'essence' (a set of qualities associated with being a woman), then perhaps 25 per cent of the XX-population in a typical social group – such as female managers in an industry or all women between 20 and 50 in a community – would *not* qualify for the label 'woman' (or, better, childbearer and primary caretaker), while a few men might do so. Similarly, if the life of 'every woman' is affected by 'the reality of male privilege', as Wolf (1992) claims, then one could argue that those subjects – irrespective of sex – not affected by male privilege are not, by definition, women.

There are, of course, other possible sources behind the construction of 'men' and 'women' (or how we label subjects), e.g. early psychosexual and object relations development, general socialization and/or role learning. It would take us too long to discuss all the claims about possible men- and women-specific characteristics. But there is no automatic relationship between body, specific processes of social constructions and a set of characteristics/orientations. And since internalization, identification, learning etc. do not stand in a one-to-one relationship to biology, emphasizing the latter criteria and defining people through their bodies is, at least occasionally, misleading. As cultural signifiers 'woman' and 'man' are often ambiguous and multifaceted: 'woman' may mean very different things in different contexts and for different groups. One possible meaning of 'woman' is a sex object for men. But this is not necessarily a consistent and uniform meaning ascribed to woman. And 'sex object' is also ambiguous. It may mean other things than the passive object and potential victim of the controlling, gazing male voyeur. The sex object can also exercise power through the capacity to evoke desire: being an object for another person's desire is a resource of power and easily makes the object a subject. The victim is not totally devoid of power – the victim has a moral right and the sympathy of any decent person, as well as the legal apparatus. This, of course, presupposes social recognition of the victim status. I am, of course, not suggesting a symmetry to treating the other and being treated as a sex object (when this meaning is viewed as a fair one), but want to problematize the ambition of ascribing a fundamental meaning to gender.

For many feminists (e.g. Chodorow 1978; Cockburn 1991) 'woman' signifies something radically different from 'man' in terms of subjectivity and orientation. For others (e.g. Kanter 1977; Reskin and Padavic 1994) 'woman' is not different from 'man' apart from being consistently and systematically unfavourably located in social structures and an object of discrimination. Here, as in most gender studies, 'woman' is given a universal, basic meaning and the category is viewed as natural, self-evident and key. The profound disagreement about the meaning indicates that there is a case for unpacking this category.

What 'woman' refers to, except certain biological equipment, is thus highly ambiguous and, in social science, it often means a problematically tight linking of biological, psychological and social characteristics.

An interesting example illustrates how social practice can be given more weight than the body in the way a subject is socially constructed. An American female director of a public relations organization, who was sent to Sudan, was invited for a meal at a businessman's home. He treated her as he would treat a man, 'brought her a cushion, served her food and washed her arms with rose water'. The female director asked him if this was not a violation of the cultural norms in Sudan. To this he replied, 'Oh, it's no problem, women do not do business, therefore, you are not a woman' (Fagenson and Jackson 1993: 311). Here the example of the Western social construction in the text of the subject as a female manager – here the female/she categorization is salient – is confronted by the Sudanese construct of the subject as a 'non-female' manager. Of course, within Western society there are variations in terms of when and how the subject is constructed as a female director. The case also illustrates other aspects; for example, that being a manager and a foreigner can wipe out signs of femininity/womanhood.

The Sudanese businessman can be read in different ways. One option is of course to see him as expressing a stereotypical, prejudiced view on women – seeing women and business as mutually exclusive phenomena. Another is to see him as a skilled constructivist, capable of discoupling essentialist ideas about gender being defined through biology, and thereby expressing insights in harmony with pomo thinking. A third option, perhaps to be preferred from a pomo point of view, is to offer both interpretations. (I treat the topic of multiple interpretations in Chapter 7.)

If the reader thinks that all this sounds strange and unfamiliar it is in line with what pomo unpacking aims to accomplish. Defamiliarization is an important part of critical research (Marcus and Fischer 1986; Alvesson and Deetz 2000). Instead of established ideas and beliefs being adapted and confirmed, they are disrupted. Taken-for-granted, commonsensical ideas are challenged. The well known, natural and self-evident should be approached in a manner that makes it appear strange, arbitrary and unfamiliar.

Critique of pomo ideas on gender

Postmodernist feminism has strongly argued that the idea of something universal or broadly generalizable about women should be abandoned. The postmodernist ideal of local knowledge is celebrated, implying an interest in the specifics of a particular group, limited to a certain time and place. But this ideal has, of course, met with strong resistance.

One line of critique maintains that the ideal of diversity and variation is strongly exaggerated. Most researchers now probably accept that it is not reasonable to consider our universalized and abstract notions of gender, reproduction, sexuality, discrimination, marriage, man, woman etc. to be adequate when they are applied to a wide range of different cultures, groups in society, historical periods etc. But this does not exclude the possibility that some generalizations could be relevant or even necessary in order to say anything of any interest.

> In our determination to honor diversity among women, we told one another to restrict our ambitions, limit our sights, beat a retreat from certain topics, refrain from using a rather long list of categories or concepts, and eschew generalization. I can think of no better prescription for the stunting of a field of intellectual inquiry.
>
> (Martin 1994: 631)

Bordo (1990) also finds the emphasis on diversity problematic, as it easily leads to a mechanical and coercive requirement that all enlightened feminist projects should take race, class and gender seriously. One cannot, however, include many axes and still preserve analytical focus and argument, she notes. In addition, the ideal of diversity would mean that research does not stop with adding class and race to gender. The list of what diversity may draw attention to is endless: sexual orientation, ethnicity, age, family conditions, occupation . . . These categories can also, and quite contrary to postmodernist ideals, be seen as unitary, macro, *a priori*. Discourses involving these variables may, from a postmodernist point of view, call for deconstruction – showing the fragile and contradictory nature of the way in which they are used – rather than being understood as positive and authoritative guidelines for what should be explored. Another objection to poststructuralism questions not the value of the approach as such, but its current relevance to feminist studies. Di Stefano (1990) finds postmodernism a valuable inspiration for reflections within academic fields that have already obtained a certain stability and strength. This, according to Di Stefano, is not the case for feminism, and the disturbance of ideas and notions that is usually the result of postmodernist reflections could therefore have very destructive consequences. Bordo (1990) also feels that postmodernism would seriously harm the critical potential and political impact of feminism, and argues that it is too soon to let our institutions 'off the hook via postmodern heterogeneity and instability' (p. 153).

There are some good reasons for sticking to the established category of woman, but it is equally if not more important to disrupt ongoing discourses that fix human identities and social relations in 'men' and 'women', thereby weakening the impact of this organizing principle. Access to an alternative vocabulary, such as the one suggested here, might be a way forward. One can argue that it is not vocabulary that matters as much as the reasoning and understanding of the words used. That is true, but what is important here is the discourse – the combination of the vocabulary and the line of thinking. Words like 'woman' and 'man' holds a strong grip on thinking and that contributes to conservativism and muddled thinking, including the strong tendency to privilege biology even if one is interested in social construction. Experimentation with words, including using a defamiliarizing vocabulary, facilitates the questioning of established frameworks and is a part of the development of new discourses.

My purpose is not, however, to claim that the vocabulary suggested here is necessarily the best or that 'conservative' signifiers such as 'man and 'woman' should be skipped altogether.[3] I am more interested in trying to show how established ideas can be challenged and rethought. I realize that talk about 'man' and 'woman' is difficult to avoid – they are too deeply ingrained in cultural understandings and in the self-identities of people. Partly as a consequence thereof, these categories have some virtues as part of a research vocabulary. One possibility is the use of alternative and varied vocabularies. One could imagine texts alternating between familiar and defamiliarizing vocabularies, between (cautiously) use of the word 'women' to encourage women-oriented demands and use of other vocabularies (bio-women, XX-persons) to encourage liberation from conventional wisdom and the conservative and stereotyping tendencies that privilege biology and the identities so forcefully imposed by it.

Implications for research practice

What would be the consequences of an unpacking approach in research practice? It would mean that dominant categories, used by research traditions as well as the subjects being studied, should be avoided in the formulation of research questions, in fieldwork, in categorizations of data and in the analysis and writing up of results. All work becomes more difficult, but the strong pressure not to reproduce traditional understandings and the established knowledge inherent in the use of standard distinctions and categories may fuel creativity and novel lines of thinking.

The researcher must then actively move away from the basic conventions and convictions that are inherent in language use and that govern intellectual activity and research practice. This is difficult, but moderate success might be a realistic objective. I continue to use the case of gender and women as my key example, but the ideas set out below aim to be of general relevance.

Sceptically follow the natives

One possibility here is to try to take an open stance and investigate when social categorizations such as man, woman, masculine and feminine appear in the talk of those being studied – in everyday life and in research interviews. Here – in opposition to when the researcher makes subjects talk about gender – the focus should be on when and how the categorizations appear unobtrusively. This would allow a better empirical picture of the constructions of gender in the setting being studied. A considerable problem is, of course, that gender constructions might not be made explicit in talk. Not all communication is verbal and explicit. Gendered meanings can also be hidden and hard to interpret. Discourse analysis and discursive pragmatism lose what is not spoken, and some space for interpretation of what is expressed in the form of subtle hints and undertones must be allowed.

A related problem is that detecting social construction processes through the study of everyday life or by listening to very open or only weakly directed interview accounts can be very uneconomical for the researcher. It may take a long time before interesting empirical material appears. This is, of course, in itself of some interest as it may indicate that gender construction processes are not very salient compared to other ways of constructing subjects, social relations and social practices. The frequency of gender categorization in relationship to other membership categorizations (age, profession etc.) might be studied. One option in interviews would be to start with relatively open questions which permit the frequency of gender categorizations to be checked and then, in the second half of an interview, to address more clearly gender-relevant issues. One might, for example, start by asking 'How do you experience your workplace?' (interactions with others, ideal job etc.) and 'How do you think people feel about working in this organization?' Later, more specific questions could be asked, e.g. 'How do you as a woman/man experience . . . ?' One could then see if and when gender – in terms of statements about men and women or male and female values, orientations etc. – emerges and evaluate its significance. The latter, more directive question may be used in the final part of an interview in order to compare answers or explore additional aspects. Of course, relatively open questions do not mean the absence of a prestructuring of responses. A feminist researcher will by her (or his) very presence probably trigger different responses from a non-feminist even if the same questions are asked.

Sceptically following the natives would be done not solely in order to discover or point at some underlying pattern or meaning, but also to point at the variations, discrepancies and variety of local, fluid meanings presumably attached to, for example, women.

Use vocabulary encouraging friction and defamiliarization

Another possibility is to use a research vocabulary that aims to cover similar terrain to the dominant categories but to do so in a strange, challenging manner. The use of vocabularies and accounts that approach the issues in ways deviating from standard scripts is here valuable. Instead of an interview subject being identified as a woman, or, following a body counting exercise, the conclusion being drawn that there were eight men and two women in a meeting, the signifier 'woman' can be replaced by something else, such as XX-person, that explicitly refers to biological criteria but nothing more, i.e. not tying any specific social meaning to this biology.

In a similar way, signifiers such as value, decision, teaching and manager can be avoided for being too strongly loaded with a universal and taken-for-granted meaning. We can talk about high wage persons and large office-holders as alternatives to managers. Instead of accepting teenagers as a self-evident category we can talk about three-quarter adults or individuals in a post-child period. Thereby we can counter the tendency to ascribe a taken-for-granted essence to subjects associated with established categories, carrying meanings not sufficiently thought through and rethought.

Consider variation and emphasize diversity and multiple meanings within a category

A third possibility is to be guided by the pomo slogan 'multiple voices'. This overlaps the first point about sceptically following natives in a discourse-pragmatist fashion, noting variation. But multiple voices can encourage more broadly embraced pluralist moves. Many researchers struggling with a varied empirical material probably feel like Acker (1989: 78) when she asks, 'how do we put together the myriad standpoints of women?' Acker may have intended to encourage a positive answer, a solution to a problem, but this would not be in line with pomo. From a postmodernist perspective this question should encourage critical reflection on how this actually is done, i.e. how order is created and fragmentation suppressed. The postmodernist avoids putting standpoints together thus hiding the diversity; instead, the myriad should come through in research texts. The ideal is a radical openness for 'women', expressing a myriad of standpoints, which are different not just between different groups, but also within a specific group. Here any categorizations (lawyers, single mothers, Turkish immigrants or voters) call for scepticism and unpacking. It should be added that the postmodernist is not satisfied with sensitivity to intragroup diversity. Within a specific individual subject there is variation in the expression of standpoints – which one would see as temporary and fluid, not fixed and integrated.

Summary

In this chapter, I have addressed the topic of unpacking important and dominant categories as a major ingredient in pomo-oriented social research. I have used gender and more specifically the term 'women' in order to exemplify what unpacking may look like.

I have made two overall, interrelated suggestions in this section: avoid privileging the use of dominant, taken-for-granted categories; and aim for the defamiliarization of established lines of thinking. This has been exemplified by the effort to discourage the use of the distinction between 'men' and 'women' based on biological criteria. It is suggested that other signifiers can be used when biology-based criteria are employed, e.g. in 'body counting' gender studies.

Both unpacking and defamiliarization try to resist the conformist pressure inherent in cultural ideas and language use. These two 'enemies' of radical openness often go together. An illuminating example, resisting conventional ideas and language use, is the Sudanese businessman who did not treat his female guest according to conservatively defined, biological criteria and refused to use conventional vocabulary.

There are two principal reasons for the avoidance of universal concepts: one concerns how such concepts create homogeneity and neglect diversity; another is that they impose stability and consistency. In the case of gender it has been emphasized fairly broadly that the idea of 'women' in general should not be addressed: diversity between different groups associated with class, age, sexual orientation, historical time and ethnicity is profound. Women must be understood locally. But also if one concentrates on a specific group at a specific time, there are no reasons, according to postmodernism, to assume stable meanings and experiences associated with this group. Even the biological sex of a woman has different and perhaps even contradictory meanings in different situations: in the gynaecological clinic, in relation to (non-)marriage and sexuality, children, various aspects of family lives. 'Women' as a signifier not primarily referring to biological sex has a variety of shifting meanings in settings in which biology/body matters less, e.g. different employment situations, political elections, equal policy situations, when being exposed to ads etc. Because of these considerations some researchers think unitary notions such as 'woman', 'feminine gender identity', 'femininity' and 'mothering' are problematic, as they imply a false unity and suppress divergence and variety (Fraser and Nicholson 1988). The pomo arguments against producing representations, knowledge creating the world and master narratives about Patriarchy, Gender and Orders, in which males and females are separated and females subordinated, are highly relevant to a challenge to dominant commonsensical and gender equality ideas.

That the meaning of 'woman' is not universal, but varies with the language contexts – discourses – in which it is used does not necessarily imply that it has to be abandoned in social studies. It appears to be difficult to avoid totally, as are other common concepts, such as masculinity, dominance, hierarchy, discrimination, division of labour. It is important to consider the trade-off between the women/men distinction as a necessary element in social and political projects that counteract prejudice and repression, and the distinction as exercising power through being made central, natural and self-evident, producing subjects who define themselves and others as 'women' and 'men', thereby implying different ways of being. The trick is to employ major categories with great care and considerable doubt, in ways that avoid indicating a misleading unity. This can be done if language use is governed by an appreciation of the local context that gives these words some temporary and precarious meaning in particular instances. This understanding is intimately connected to the postmodernist understanding of language, as something more and other than a neutral and simple reflection of reality.

Postmodernists question the very idea of finding a universal ground for reason, science, progress or even the subject. The feminist search for Truth – or the Genuine female standpoint – is seen as just one more attempt to conquer reality, and it prevents researchers and those consuming their texts from understanding ambiguities, diversity and fragmentation, and how reality is rhetorically constructed rather than discovered by social researchers. Rather than the development of valid knowledge based on a firm methodological standpoint or a strong political commitment, sensitive listening and the provision of space for alternative voices are celebrated. Rather than broad generalizations, local theory – emphasizing the uniqueness in a specific case – is to be privileged.

Three research methods for accomplishing this have been addressed in the chapter. One is to refrain from using theoretical vocabularies and ways of reasoning built on established categories, and instead carefully to follow the language use of those being studied. The discourses produced by those being studied can then be followed and the fluctuating and ambiguous meanings indicated. One can, for example, explore the variety of subject positions that various subjects in various micro-situations place women in. This approach follows a discourse-analytical or, less strictly, discursive pragmatism approach to the subject matter.

A second approach is to use a research tactic of defamiliarization. Here the researcher actively tries to avoid well known established categories and ways of structuring a field. Defamiliarization can take a variety of different expressions, partly related to literary form and style of writing. Here I have pointed at how core categories can be replaced by vocabularies that: (a) mean the use of a slightly different distinction; and (b) involve an element of making the well known alien and strange. As an example I suggested the use of XY- and XX-subjects for 'men' and 'women', thus pointing out that the base for the distinction is certain ideas about biological characteristics, rather than some combined biological and social 'essence'.

A third approach is the conscious use of multiple voices, with an emphasis on diversity and multiple meanings. This can to some extent be accomplished in a discourse analysis type project, but this is restricted to a detailed and rigorous reading of accounts. It is possible to embrace a diversity/multiple voices approach more strongly, actively to search for and encourage the expression of diversity, e.g. in the choice of informants, the encouragement of these taking different subject positions (you as a mother, a mother of teenagers, as a female colleague, in your relationship with older/younger men . . .) or the choice of observational settings. The analytic strategy emphasizes diversity rather than patterns.

As many feminist critics of pomo have argued, a strong emphasis on these kinds of ideas may well weaken any project's efforts to explore broader patterns of gender inequality and forms of repression. By emphasizing the unique example and arguing against the interest of what some people think are broadly shared experiences, pomo thinking may well discourage political and social projects of widespread relevance, and thus leave current gender relations intact, thus serving dominant groups. The risk of such an impact, at least with a very strong version of pomo thinking, should not be underestimated. A similar reservation with regard to defamiliarization can be mentioned. It might lead to feelings of alienation for groups of people not used to such tricks, and appeal mainly to fairly sophisticated people. Work with pomo ideas calls for careful consideration of their effects and possibly the use of pedagogical skills, if one does not wish to face a narrow reader-ship and a limited social and political impact. I come back to the topic of writing in Chapter 7.

Notes

1 Inconsistencies are, of course, hard to avoid. Too much demand on rigour may lead to narrow and uninteresting work. Postmodernism would have it that incon-sistencies cannot be avoided. All texts are full of loopholes. Sometimes, however, they need to be addressed critically.
2 In this chapter I treat body and biological criteria for separating men and women as unproblematic, which is far from a self-evident position. The body is, of course, not pure, objective nature. One may, for example, say that there are a large number of biological sexes, depending on what criteria one is using (see Kaplan and Rogers 1990 for a review). Still, in the majority of cases there is not much ambiguity as to whether a person is biologically male or female.
3 To repeat, there is no automatic relationship between certain biological (sex) equipment and the social construction of sex. That this is so is evident if we con-sider cultural, class, racial etc. variation, but even in a specific social group a particular body is not an object of standardized social construction processes. Not all carriers of female bodies become secretaries, nurses or kindergarten teachers, become subordinated to men or are understood by others and/or see themselves as oriented towards relatedness, empathy and nurturance. There may be strong ten-dencies that a female body triggers processes of this nature, but a specific person, with a female body, may well depart from this path.

6 Postmodernism and interviews

It is now time to discuss what perhaps most people understand as the core issues of social research: methods for the generation of the empirical material through which knowledge is created. As noted, postmodernism encourages us to downplay their significance: how we work with language – including how we relate to dominant concepts and discourses – and how we write are seen by most pomos as more decisive elements in research work. The literature on postmodernism is not very informative about specific practices for data generation: it doesn't provide much guidance for what to do in the field. It provides mainly 'negative' lessons of the futility of representation or how knowledge claims exercise power by ordering the world targeted. There seems to be more talk about the case for postmodern ethnography than successful examples of such work. As this book does not follow a 'faithful' pomo route, but draws upon pomo ideas to inspire empirical social research, my task is a bit simpler than that of those defining their projects as postmodernist.

This chapter addresses qualitative interviewing, although many of the themes have broad relevance for research in general. Why do I pick interviews as my example of research practice? Qualitative research has become increasingly common in social studies. This is often exclusively or mainly based on interviews, which appear to be the most frequently used technique in qualitative work. In ethnographies, interviews are typically an important part of the arsenal of techniques employed. There are many comments on ethnography from a postmodernist perspective, but such texts often relate largely to basic problems with conventional understandings of culture and/or the need for new ways of writing, and I draw upon this in other chapters. In the present one, I am interested in the more specific aspects of data generation.

The chapter starts with a brief overview of common ways of understanding interviews, followed by a proposal for how to rethink the research interview based on some postmodernist ideas. Then follow sections on the implications of such a rethinking for technique, for interpretation and for the research questions that it is possible and productive to study.

Major positions on interviewing: neopositivism and romanticism

'Interview' has – like everything else – no distinct meaning. The focus of this chapter is on interviews that aim to get 'rich accounts'. They are typically relatively time-consuming to carry out and lead to varied responses from interviewees. Qualitative interviews – in opposition to 'talking questionnaires' (Potter and Wetherell 1987) – are relatively loosely or semi-structured and open, to some extent, to what the interviewee feels it is relevant and important to talk about, given the interest of the research project. Interviews are beneficial in as much as a rich account of the interviewee's experiences, knowledge, ideas and impressions may be considered and documented, advocates of interviews typically argue (Bryman *et al.* 1988; Fontana and Frey 1994; Holstein and Gubrium 1997). Two basic positions on interviews – positions that can be found in relationship to qualitative research in general – can be identified.

The *neopositivist* is eager to establish a context-free truth about reality 'out there' by following a research protocol and getting responses relevant to it, minimizing researcher influence and other sources of 'bias'. Here, 'the interview conversation is a pipeline for transmitting knowledge' (Holstein and Gubrium 1997: 113). The interest is typically in how things are: 'facts' about structures, processes, relations etc. are studied. This is at least often the intention. Most interview-based research that gets published in disciplines and journals dominated by conventional research standards tend to be neopositivist. Researchers imitate quantitative ideals for data production, analysis and writing. Rules, procedures, avoidance of bias, detailed coding, large quantities of material etc. are emphasized in methodological texts as well as empirical writings (e.g. Glaser and Strauss 1967; Eisenhardt 1989). The ideal is a maximally transparent research process, characterized by objectivity and neutrality.

The *romantic*, advocating a more 'genuine' human interaction, believes in establishing rapport, trust and commitment between interviewer and interviewee in the interview situation. This is a prerequisite in order to be able to explore the inner world (meanings, ideas, feelings, intentions) or experienced social reality of the interviewee. The typical ambition of interview studies is to accomplish 'deeper, fuller conceptualizations of those aspects of our subject's lives we are most interested in understanding' (Miller and Glassner 1997: 103). Words like deep, full experience, definition, meaning, view and intersubjective dominate these texts. Romantics emphasize interactivity with and closeness to interviewees. Romantics take seriously the risk that interviewees are guided by expectations of what the researcher wants to hear and social norms for how one expresses oneself. They believe, however, that establishing close personal contact with respondents – who are seen as 'participants' instead – might minimize this problem. Fontana and Frey (1994: 371), for example, suggest that the researcher may reject the 'outdated' technique of avoiding getting involved or providing personal opinion, and instead engage in a 'real' conversation with 'give and take' and 'emphatic understanding': 'This makes the interview more honest, morally sound, and reliable, because it treats the respondent as an equal, allows him or her to express personal feelings, and therefore presents a more 'realistic' picture that can be uncovered using traditional interview methods.'

Here emphases on empathy and the development of trust are assumed to 'solve' the problem. Other advocates of interviews talk about 'active interviewing' as an ideal form (Ellis *et al.* 1997; Holstein and Gubrium 1997). Here, the idea is that the researcher's interventions transform the interview subject 'from a repository of opinions and reasons or a wellspring of emotions into a productive source of knowledge' (Holstein and Gubrium 1997: 121), as 'the subject's interpretative capabilities must be activated, stimulated and cultivated' (p. 122). The interview subject has much of value to say, but this calls for the researcher to lead the subject into intelligent talk. One could say that some interview proponents have responded to the critique of the more cool, minimalistic versions of interviewing – aiming to avoid bias – by advocating hyperromanticism, i.e. escalating efforts to accomplish 'depth' and authenticity by turning the interview into a moral peak (as in the quotation from Fontana and Frey above), or by activism, turning the interviewee into a focused and systematic knowledge producer.

The state of the art: moderate doubts?

The development of interview methods has moved from neopositivist conceptions to an increased awareness of the complexity of the interview situation, including the need to get the full cooperation of interviewees. Most of the literature on interviewing still deals at length with how this practice may be utilized as effectively as possible to get the interview subject to talk a lot, openly, trustfully, honestly, clearly and freely about what the researcher is interested in. In general, interview accounts are presented as data pointing at a particular reality, and very little space is typically used to discuss the weaknesses and problems of linking accounts with some interior or exterior reality.

A still relatively small, but growing, stream on interviewing breaks with the assumptions and purpose of neopositivists and romantics, including discourse analysts and like-minded language- and conversation-focused researchers (e.g. Silverman 1993). As addressed in Chapter 4, there are some similarities with pomo but also significant differences. This approach, which can be referred to as *localist*, emphasizes the point that interview statements must be seen in their micro-context. An interview is an empirical situation that can be studied as such, and should not be treated as a tool for the collection of data on something existing outside this empirical situation. Localists do not see the interview as different from other events and situations. People talk with their bosses, they visit cinemas, they drive cars. They also participate in interviews – although research interviews, at least for the majority of people, are rare events and thus differ from more typical conversations. Behaviour in research interviews can be studied in similar ways to these other phenomena, but is not necessarily seen as a very interesting phenomenon owing to its special character. Interview talk does not, from this position, offer valid knowledge of other settings, it just informs us how people behave in the interview situation: what stories they tell etc. The interest of postmodernist authors in interviews have been fairly limited. One exception is Scheurich (1997), who argues against the romantics' ideal of the interviewer and interviewee working together in an open and productive manner to co-construct meaning. Scheurich claims that 'Interview interactions do not have some essential, teleogical tendency toward an ideal of "joint construction of meaning"', irrespective of the intentions and skills of the researcher (p. 66).

The popularity of postmodernist, localist and other sceptical ideas on method in general has had some effect on researchers using interviews for conventional purposes. Increasingly authors include remarks signalling caution about the validity of interview material, e.g. they use expressions such as interviewees 'reported such feelings' (Martin *et al.* 1998: 449) or 'gave me this account' (Barker 1993: 408). However, formulations such as these only marginally soften the impression that the data and results presented are robust and authoritative, and the reader is not encouraged to reflect upon the meanings of the interviews made and what the accounts really are about.

The literature seldom incorporates any ambitious theoretical ideas on this subject matter and tends to treat them as biases to be overcome with techniques or as something to be aware of in analysis. Most writers on interviews assume that skills can be developed and an approach taken in which errors are minimized and qualified empirical material is produced (see, for example, Whyte 1960; Easterby-Smith *et al.* 1991; Fontana and Frey 1994; Kvale 1996). There is a limited appropriation in the interview literature of localist ideas oriented towards going beyond studying the setting. Holstein and Gubrium (1997), for example, suggest that 'understanding *how* the meaning-making process unfolds in the interview is as critical as apprehending *what* is substantively asked and conveyed' (p. 114). The interest in local circumstances and processes ('how') does not prevent these authors from believing in the ability of interview answers 'to convey situated experiential realities in terms that are locally comprehensible' (p. 117) and interview subjects from holding facts and details of experience, although in the interview the subject 'constructively adds to, takes away from and transforms the facts and details' (p. 117). The interview then appears, on the whole, as a valid source of knowledge production, although the social process and local conditions need to be appreciated and actively managed by the interviewer in order to gain valid results.

Still, interview accounts are seen as providing clues – perhaps indirect and uncertain, but still clues – to the 'interiors' of the interviewees or the exteriors of organizational practices. In order to be more open to the idea that interview statements reveal less about these phenomena and more about something else, I will suggest a couple of theoretical conceptualizations of the research interview and its dynamics. My approach differs from the preoccupation with the researcher's subjectivity, and ways of dealing with this, that dominates efforts to reflect upon the complexities of the research interview and its outcomes. I emphasize the research interview and the multitude of forces acting upon it and the interviewee, competing with 'reality out there' and 'genuine experiences' in influencing talk.

An example of interview research: interpretive and postmodernist views

Jorgenson (1991) provides a good example of the need to go beyond conventional approaches to interviews. Her research project was to understand how family members see themselves in families and to get a sense of people's relational selves as members of a 'family'. Rather than leaving it to the researcher (family therapist, social worker etc.) to define what is a family, it was seen as important to pay attention to how families understand themselves. This is a typical project for interview research, paying attention not to what the expert decides to be 'objective properties', but to the meanings and views of the subjects to be understood. Jorgenson learned, hardly surprisingly, that individuals – including those who see themselves as members of the same 'family' – vary in terms of how they draw boundaries between 'family' and 'non-family', and also in the criteria they use in order to account for their distinctions.

One could end the story there, but Jorgenson notes and reflects upon some basic complexities in the research that make it difficult simply to claim that people have some ideas about 'family' and the research showed these.

The conceptualization of 'family' is, here, bound up in the process by which interviewer and respondent negotiate a sense of mutual understanding out of initially ambiguous questions and terms; and how they accomplish this cooperative construction, I would argue, depends on how they come to interpret each other as social actors.

(Jorgenson 1991: 215)

The respondents, then, produced accounts based on their shifting perceptions and understandings of the interviewer. Inconsistencies and apparent contradictions within specific interview accounts could be understood not as 'errors', but as indications of the interpretive repertoires respondents use when making sense of the person they are talking to. As the interviewer does not remain a constant during the interview – the questions asked and the lines followed up, personal viewpoints expressed etc. all affect the construction of the person the respondent is talking to – variation comes through.

From a postmodernist position this could be seen as an illustration of the futility of establishing fixed meanings, ideas or understandings that emerge from a stable relational self as a family member. 'Family' must be decentred. There is a multitude of temporal, varying, sometimes inconsistent or even contradictory meanings in motion as 'family' is constructed and reconstructed in different situations. This variety and fluidity are not restricted to the interview situation, but can be traced in all kinds of situations and relations where 'family' becomes a topic.

Rethinking interviews: postmodernist inputs

The dominant ideas about the research interview seem to be: (a) that the interview is an *instrument*, to be used as effectively as possible in the more or less capable hands of the researcher; and (b) that this is employed in a *human encounter*, where the encouragement of the interviewee to reveal her authentic experiences is crucial. Often these are combined – the instrument is in the service of messy social engineering rather than surgery, and this calls for interaction with a human touch in order for the interview tool to work. Arguably, these ideas are pragmatically helpful and fit into neopositivistic and romantic epistemologies, but draw attention away from significant aspects of the interview as a complex social situation.

The interviewer and the interviewee as sources of 'problems'

There are at least three obvious problematic issues undermining the interview as a knowledge-producing situation: the interviewer, the interviewee and the social situation. As Scheurich (1997: 62) points out, 'the researcher has multiple intentions and desires, some of which are consciously known and some of which are not. The same is true of the interviewee.' Most researchers probably think that this sounds deeply problematic and tend to construct the researcher-interviewer (i.e. themselves) as well as the interviewee in more positive terms, assuming that they are both engaged in the knowledge-pursuing project and capable of mobilizing a reasonable degree of rationality. Some researchers would agree with the view that the subjects involved in the interview are far from rational, but assume the intellectual and theoretical capacity of the researcher to master the situation: 'We intend to construe both researcher and researched as anxious, defended subjects, whose mental boundaries are porous where unconscious material is concerned. This means that both will be subject to projections and introjections of ideas and feelings coming from the other person' (Hollway and Jefferson 2000: 45). Here it is assumed that psychoanalysis and narrative analysis make it possible to understand the research relationship, and paying attention to the researcher's own feelings becomes a valuable aid in interpreting the subject matter. While postmodernism would applaud the recognition of the role of feelings and the recognition of the complexity of the research situation, it would be very doubtful about the possibility of interpreting the situation, as well as the use of psychoanalytic and narrative theory as means of clarification.

There is a considerable focus in the method literature on how to make the interview situation as rational and productive as possible by effective interviewer behaviour. Eisenhardt (1989), for example, recommends that there be two interviewers present, one asking questions and the other making observations of what is happening, in order to reduce interviewer subjectivity and bias. The interview with one active interviewer and one passive observer is similar to a police interrogation – which nicely illustrates Foucault's view on the power–knowledge connection in social inquiry.[1] Eisenhardt misses the impact of the social setting on the interviewee, a complex setting with consequences for the responses that are partly outside the researcher's control. The interviewee's response is mainly seen as an outcome of how the researcher frames the situation, asks and follows up questions, establishes confidence etc.

But the interviewee may be far less compliant or able to mobilize for truth-seeking projects. The romantic view on interviewing is grounded in an image of a potentially honest, unselfish subject, eager or at least willing to share his or her experiences and knowledge for the benefit of the interviewer and the research project. The interviewee then supposedly acts in the interest of science. The view of the interviewee as an informant illustrates this assumption. However, interviewees may have interests other than assisting science by simply providing information. They may be *politically aware and politically motivated actors*. Many people have a political interest in how socially significant issues are represented. This does not necessarily mean that they cheat or lie. Honesty and political awareness do not necessarily conflict.

Willing respondents not using the interview mainly for their own political purposes might very well tell the (partial) truth as they know it, but in ways that are favourable to them, and not disclose truths unfavourable to them and their group (Alvesson 2001).

However, apart from pointing out basic 'shortcomings' of the interviewer as well as the interview in relationship to the ideal of subjects engaged in the research-guided or participative project of knowledge-seeking, it is perhaps more fruitful to look less narrowly at specific actors and focus more on the social situation as well as on the ordering principles – Discourses with capital D – that construct subjects. This would be more in line with postmodernism – which discourages an interest in the level of the subject as the origin of motives and capacities – and is what I do next. The first section – adopting a discourse pragmatism view – takes a look at the local setting, the second addresses, in a more Foucauldian manner, Big Discourse operating behind and on the subject.

The interview in its local context

An interview is a social situation in which two persons (or more) who are typically unfamiliar to each other meet for a short period of time, on average around one or two hours. The interviewer has set up this situation 'in order that the respondent speaks openly, authentically or truthfully, to produce valid reporting on some interior or exterior state of affairs' (Baker 1997: 130) so that the interviewer can use this speech as 'data' in a research publication. In interviews, localists argue, people are not reporting external events but producing situated accounts, drawing upon cultural resources in order to produce morally adequate accounts. Against the neopositivist and to a considerable extent also the romantic view on the interview as a technique, localists see it as situated accomplishment (Silverman 1993: 104).

What takes place during the interview may be seen as a complex interaction in which the participants make efforts to produce a particular order, drawing upon cultural knowledge to structure the situation, and to minimize embarrassment and frustration, feelings of asymmetrical relations of status and power etc. Making the other comfortable, saving face, making him or her open up and engage in 'relevant', productive talk through a mix of means, including providing clues as to what is interesting and what is not, calls for activity on behalf of the interviewer. There are different opinions in the literature concerning the optimum degree of friendliness versus neutrality and interviewer activity versus the avoidance of the creation of bias through too much interference. The dilemma is a classical one (Cicourel 1964).

Irrespective of preferences here, complex social interaction that aims to establish a functioning micro-order takes precedence over the researcher triggering productive responses through certain techniques. The interplay between two people with their own gender, age, professional background, personal appearance, ethnicity and so on makes a deep imprint on the accounts produced. Parker (2000), for example, notes how age had strong significance in his interviews with managers: in some cases, with older interviewees, he was addressed as junior, as a novice: in others, with people close to his age, he was used as a confidante; and in a third type of relation, with very junior and/or marginal people, he was seen as an expert (management consultant or even management spy). Jorgenson (1991), while presenting herself as a communication researcher interested in how families think about family life, was perceived as a research psychologist by some interviewees and as a family expert by others. (As she was visibly pregnant during the last part of the research, her position as 'soon to be a parent' became salient for some interviewees.) As an 'expert' she was more often seen as a potential critic who would evaluate participants' responses with reference to what is normal or appropriate. She argues that 'the person to whom a research subject speaks is not the person an interviewer thinks herself to be' (p. 211).

More mundane issues, such as physical location, may also matter in the framing of the interview. Some researchers note different responses when interviewing managers in their offices and in other settings (parking area, home, canteen) (Easterby-Smith *et al.* 1991).[2] The specific words used by the interviewer, his or her gestures, writing behaviour (accounts may be followed by more or less intensive note-taking) and so on affect the responses of the interviewee. Carrying the point a bit further, Schneider (2000), in a study of interviews in an educational organization, shows how interviewers are not 'simple conduits for answers but rather are deeply implicated in the production of answers' (p. 162). Accounts produced are in themselves empirical phenomena calling for explanation, not reflections of other empirical phenomena or 'proofs' of explanations of these, localists argue (Silverman 1985, 1993; Baker 1997).

The significance of the interview as local accomplishment makes it more reasonable to see interview accounts as contingent upon the specific situation and too local to be taken as reflections of how the interviewee thinks, feels, talks and acts in situations that are totally different from the interview situation. The interviewee becomes different persons in different relationships – a person is not the same when interviewed by someone perceived as a consultant reporting directly to her superior in an organization as when interviewed by a young person who needs her help in order to produce a dissertation. Different identities come forward when one is interviewed by someone perceived as a research psychologist, a family expert, a communication researcher or a soon-to-be-first-time-parent, to refer to the case of Jorgensen noted above. This calls for an appreciation of the local nature of interview talk and the specific identities that come forward in this specific situation – which may be loosely coupled to the identities that are constituted and expressed in other situations.

Big Discourse constituting the interviewee – the interview as a play of the powers of discourse

To repeat one of the main points of Chapter 3, postmodernists – and many others for that matter – challenge the idea of the conscious, autonomous, holistic and clearly defined individual as the bearer of meaning and as an active and 'acting' subject around which the social world rotates (e.g. Foucault 1980; Weedon 1987; Deetz 1992). Assumptions about the individual as a coherent, unique and, in terms of motivation and cognition, more or less integrated universe – a dynamic centre for consciousness, emotions, evaluations and actions – are viewed as problematic (Geertz 1983: 59). Of course, this critique goes to the heart of the neopositivists' and romantics' conception of the interview subject and rejects the idea of interviewee accounts saying something specific about the thoughts, feelings, intentions or experiences of him or her.

The postmodernists want to shift focus from the autonomous individual to a linguistic and discursive context, which socially creates forms and expressions of subjectivity limited in time and space.[3] Language is not an expression of subjectivity; instead – it is claimed – it is what constitutes subjectivity. From this it follows that subjectivity is frequently unstable and ambiguous – a process rather than a structure. Thinking and actions 'depend on the circulation between subjectivities and discourses which are available' (Hollway 1984: 252). The presence of a powerful Discourse might stabilize subjectivity, but the plurality of discourse in people's lives typically encourages varied and fluctuating subjectivities.

Discourses are not produced or mastered by the individual: they speak him or her, in that available discourses position the person in the world in a particular way and at a given time, prior to the individual having any sense of choice. In terms of interviewing, this understanding would see the situation as an outcome of the discourses that are present, constituting the subject and her talk. The accounts produced are mainly of interest as indications of the discourses at play and the powers over the individual subject (Foucault 1980). Prior (1997: 70) argues that 'a representation should be understood not as a true and accurate reflection of some aspect of an external world, but as something to be explained and accounted for through the discursive rules and themes that predominate in a particular socio-historical context'.

If a subject is asked about, for example, her motives for taking a particular sort of education, the motive talk would be viewed as an indication of socially dominant discourses about how the normalized subject thinks, feels and functions. Any reference to self-actualization, personal development, career or intrinsic motivation – not necessarily formulated in these terms – would be seen not as anchored in the subject, but as an expression of the Discourse in operation, placing the person interviewed in a particular, temporal subject position. Postmodernists would be sceptical of any claims of true motives being reflected in talk, but also of the very idea of subjects having clear motives guiding their actions.

The Discourse power play view, then, explores how discourses make themselves present in the interview situation, work on the subject and give primacy to how he or she 'carries' certain constitutions of the social world. The interviewee is then seen – almost – as a puppet on the string of the discourse(s). This metaphor can be criticized for ascribing too much strength to discourse and assuming too weak a subject (Newton 1998; Alvesson and Kärreman 2000). As a potentially inspiring countermetaphor to dominant conceptions, it might, however, like the others here proposed, be productive. Upon reflection, it is perhaps less exaggerating or 'biased' than the dominant views of the interview as an instrument controlled by the researcher, or as an encounter in which interviewer and interviewee openly participate in order to produce joint meaning and knowledge.

Implications for methodology

Pragmatic response

The reader interested in exploring meaning, experience and complex social practices might now feel at some unease and even ask what the point of doing interviews is. Such a feeling about how much, even if, social life can be explored is of course a consistent feeling when one is confronted with pomo ideas, but is perhaps even more acute and distinct in the context of interviews. It is *not*, however, my intention to make an extremely strong case against an instrumental use of interviews. While postmodernists and others (localists and advocates of observational methods) have delivered important critiques of neopositivist as well as romantic notions of interviewing, it would be premature to ban this method or to use it exclusively in 'minimalistic' ways. As with all scepticism and critique, it may be too harsh and taken too far. Studying interview talk solely as local accomplishment and treating accounts as the object of study, or viewing these as indications of the Discourse, are important and somewhat novel options, but they exclude too many interesting research themes. There is a trade-off between relevance and rigour, and localists perhaps put too much emphasis on rigour. Privileging this virtue over relevance would mean that rather narrowly focused observations or tape-recordings of talk would be the only valid approaches, while questionnaires and interviews as means of obtaining data on phenomena 'outside' what is the direct focus – interview talk – would hardly do. Even an ambition to study Discourse is tricky, as one is here making speculative claims about interview talk – discourse in a micro sense – as saying something about Discourse, i.e. a mode of reasoning about and shaping the world that structures language use and experiences. Critique needs to be balanced against dimensions and virtues other than the particular yardstick from which something is judged to be insufficient.

Taking postmodernist and other critiques 'reasonably' seriously – some may say halfheartedly – can lead to interview material being seen as difficult, but not impossible, to use for 'conventional' analysis, i.e. saying something about the views, meanings or beliefs of people and/or about their behaviours and practices (i.e. 'material practices'). The researcher should provide good reasons for giving interview material a particular ontological status, in particular if it is seen as referring to social phenomena out there or the interior (level of meaning) of the interviewee and his or her likes. While a moderate acceptance of the postmodernist views would lead to caution and scepticism, one can imagine a more 'optimistic' or 'constructive' reading where implications for methodological practices and greater care in the interpretation of interview accounts can be developed.

The co-option of pomo ideas by perspectives on the research interview that aim to use it to create social knowledge can lead to at least three different responses:

1 Regarding the interview as an instrument or encounter for knowledge production.
2 Regarding the understanding and interpretation of interview material.
3 Regarding the kind of research themes in which the shortcomings of the instrumental view of the interview may be 'less problematic'.

Implications for interview practice

The idea of using pomo insights to improve methods (techniques) might seem odd – and it might be only because I operate within the covers of a text on 'Postmodernism and social research' that this idea is possible. But some of the stuff put forward under the label postmodernism (or poststructuralism) includes insights that are useful in interview situations. Qualifying thinking on method by incorporating scepticism about conventional views may encourage more informed ways of fieldwork. Ideas about the language-sensitive and fragmented subject might, for example, have clear and strong implications for the interview.

An awareness of how dominant Discourses and conventions for expression can lead to script-following might, if one is not interested in studying that aspect, lead to interview interventions in which familiar, institutionalized ways of talking about things are discouraged. Here it is important that the researcher has done some work in advance and continues during the fieldwork to unpack dominant categories that define the initially formulated research theme, but also the notions that emerge as important during the research process. A simple technique is to ask questions such as 'Can you explore that using other words?' when interviewees use standard jargon.

This may trigger responses that are not caught in script-coherent expressions contingent upon Big Discourse or other norms for how one talks about certain matters. Restarting and coming back to a particular theme using different vocabularies (points of entry) at later stages in an interview might also be useful.

Some encouragement to use words other than those belonging to the dominant Discourse might loosen its grip on the accounts produced. The interviewer can explicitly encourage the interviewee to approach a subject such as 'leadership' from a different angle by not using this signifier – which incorporates a particular 'leadership' Discourse. One can, for example, ask about coordination, power, hierarchy, subordination and social relations between people with different formal positions, or managerial work, instead of, or in addition to, 'leadership'. Or one may consciously and explicitly position oneself and the research project in different ways, either for the same interviewee subject or for different subjects in a 'sample', thus investigating how different kind of assumptions or framed contexts for interviews affect the accounts produced. Jorgenson (1991), for example, could present herself as a 'research psychologist', a 'family expert' and 'soon to become a parent for the first time', and Parker (2000) could have emphasized his youth, his expertise, his pro- or anti-management orientations in presentations and in questions asked and comments made, and then seen if and how the responses varied. This might be seen as manipulation and involves an ethical problem. But most interviewers are not homogeneous and one-dimensional in their identities and orientations, and can 'honestly' express different self-images in different ways. And all forms of interviewing include an element of manipulation. Neopositivist ideals of remaining detached and neutral, at least if the researcher feels that the questions and responses are engaging, and the romantics' ideal of closeness, empathy etc., can both be seen as efforts to camouflage the situation: one stranger trying to exploit the 'inner life' of the other for his or her own research purposes. Occasionally, with a skilled, politically oriented interviewee, the exploitation might be in the other direction: what the researcher and her audience perceive to be the transmission of facts or the expression of authentic experiences masks the careful placement of interest-laden 'truths' into the legitimated sphere of scientific knowledge.

Implications for more rigorous interpretations of interviews

A second possible lesson from pomo-inspired ideas on how to understand interviews concerns how the interview accounts relate to the themes they address. Here one can imagine interpretations other than those favoured by most pomo writers – for whom any rigorous approach would be confined to deconstructive readings of the accounts as texts. One option for those inclined to maintain conventional concerns – using interviews to study phenomena other than local accomplishments in interviews – is to try more carefully to evaluate the 'nature' of the empirical material. One could try to scrutinize the interview material in terms of local accomplishment and as an outcome of Big Discourse, and think through whether it makes more or as much sense in these terms as a reflection of social practices or the 'inner life' of the interviewees. (There are, of course, also other ways of understanding, but I concentrate on the key 'rival' interpretations of interest in this chapter.) If local accomplishment or Big Discourse interpretations make most sense, then it is a bad idea to use the interview material to study the social outside the interview situation and outside the interview text. Incorporation of pomo ideas can then be seen as useful as a way of developing tougher criteria for the use of interview material than are conventional.

The empirical material that withstands the acid-bath of critical scrutiny – i.e. does not seem to be best understood through pomo or localist readings – can potentially be used in a conventional way. Some pomos believe that nothing, or only trivial statements, would withstand the bath, but one can imagine a more open approach, looking at the interview and finding out what it tells us rather than defining it *a priori* as local accomplishment or the expression of Big Discourse. For many people a source of worry is probably the difficulty of assessing interview statements in terms of competing under-standings: does it make most sense to see a specific interview account as local accomplishment, the outcome of Big Discourse, a reflection of the inter-viewee's beliefs or even external reality 'out there' (behaviour, practices)? It is seldom easy to tell which interpretation is 'the best' in an individual case.

Although problems regarding how interviews can best be understood should not be underestimated, judgement is key to all research activity, and more or less good reasons for a particular view on the status of the interview material can be advanced. This means that one argues for the possibility of substantiating the case for using interview accounts in order to make state-ments on phenomena 'out there' (outside the interview situation/text). In the conventional view on empirical material, the interviewee is assumed to have provided the researcher with reliable data about a phenomenon, as long as there are no apparent reasons to believe otherwise. Rules for coding and conventions for the presentation of data generally imply this kind of stance.

A more reflexive approach, using pomo ideas to a moderate degree, would replace this assumption with scepticism, but not *a priori* rejection. It would assume that there is a lot more than truth-telling – or co-construction of meaning – involved (as suggested above), but that these other elements or 'logics' do not necessarily dominate. It is only when it can be credibly argued that specific interview accounts have validity beyond the local context, beyond the reproduction of Discourse etc., and indicate something 'out there', that statements can be treated in this way. If accounts deviate from Discourses or scripts about how people should express themselves in certain situations, then some of the pomo arguments are weakened and the researcher can perhaps see them as strong indicators of how the interviewee experiences the focused social world. This needs to be thought through and shown; for example, by explicitly comparing the plausibility of this kind of interpretation with that of the alternative ones (e.g. local accomplishment and Big Discourse). Sometimes the trustworthiness of interview material can be strengthened with observational material, although it is normally not possible to compare different methods directly, due to variations in context (Potter and Wetherell 1987; Denzin 1994). From a pomo point of view, observations are not more reliable than interviews and are seen as the observer ordering and imprinting his or her language use on the world targeted for gazing. One should not accept such a categorical dismissal of observations, but it is important to recognize that observation is no safe way to superior knowledge either.

The point is that it is insufficient just to present, or refer to, a number of interview accounts or the use of a particular tactic for managing inter-viewees in order to claim trustworthiness. A common tactic is to emphasize the quantity of the empirical material and the technical rules for coding it. A large and varied range of empirical material might facilitate informed judgement, and rules for data management are sometimes practical, but there is a risk that large volumes and a reliance on technical procedures can draw attention away from, and reduce time and energy for the consideration of, problems of representation and interpretation. A misleading impression of robustness might be given. Interview reports from several people are not necessarily an indication of high validity – they might all follow the same script or Big Discourse.

Of course, there are several problems with interviewing besides those pointed out here: interviewees may cheat or lie, misunderstand what is at stake, feel uneasy and inhibited in the interview etc. There is also the compli-cation that 'local accomplishment' or 'Big Discourse' and a 'reflection of the world out there' interpretations are not necessarily mutually exclusive – an account may be an effect of Big Discourse and say something valid about reality out there or a person's 'genuine experiences' at the same time. But this means that the researcher is free to choose the interpretation she finds most interesting. The 'rule' of comparing conventional and pomo-inspired interpretations is thus only one element in the struggle over how to use inter-view material, but it provides guidelines for how to use empirical material in a way that is conscious of pomo viewpoints without necessarily privi-leging them.

Revisions of research questions

A third implication of scepticism about the instrumental view of interviews is that more carefully chosen research questions are needed. Recognition of the futility of many conventional research tasks, and of the problems of assuming that interviews reflect something outside themselves, means that asking questions that simply cannot be answered through empirical inquiry might trigger a reorientation of research. It may be that interviews can be conducted if the interpretation stays close to the interview as an empirical situation, and the researcher sees this as a productive site for studying phenomena not very dissimilar to it. The idea is that researchers must be prepared to revise research questions so that they adapt to the (severe) shortcomings of the interview method and do not take the naive view of the mirroring capacity of language and of the interviewee-subject as the centre of meaning and experience. As argued in Chapter 4, to treat interview material as discourse – examples of language use in which a particular view on social reality is constructed (not revealed) – is, of course, a possibility; or a *set* of possibilities, as there is a variety of discourse approaches to any text material (Alvesson and Kärreman 2000). A Foucauldian Big Discourse analysis is one possibility. A more rigorous, detail-focussing discourse analysis is another. A discursive pragmatism approach gives a somewhat wider set of possibilities. It makes it possible to view interview materials as examples of 'broader' social patterns related to language use. Interview material might, for example, throw light on vocabularies of motives (Mills 1940) or, as illustrated in Chapter 4, identity work (Alvesson 1994). Of course, it is then important to give good reasons why, and/or some indications that, talk during interviews says something about talk in everyday life. As Boje (1991) argues, interviews about stories in organizations might give a rather different impression from observations of story-telling in 'real life' – here the performance of story-telling and the specific context and readings of the listeners are vital aspects. It is very important to appreciate the dynamics of the situation in order to understand how stories are told and how they work. The key features of stories and other forms of language use might, however, also allow interesting investigations (e.g. Martin *et al.* 1983).

Of course, another possibility is to place less emphasis on empirical material, as introduced in Chapter 4 as 'grounded fictionalism'. The basic question in the present chapter – and in the book as a whole – is how to use empirical work in a sophisticated and ambitious way and let it play a larger role than that of a source of inspiration for fiction. But sometimes interesting research questions and strong theoretical ideas do not play well with what we are able to study empirically. Perhaps we should be more prepared to let data abdicate from their privileged position and put more emphasis on interesting ideas than on empirical support.

According to Astley (1985), a theory's influence has very little to do with the degree of empirical support it has received. Gergen and Gergen (1991), taking the idea that language cannot mirror reality seriously, and arguing that there consequently cannot be a 'fit' between theory and data, suggest that empirical work can be used for generating vocabularies useful for understanding, but no more than that. I don't think we should go that far, but perhaps we should be more modest about empirical claims in some cases. We should perhaps realize that the shoulders of interviewees are narrow and the capacity of interview talk to mirror, or say something valid about, reality is limited. The ability of interviewers to grasp what is said and what is going on around them also has its shortcomings. For example, can we, during interviews over one or two hours, seriously expect managers to give accounts of their 'leadership' that actually reflect their work days, or 'unemployed' people to relate their life situations?[4] And can we expect the interviewer really to understand what these accounts are about? It is possible that careful methodological reflection on what interviews (and other practices) can do might limit our hubris and encourage the use of empirical material for inspirational or illustrative purposes or as an ambiguous corrective (counterpoint) to bad ideas, rather than as a robust basis for the determination of the truth or development of (grounded) theory.

My own position is that I think it is important to be very clear about our ambitions and claims: if we claim that empirical work and results are important in a study, they must be in tune with a reasonable idea about what we can expect from language, the interview and the interviewee subject. If what one wants to explore goes beyond this, then empirical material should be treated accordingly – e.g. as ambiguous illustrations – and the pressure to develop really interesting theoretical ideas becomes stronger.

An illustration

In this section I present an extract from an interview and then discuss some possible interpretations in the light of the understanding of interviews outlined above.

The interview is with a senior consultant and project manager in a very large management consultancy company. The topic is on project work and how the company controls it. The interviewee says

> Well, I have a large degree of freedom in what I do so that we deliver what we should, and absolutely the most important is quality, and then economy comes in second. We are very eager to avoid a bad reputation, as in this project where we had one person where the client felt a bit uncertain whether he really had the necessary qualities and then we put in a more senior person some days providing extra support so that the client would feel more comfortable. This means extra cost that you have to take . . . but this is acceptable.

While this account might seem to indicate the significance of 'quality', one can point at the uncertainties regarding what this term is supposed to refer to. The interview account seems to indicate that quality is making the client happy and removing any doubt or worry on his or her behalf. On the other hand, quality can be seen as a guideline that is central, and there are signs that quality problems are anticipated, calling for measures to improve the situation.

Later in the interview, when budgeting and planning is addressed, the interviewee claims that the company is fairly accurate in its estimations.

> I think we are fairly accurate . . . in a systems project then the system has to work and you can't do any tricks anywhere, but if it is softer areas where you work with organizational development or employee education and so on, then you can 'cheat' so that you stick to the plans, in terms of how deeply or broadly you do things.

This account points to how quality matters differ with respect of the degree to which errors and suboptimal solutions are detected. Quality is the most significant value for the company, according to the first, general account, but if it is possible to get away with certain tricks and save money then quality appears to be less important than keeping to the budget, according to the second account. Arguably, something is done 'less deeply or broadly' at the expense of 'quality', if 'quality' is defined as doing a very good job. If quality is defined as the client being happy and not noticing errors or slightly suboptimal solutions, then the two parts of the interview are well in line. But then quality refers to 'what you can get away with', without dissatisfying the client or getting a bad reputation. But what quality stands for, in this account and in most others, is very unclear and highly ambiguous. Despite, or rather because of, this, quality is talked about and its significance underscored. This is of course the case not only in this company but in organizations in a variety of situations. It is a kind of standard talk that people produce as self-evident in interactions such as interviews with researchers and conversations with clients. It fulfils a legitimating role.

The second quotation indicates that quality is not always that important, after all. Here keeping to the budget sometimes seems to be the first priority. The discrepancy between the accounts can be seen in terms of different economic contexts and discourses. The first account circles around client relations and 'quality': here quality is absolutely the most important ingredient. The second deals with management control and financial results: here quality is less important in relation to keeping the budget. The discourse invoked here produces a different version of the corporate world and priorities from the client orientation discourse: according to the latter 'quality' is 'absolutely the most important', while the former says that keeping to the budget sometimes ranks higher.

This case illustrates the problem of viewing interviewees as integrated and stable sources of knowledge.[5] The discourses being invoked in the situation in a sense take over and produce certain kind of statements. The case also illustrates difficulties in nailing down social reality. Quality talk and various more or less symbolic acts that try to communicate a serious commitment to 'quality' can be registered, but there might be no stable and integrated ideas and meanings held by subjects or specific objective quality characteristics that we can determine. Expressing concern for quality can be seen as a political act. The variation of the accounts in the interview might reflect social interaction: the different themes during different parts of the interview create different local contexts of talk, different rankings of guiding values. Assertions based on the interview material are thus difficult to make. If a number of people say something similar that does not mean that one comes any closer to robust knowledge about the orientations of people or the objective practices of the company.

The example illustrates some of the problems of taking interview material as given and the need to consider it in relation to the local social context as well as to the more or less conscious political orientations of people interested in portraying themselves and their organizations in moral and rational terms (however, these orientations do not fully come through in the less 'sensitive' area of keeping to the budget). Carrying out interviews so that a topic is framed in different ways might be helpful – talking about clients and management control means that 'quality' appears differently – in order to check for incoherence and fluidity of meaning. Interpreting the interview accounts more carefully, and considering postmodernist aspects, can lead to an appreciation of the shakiness of the idea that accounts 'mirror' meanings or facts. New and perhaps more interesting research questions, such as the tactics and contingencies of quality claims, may be triggered to replace more conventional questions.

My illustration was not picked carefully to fit into postmodernist ideas on the difficulties of fixing meaning. My experience is that it is common that a careful look at interview material – and many other kinds of 'data' – will display incoherencies and instabilities (Alvesson and Deetz 2000: Chapter 6; Alvesson and Sköldberg 2000: Chapter 7). In Chapter 8, I illustrate this further and at length.

Conclusions

Dominant understandings of interviews circle around a metaphor of the interview as a tool, and the outcome of the skilful use of it is treated as a pipeline to the interiors of interviewees or the exteriors of social reality. Only recently and to a modest extent have interview methodologists outside the postmodernist and localist camps begun 'to realize that we cannot lift the results of interviewing out of the contexts in which they were gathered and claim them as objective data with no strings attached' (Fontana and Frey 2000: 663). But this emergent insight is mainly restricted to acknowledging this complication and a general call to be aware and recognize it, and there have not been many efforts to develop a theoretical framework for understanding context issues. This chapter tries to take some small steps in this direction and has proposed a rethinking, so that what are conventionally seen as sources of bias to be minimized through various techniques are instead viewed as key features of interviews that call for an ambitious theoretical understanding, incorporating some pomo ideas.

Two pomo-inspired ideas on how to conceptualize the interview theoretically have been expressed in the chapter. One is to see interviews as complex social settings in which accounts can be viewed as local accomplishment, constrained by, sensitive to and understandable given the local, interactive context. The other is the view of the interview as the play of powers of Big Discourse. Here interview talk is seen as governed by and thus as a potential indication of the socially dominant modes for constituting, reasoning and shaping various objects of knowledge.

Instead of a heavy reliance on the researcher optimizing the interview as a technique or tool and/or working hard in interview encounters in order to get interviewees to be honest, clear and consistent, the message expressed in the present chapter is that the ideal of the good interview producing robust knowledge is problematic. The interview setting is a complex social interaction involving much more than a skilful researcher enrolling an interviewee in the service of science to produce information and insights. Making sense of interview accounts is not primarily a matter of coding and processing data in an objective way. Pomo suggests that we understand the entire interview project as inherently shaky, and this insight should guide any reading of the process and the outcomes:

> We can foreground the open indeterminacy of an interview interaction in itself. But merely announcing this indeterminacy in an introduction and then proceeding to name 'reality' is not sufficient. As we conduct the interview and interpret the interview 'data', we can illustrate, though never completely, the shifting openness within the interview itself.
>
> (Scheurich 1997: 74)

The shakiness of interview material should not necessarily prevent us from using it as an indication of people's beliefs and meanings or of social practices and conditions. Interview material will be more or less ambiguous depending on the topic and the researcher's treatment of it.

This chapter addresses three possible implications of the pomo critique of neopositivist and romantic views on interviews:

- Interview practices can be modified so that it becomes possible for the researcher to assess better the significance and impact of how issues are framed, the various relationships and interaction effects characterizing the interview and the responses.
- Interpretations should carefully consider various ways of understanding the produced interview accounts, including different logics from seeing

the accounts as expressions of the interviewees' knowledge of the world out there, or their subjective ways of relating to it. These logics include, for example, the interview talk as local accomplishment and as expression of Big Discourse.

- It is important to rethink research questions so that they are realistic, given the complexities of the interview situation, and guided by a framework taking the active, functional and context-dependent character of language into account.

Notes

1 I am grateful to Robert Grafton-Small for this insight.
2 Female researchers frequently use private settings in order to establish better contact (e.g. Martin 1992; Skeggs 1994).
3 Subjectivity refers to the individual's conscious and unconscious thoughts, emotions and perceptions, the individual's self-insight and attitude to the surrounding world.
4 This comment is, of course, even more valid about questionnaire research (Alvesson and Deetz 2000).
5 Some pomos would probably think that it also illustrates the indeterminacy of the social world, but one can say that financial results and client-perceived quality seem to be important, and that although core objectives may be difficult to rank, there is little doubt that these are more significant than values like workplace democracy or job satisfaction in this company.

7 Interpreting and writing

While the first chapters of this book outlined some broad principles and options for social researchers who want to incorporate responses to the critique and insights produced by postmodernism (and sometimes other streams), and Chapter 6 discussed some implications for the fieldwork in which empirical material is produced (some would say collected), the present chapter deals with post-fieldwork issues. It does not, however, do so in an exclusive way, as the various moments or phases of the research process cannot be fully separated. Of course, the overall themes of postmodernism – around representation, the power–knowledge connection etc. – provide much of the inspiration also for how to deal with the post-fieldwork moments, so to some extent issues of interpretation and writing have already been covered.

There is, of course, much more to say on these topics. In this chapter I treat the theme of voice and go on to problems of interpretation or – as many postmodernists prefer to put it – reading empirical material, and after that devote a section to issues of writing. Many advocates of pomo seem to view this as the most important element in research.

Voice

One of many keywords in certain postmodernist circles is 'voice'. There is a variety of viewpoints depending on whether voice refers to a preoccupation

with the researcher or with those being studied. 'Following a poststructuralist emphasis on contradiction, heterogeneity, and multiplicity, we produced a quilt of stories and cacaphony of voices speaking to each other in
dispute, dissonance, support, dialogue, contention, and/or contradiction'
(Fine *et al.* 2000: 119). This is what it should look like, according to many
advocates of postmodernism (although Fine *et al.* use the term poststructuralism). Hertz (1997: xi–xii) views the theme 'voice' as a matter of 'a
struggle to figure out how to present the author's self while simultaneously
writing the respondents' accounts and representing their selves'. It focuses
more on the post-fieldwork problem of interpretation, representation and
writing than on problem formulation and data gathering. Richardson
(2000: 936) emphasizes the researcher-author, not the subjects being
studied, and wants to 'encourage individuals to accept and nurture their
own voices' as part of the development of self-knowledge and knowledge of
the topic. Compared to Fine *et al.*, who focus on representations of the field,
Richardson views voice as a matter of the expression of the researcher. The
former is more common when voice is focused. All the authors cited do,
however, emphasize writing.

The preference for the signifier 'voice' is slightly peculiar, as pomos are
often more preoccupied with text and writings. Derrida objects to the privileging of the spoken as more genuine and original, and emphasizes the (written) text, instead. The notion of voice might also lead to the idea that
subjects can and should express a kind of authentic experience and insight,
emerging from their deepest selves. This is what Richardson seems to have
in mind. This kind of humanistic idea clashes, of course, with what most
people see as postmodernism. The theme of voice addresses a more interesting problem when used as formulated by Fine *et al.*, i.e. when related to
issues of multiplicity, contradictions and representation. Particularly in postmodernist research, voice is more relevant in relation to these issues than as
an aspect of the ability of researchers to 'accept and nurture their own
voice'.

Postmodernists often relate voice to issues of marginalization and multiplicity. Through a careful treatment of the rich variation of viewpoints and
signals, postmodernists aim to avoid the mainstream interest in finding a pattern, discovering or creating an order or a system or working with a 'deeper'
meaning, mechanism or logic that explains contradictions and inconsistencies. The idea is that the variation and plurality of voices in any empirical
material – be it interview accounts, documents or observations of events –
should be carefully nurtured and presented in research reports with minimal
interference from the researcher. The term voice can be seen as a sensitizing
term encouraging the researcher to show utmost care in confirming the 'contradiction, heterogeneity and multiplicity' and similar qualities that pomos
assume to characterize the kind of reality – or texts – being studied, and/or
that they think deserve to be brought forward in research writings.

Sceptics have not hesitated in producing harsh critiques. Thompson (1993: 197) complains that there is nothing inherently 'useful in a multitude of voices or "carnivalesque discourses" (Jeffcutt 1993), if any sense of organizational reality is lost in the babble'. Of course, sometimes reality may for good reasons be viewed as having these characteristics. Wolf (1992) argues that it is the task of the researcher to sort out nonsense material from more valuable pieces of information and insights. In a large body of empirical material, there is a wide diversity of statements, some providing valuable information and many deserving less attention, contingent upon the informants' interests, experiences, verbal skills, openness, motivation to participate in the research project etc.

There is, of course, a significant, in some fields almost dominant, tradition of taking the side of the (comparatively) weak, marginalized and powerless in social research: shopfloors have been studied and the voice of the workers raised by academic texts, women have been the topic of many studies and their experiences and viewpoints have been presented with considerable force etc. This is often a kind of 'loud-voice approach', where the researcher takes the position of a (self-appointed) representative of a group of workers (or the working class), a specific group of women (or women in general) or any other category that deserves moral and political support, acting as a facilitator of the group's assumed interests and viewpoints. This research is guided by an emancipatory cognitive interest.

Advocates of a postmodernist voice position are not, however, happy with an approach that takes the singular voice of a broadly recognized group as its point of view, and resist the idea of there being one single alternative voice that needs to be brought forward (labour, women's perspective). As subjects are assumed to be fragmented and varied, their claimed experiences, viewpoints and interests are also contradictory, heterogeneous and multiple. Single subjects also express a multitude of voices and these should be read and represented in research texts. For many pomos the idea of grounding research in an emancipatory cognitive interest is a source of suspicion – it stands for elitism and masks a will to power. However, others sympathetic to postmodernism combines this with a critical orientation that aims to support emancipation/resistance against dominant social forces (e.g. Agger 1991; Boje 1995; Alvesson and Deetz 2000).

Acting on the idea of multiple voices and being sensitive to them is often a difficult enterprise. Fine *et al.* (2000) write about the difficult considerations with regard to their research, which tried to capture the everyday life, experiences and viewpoints of people who were extremely poor and living on the streets of New York. The authors agonized a lot about whether and how to represent statements that were very pejorative to various groups, sometimes including racist opinions, contempt for people living on social welfare etc.

Another problem concerns how to deal with subjects who mainly express one voice, but occasionally air other standpoints and show some, but not much, variation. From a hardcore pomo perspective one might simply assume that subjects are fragmented or multiple, and that any indication in line with this credo should be taken very seriously. Another extreme is that one goes for a kind of statistical representation, so that consideration of a multitude of voices should be balanced against a reflection of the frequency of the expression of various voices. Either version – just noting variation in order to present as many voices as possible or working with some kind of statistical idea of the prevalence of the subject positions or voices coming through – appears unsatisfactory, so the handling of this problem may call for some thought. The pomo is saved from this dilemma if more than one voice can be traced in the subjects observed or interviewed and if the pluralism is not too trivial. But if the subject – or group of subjects – appears to talk in a fairly unitary way, the postmodernist might feel some worry as to what do to about this.

Interpretation

Interpretation – a pro-pomo or non-pomo signifier?

The question of interpretation is interesting in the context of postmodernism. So, for the moment, we can leave aside the 'sceptical' or hardcore pomos interested in deconstruction or 'anti-meaning' projects, and discuss a more moderate pomo position.

Even within the pomo literature there are various positions in relation to the term 'interpretation'. Emphasis on interpretation as a crucial aspect of research may be a part of the critique of 'modernism' and authoritative science: one can argue that there are no facts, only interpretations within the bounds of a common language. This underscores the uncertainties and subjectivities involved. But interpretation can also be associated with hermeneutics and a research orientation that searches for an underlying meaning behind surface manifestations in written texts, interview accounts or observed behaviours. Denzin and Lincoln (2000: 3) write that 'qualitative research involves an interpretive, naturalistic approach to the world . . . and interprets phenomena in terms of the meanings people bring to them'. This is at odds with postmodernism, which tends to avoid the idea of meaning, at least meanings that are stable over time and space and that people ascribe to phenomena. Pomo expresses the orientation that there is no 'depth' behind the 'surface' to be located through hermeneutic of phenomenological procedures. Some pomos prefer to talk about readings rather than interpretation. The researcher can thus contribute with more or less interesting readings, rather than more or less true or more or less insightful interpretations of the empirical material studied.

The notion of voice can be viewed as discouraging interpretation.

Interpretation means going beyond what is expressed. A sensitive way of dealing with the voices of those being studied will call for some caution about the researcher imposing his or her meaning upon them, about the voice of the researcher taking over the voice over the subjects. But frequently the researcher feels that the views of the people being studied cannot just be accepted, but call for challenge, even rejection. Skeggs (1997), for example, studied young working-class females who rejected the role of class for their situation and orientations. Skeggs did not accept this understanding and thus rejected the rejection of class as vital for the women.

Even if one takes a serious and ambitious pomo stance, it is not necessary to ban the term interpretation. One can adapt a more relativistic or open-minded attitude, viewing interpretation as the best shot – or some good shots – rather than as a rational and authoritative project. If the uncertainties and language-dependent nature of interpretive work are emphasized, and the text stimulates active reinterpretations of the text, then the idea of interpretation is less pomo-alien. In relationship to the voice theme, cautious interpretations might be necessary in order to identify, situate and give space to various voices and to give some clues as to how to understand where a particular subject or subject position comes from.

All interpretation is sensitive to social context. We cannot understand observed behaviour (talk), interview accounts or written texts (documents) abstracted from historical period, society or even specific social micro-context. Postmodernists tend to emphasize micro-situation, i.e. to point at the local character and not interpret anything as an indication of broader phenomena or meaning patterns transcending the specific, local setting. Interpretivists – hermeneuticians and other people with a strong interest in interpretation – work with a more wide-ranging and/or depth-oriented notion of interpretation. Here subjective in-depth meanings (phenomenology, psychoanalysis) or socially established structures of meaning (anthropology and other culturally oriented disciplines) are assumed and studied. In addition, postmodernists emphasize that meaning is unstable, temporal and constituted within discourse (possibly Big Discourse) – strongly language-driven and dependent – while interpretivists assume that meanings are 'grounded' in a broad set of forms of communications and expressions, but also in the cognitions and emotions of individuals and/or communities.

Multiple interpretations

Perhaps one of the most valuable lessons from postmodernism is that the ideal of a well integrated theoretical frame of reference should be treated with caution; it should also be recognized that such frames of reference can impede understanding and mislead the researcher or reader, as a result of their totalizing effect and their tendency to present reality as unambiguous and accessible to representation in the chosen theoretical idiom. Rorty

(1989: 73) warns against an approach in which a 'final vocabulary', a language providing the ultimate knowledge or wisdom, is used. Instead he proposes a position in which the researcher

> (1) has radical and continuing doubts about the final vocabulary she currently uses, because she has been impressed by other vocabularies . . . (2) she realizes that argument phrased in her present vocabulary can neither underwrite nor dissolve these doubts; (3) insofar as she philosophizes about her situation, she does not think that her vocabulary is closer to reality than others, that it is in touch with a power not herself.

An openness to the values and limitations of different vocabularies and understandings is thus well motivated. There is something to be said for caution when it comes to 'monologic texts [that] employ a consistent and homogeneous representational style . . . and express a dominant authorial voice' (Jeffcutt 1993: 39). This lesson can lead to a certain humility in face of the idea that truth, or the 'right' or 'best' interpretations, can be produced. In such a case a greater willingness to allow diverse vocabularies, interpretations and voices to make themselves heard in research texts appears desirable.

It is important that researchers primarily use theories they grasp well and for which they feel an emotional preference. Very few researchers can successfully move between theories with different paradigmatic roots. It is possible to operate within a particular intellectual horizon, which may incorporate some related intellectual traditions. If we broaden our horizon in one direction, it is not unlikely that we narrow it in another. However, researchers can make secondary or complementary interpretations using frameworks or positions taken from the set of theories to which they are mainly committed. When comments from alternative positions are made, it becomes possible to throw critical light on the set of perspectives favoured, and to encourage the reader to consider yet other alternative interpretations, thus further counteracting the totalizing element that is more or less pronounced in all research, and about which postmodernists are with some justification so worried.

It is my experience that it is necessary to concentrate work within a particular theory, in order to be able to exploit its interpretive powers (Alvesson 1996). I think it is difficult to move freely and immediately between different positions in multiple interpretive work. 'Intellectual jumping' is not easy, even if one restricts oneself to work with theories and vocabularies based on the same paradigm. Moving to a new position calls for 'unfreezing' and desocialization from the previous position. It is necessary to distance oneself temporarily from the theory in which one was previously engaged. Perhaps the research process should be divided into distinct phases. Paradigmatically related theories make changes possible, but might also make it difficult to exploit the differences to the full. (It is like talking two similar languages. The similarities make it easier to get a fairly good under-standing of both of them, but they also often make it more difficult to master either altogether, as it is so easy to mix and confuse the two.) Even if one is well read in the particular theoretical positions used in a multiple interpre-tation framework, it still takes a lot of re-reading to change from working with one theory to another. The exposure of gaps within a particular, favoured line of inquiry is also often time-consuming and stressful. Never underestimate the hard work involved in using several theories! I should also add that the very point of using multiple interpretation is that each should add some potentially good or interesting idea. It is unsatisfying just to add more theories and vocabularies in order to introduce possible ways of understanding a subject matter – each proposed understanding must include a creative idea. As it is sometimes difficult to come up with a single really or even moderately good idea when working with an empirical material, it is clear that multiple interpretations not only involve quite a lot of theoretical and analytical work, but also call for a lot of inspiration and luck!

Writing

One of the distinguishing features of postmodernism is its heavy focus on the research text as a key element in social research. This is especially the case in anthropology and in other fields working with ethnographies. Here titles like *Writing Culture* (Clifford and Marcus 1986) and *Tales of the Field* (van Maanen 1988) and subtitles like *The Anthropologist as Author* (Geertz 1988) have aroused great interest. There are different views on what an ethnography is, but it is primarily in the sense of a study of social settings from a cultural perspective based on the researcher's extended presence in the setting that the textual features of the ethnography have been empha-sized. Wolf (1992: 1) uses the label pomo to identify 'academics who are currently more preoccupied with the way ethnography is written rather than with the way it is carried out'.[1] The term ethnography usually refers to both the research process and the completed text – process and product. There is, in anthropology, but also to some extent in other social science disciplines, a change in focus from the research process to the text, from the content of culture to the format and the ways culture is constructed in writing. Textual features, such as genre, structure, rhetoric and various literary devices used in order to produce a credible representation of the phenomenon being studied, have become targets of interest and are viewed as equally or perhaps even more important than the fieldwork preceding the writing up of results. The term 'faction' has been coined: 'imaginative writing about real people in real places at real times' (Geertz 1988: 141). The argument is that a 'fiction form is laid over a "fact oriented" research process' (Agar 1995: 114). The position taken is similar to the 'grounded fictionalism' response to the linguistic turn in philosophy and social science briefly addressed in Chapter 4 – although this is seen as a possible research direction, while a lot of the pomo interest in writing and texts sees the 'faction' theme as a central problematic for all social science writing.

This textual move is partly grounded in critiques of earlier (and still) dominant modes of producing academic texts. These are seen as placing the researcher and the researched in a highly asymmetrical relationship. The researched are exposed, their voices are domesticated, the researcher hides and is in control, neutral and detached. The research process is, then, presented in a dishonest and ethically problematic way: concealing the role of the researcher and hiding his or her subjectivity and often arbitrary moves. Another problem is that the texts are often very disengaged and fail to offer a deeper feeling for what the theme being researched is all about. Indeed, texts are often boring to read. Richardson (2000: 924) complains that she often found books on topics she was very interested in boring because of the style of writing: 'acute and chronic passivity: passive-voiced author, passive subjects'.

Postmodernists and poststructuralists reject the traditional Western dichotomy in science, which excludes certain expressive forms from the legitimate repertoire: rhetoric (by referring to well defined, transparent linguistic forms), fiction (which is defined in negative relation to facts) and subjectivity (which must be eliminated in order to achieve objectivity) (Clifford 1986: 5). As these excluded elements are both unavoidable and central constituents of social and humanist science, they must be subjected to reflection and expressed explicitly in the text, but without constituting the only feature of an ethnography.

> [T]he maker (but why only one?) of ethnographic texts cannot avoid expressive tropes, figures and allegories that select or impose meaning as they translate it. In this view, more Nietzschean than realist or hermeneutic, all constructed truths are made possible by powerful 'lies' of exclusion and rhetoric. Even the best ethnographic texts – serious, true fictions – are systems, or economies, of truth. Power and history work through them, in ways their authors cannot fully control.
>
> (Clifford 1986: 7)

The fiction element in ethnography and other versions of social science is not necessarily emphasized in all efforts to address the question of style and narrative. It is not uncommon to downplay or sidestep the fact–fiction relationship and take an interest in the kind of writing that exists in social science texts, and perhaps encourage new styles and ways of dealing with the representation problem. Van Maanen (1988) discusses three broad narratives in social science writings. The predominant one is what he refers to as *realism*. In ethnography this is marked by 'the swallowing up and disappearance of the author in the text' (van Maanen 1995: 7), an emphasis on an average or common cultural meaning and a validity claim based on the researcher having been there. Sometimes it creates the impression that ethnography offers a clear, straigthforward, objective account of a knowledgeable world. Two other styles of writing appear to be more to the taste of the pomo. *Impressionistic writing* builds on a scenic method in which the writer shows rather than tells. Situations are (re)created for the reader to get a lively feeling of what goes on. 'Detailed scenes pull the reader in, involve him or her in the immediacy of the experience' (Agar 1995: 118). In *confessional* ethnography the researcher-author stands in the forefront of the text. The experiences of the researcher when trying to develop knowledge about a social setting offer the medium for the reader's learning. The research process becomes the focus of the text. 'Its composition rests on moving the fieldworker to center stage and displaying how the writer came to know a given social world' (van Maanen 1988: 8).

It is, however, possible to be more specific and to look at how different texts or streams within a field adopt elements of different literary genres. Jeffcutt (1993), for example, shows how heroic, tragic and romantic styles characterize a variety of examples of organizational culture research. Texts narrated in a heroic style typically emphasize how a top executive creates radical organizational change to get a company in bad shape on to its feet. Tragic texts emphasize irrationalities, inertia, domination and other less positive features of organizational life. A romantic style emphasizes the possibility of harmony and unity through shared beliefs and values, and forms of symbolism – myth, tradition, identity – that facilitate social integration.

Apart from taking an interest in styles of writing and looking at how texts are structured, and thus encouraging either critical reflections on the rhetoric and other tricks involved or more informed choices of what route the researcher may follow, there are also themes of text production that focus more on how researchers can do their jobs as authors in more productive ways.

One important theme is how one relates to writing, i.e. how one conceptualizes what writing is about. Richardson (2000: 923) considers writing as a 'method of inquiry':

> Although we usually think about writing as a mode of 'telling' about the social world, writing is not just a mapping-up activity at the end of the research project. Writing is also a way of 'knowing' – a method of discovery and analysis. By writing in different ways, we discover new aspects of our topic and our relationship to it. Form and content are inseparable.

This point is a bit different from many other points about writing, which focus on the author communicating or representing something in a particular way for an audience, i.e. how the researcher-author mediates between the field (object of study) and the reader. Richardson emphasizes writing as central for the knowing project of the researcher. It is not necessarily the final text that is of interest here, but writing during the research process. It is here that much of the knowing takes place, when text drafts are written and rewritten. This is not necessarily a pomo-specific theme – fairly conventional researchers may also do much of their thinking and creative work when writing. This is normally not something brought forward very much. Postmodernism may, however, emphasize and legitimize this important element in a more powerful way than has previously been the case.

Another theme concerns the issue of how to deal with the problem of representations, i.e. how to produce a text that provides a fair description of and a good feeling for the object being addressed, and avoids alienating the reader and the subjects addressed in the study. This problem is particularly significant when deeply personal experiences and meanings are being studied, e.g. sexual abuse, poverty, discrimination, illness and pain. This calls for transcending the traditional norms for writing social science. Some people argue for highly unconventional modes of expression, including using poetry and mixing fiction and science (Denzin 1994; Richardson 2000). Perhaps a more productive way is to avoid mixing very different genres, calling for very different skills and modes of reading, and try to develop social science text productions rather than borrow from other fields. I will give one illustrative example. Charmaz (2000: 527), writing about people living with chronic illness, tries to evoke experiential feeling in writing. 'This means taking the reader into a story and imparting its mood through linguistic style and narrative exposition.' She uses analogies and metaphors. She frames key definitions and distinctions in words that reproduce the tempo and mood of experience. For example, existing from day to day is an important concept, defined as occurring when a person plummets into continued crises that rip life apart'. This way of writing is not necessarily distinctly postmodernist, but it does take on board its emphasis on the significance of writing and the need to be more careful about it.

There is much to be said about writing. Perhaps too much, according to some critics, whose voices we listen to in the next section.

The fieldwork – text writing trade-off

After worrying for so long about the problems of fieldwork, it is now time for anthropology to take the problems of authorship seriously, Geertz (1988) argues. But after a decade or so of this reshuffling of worries, the pendulum swings over and other problems enter. Now anthropologists worry about this strong textwork focus and feel that 'the text-oriented celebration of the neglected product will cause us to lose sight of the process side' (Agar 1995: 113). There are other worries contingent thereupon: lack of credibility, a shift in focus from those one wants to study and understand to the researcher and her writing and text. Efforts to avoid the problems of the conventional style of writing may lead to texts that are difficult to access and appreciate for other than a small group of academic writers. This critique is hardly, of course, valid for the people who argue for a focus on writing precisely in order to avoid academic writings being experienced as esoteric and alienating due to the conventions for style (addressed in the previous section). But these people do take pomo ideals only moderately into account, and many pomos would be sceptical of the rhetoric involved and of claims made to, for example, communicate the experiential reality of a chronically ill person in an academic (or any other) text.

Critics argue that if we attend more to format, style and the text, then it is at the expense of fieldwork and content. Experimental texts in anthropology 'have been praised more for being experimental than for the new insights they provided into culture' (Wolf 1992: 51). Some critics worry that the emphasis on writing will encourage authors to become more oriented towards making what has been studied fit into the requirement for a text that is engaging and entertaining to read. When emphasizing the significance of the text and the style of writing, researchers might feel encouraged to downplay the attention given to the constraints of the empirical material and to write texts that score high in terms of entertainment, aesthetics or novelty. People in the setting being studied might be reduced to interesting characters in a plot that is part of the researcher-author's narrative. A pomo would argue that this is always the case, but a more conventional researcher would probably claim to be prepared to sacrifice a good plot, at least to some extent, in order to be 'fair' or 'faithful' to the empirical material and social reality. One might, for example, include boring and mundane details and not just emphasize dramatic elements in the text. One might devote a lot of space to nuances and reservations about validity and interpretations that do not add much to the quality of the text in terms of aesthetics.

The increased focus on the text does not necessarily imply using literary tricks in order to make the text more enjoyable to read. Pomos sometimes emphasize that the forgotten, the marginal, should receive attention. Mundane details of daily living 'are typically left out of ethnographic descriptions of life in poverty. They don't make very good reading, and yet they are the stuff of daily life. We recognize how careful we need to be so that we do not construct life narratives spiked only with the hot spots' (Fine *et al.* 2000: 118). An attention to the text can thus lead to reflection going in the opposite direction to what most critics seem to fear, but this would call for a careful watch on the empirical reality one is supposed to talk about, and would suggest a closer relation between reality and text than most postmodernists assume.

A strong focus on the text might lead to a lack of, or at least reduced, attention to standards of fieldwork and analysis. Even if very few, if any, anthropologists are suggesting an 'anything goes' attitude to data collection and analysis, they may be read as signalling a *laissez-faire* attitude in this respect.

Although most commentators point at the tension and trade-off between the focus on the object of study, fieldwork and evidence and the focus on writing conventions, textwork and rhetoric, some downplay the contradiction. Hammersley (1993) argues for a realist approach – although not a 'naive one' – but thinks that it can be combined with the textual strategies advocated by postmodernists and others who emphasize rhetoric in research and writing. He suggests that there is nothing wrong with, for example, evocative narratives or fictional constructions of average or exemplary types. However, the use of these techniques should be 'subordinated to the goal of presenting clearly the claims made and conclusions drawn, and providing sufficient supporting evidence and information about the research process to allow the reader to assess the plausibility and credibility of these claims and conclusions' (Hammersley 1993: 32). Of course, this formulation expresses a general understanding of the research process and its textual outcome that is rather far from most postmodernists' scepticism about all the ingredients valued by Hammersley. His view clearly privileges the idea of representing reality, even though such claims are fallible constructions that are selective representations of the phenomena to which they refer. One can, however, note the (highly) partial acceptance of the role of rhetoric and textual strategies within the ideal of a realist approach, as formulated by Hammersley.

Agar (1995) argues that there is a form between fieldwork and textwork – fieldtexts, i.e. writings done in the field and close to the observations and experiences of empirical (ethnographic) work. Agar suggests that 'the structure of the ethnographic text grows out of the structure of data gathered during ethnographic research. By and large the process and product are more intimately related than contemporary discussions of textuality suggest' (p. 126). But even if fieldwriting predicts the completed published text this does not necessarily mean that the final text stands in any clear relationship to the social reality it is intended to address. I would here like to remind the reader of my imagined example in the introductory chapter and the wealth of transformations that interview transcripts, observation protocols and diary notes go through on their very long travel to the final form. An important argument against Agar's idea that data structure the published research text is that typically only a tiny minority of all the empirical material is inserted in the ready text. A given set of data can be structured and presented in an indefinite number of different ways.

There are thus good reasons to consider the research text carefully – how it is composed and how it uses a particular genre and a certain rhetoric in order to produce effects. Of course, all research is a compromise between different ideals. In the best of worlds, the researcher devotes a lot of work and skills to fieldwork *and* to writing *and*, of course, to all the other necessary ingredients (reading the literature, analysing and interpreting the data, developing ideas, reflecting upon them etc.), but trade-offs must be made. Placing writing at the centre of attention and assessment means less time and energy for the other elements of work. Given how poorly written many dissertations and research papers are, one is sometimes hesistant in suggesting that one should be too ambitious in producing texts that deviate from the established templates – after all, what one is familiar with is easiest to copy. However, devoting more than common care to textual form, and trying to address the problems of the realist style of writing and the more general norms of communicating robust research results to the reader, must be applauded as an ideal worth pursuit, at least for those with surplus energy and more than average writing skills.

The author–reader relationship

Another important theme is the way texts are read and consumed. It can be argued that the author is not interesting, that the text does not stand as such without a reader and that it is the way the reader relates to the text that is of interest. This is so partly because of the undecidability of meaning: the text is not just a medium for the transformation of certain intentions and a clear message, but is open to a variety of readings. Van Maanen (1995), for example, identifies three distinct activity phases or moments associated with ethnography (but not restricted to this method): data collection, the construction of a report and the reading and reception of the report.

Postmodernism is interesting as 'it' – i.e. the label – is connected to the problems and dangers of authorship and what the text expresses, on the one hand, and a change of emphasis to the role of the reader-consumer of texts, on the other. The power–knowledge connection and the centrality of discourse and language make the research text a vital source of power: social scientists are very much in the discourse distribution and reinforcement business. But the pomo emphasis on the ambiguities, fluidity of meaning and undecidabilities of the text encourages a shift of emphasis to the reader and her creativity on the other hand. There is a contradiction between the emphasis on the creative activity of the reader and the great worry about the authority of the author(-ity) and the power she can exercise through the text. However, pomo is not a coherent tradition and under its flag a lot of different things are being said. It is possible to emphasize the creative reading of the text as an ideal to be encouraged as a solution to the problems of the danger of the text, although the danger does not seem to be that great if this solution really is workable. The majority point of view associated with pomo seems to be that, because it is not possible to mirror what exists or to tell the truth, the particular order constructed and norms expressed in texts (such as the present one) call for careful scrutiny.

The pomo ideals of play, irony, variation etc. can to some extent be seen as defensive measures, intended to disarm the danger of social science texts creating the truth and expressing disciplinary power. The idea – or the possible effect – seems to be to loosen up the text and weaken its directive powers.

The role of the reader may seem to have little immediate implication for the researcher and the text. It seems simply to reduce their importance – if it is the reading that matters, then one can be more relaxed about writing. However, the reading still depends on the text and one can imagine an authorly ideal in which the researcher tries to mobilize the reader and encourage her creative capacities. What would such a text look like? Activating the reader would call for something that is engaging and interesting. Challenging the reader, trying to make him or her think and rethink favoured positions and taken-for-granted assumptions, is perhaps the ideal. Unpacking established and cherished categories might be one option. More engaging styles of writing, such as confessional and impressionist narratives, might also be beneficial. These can conflict with another option, and that is the presentation of empirical material in a way as complete and open as possible, making it possible for the reader to make her own interpretations and readings. The ideal of producing multiple interpretations can also reduce the reader, subordinating her to a particular truth or way of thinking. It can also make it more difficult for her to come up with alternative readings to those the author has proposed. The author's grip on the reader might be reinforced. The space occupied in the text to present all the interpretations and the time it takes for the reader to grasp them can reinforce the author element in the author–reader relationship, compared to that in texts less full of the author's interpretations.

A general piece of advice for the author interested in activating – or avoiding passivizing – the reader is to resist the urge to persuade and control the reader's response by making the case and writing as watertight as possible. The norm is to present arguments and support for one's case that are as strong as possible, and to minimize revealing the loopholes and weaknesses that one does not expect the reader to discover. A more generous style, where one points out debatable issues – within the favoured line of reasoning – and opens up the text for dialogue, is one option.

The author–reader relationship is a tricky issue. It is well worth taking seriously, but as with so many other issues in the field of this book, there are no straightforward, authoritative guidelines to propose. Apart, of course, from the very general one of careful consideration of the reader as a potentially active and creative subject, a partner in dialogue, whose activity and creativity can be seriously obstructed by research texts written as if they were just a medium for the transmission of research results.

Summing up: dilemmas of pomo-inspired work

The three themes of voice, interpretation and writing hang together but cannot be reduced to the same issue.

Fine *et al.* (2000) write about the triple representation problem: how to present (a) the researcher, (b) the narrator (interviewee) and (c) the 'others' (clients, bosses, authorities, ethnic groups, men etc.) who are represented by the narrators in particular, sometimes pejorative, ways.

To what extent should the researcher be present in the text. And in what capacity? As the fieldworker, having been there and struggled to do observations, 'co-constructing reality' in interviews, trying to learn culture? Or as an interpreter, working with empirical material in the post-fieldwork phase, trying to make sense of them and producing creative ideas and revealing insights? Or perhaps as the author, preoccupied with writing a text, self-conscious about rhetorical tricks, conventions for writing and pressure to conformity, and/or trying a variety of literary experiments – poems, pictures, impressional tales, self-confessional passages – in order to give the reader a chance to engage with the material in novel ways?

While it is appealing to ask the author to be present in the text and not concealed by a writerly convention pretending that it is science that produces the text, too much concern with the researcher and/or author and too much elaboration with format may draw attention away from the subjects the research is supposed to say something about. These subjects can be represented in a variety of ways. To whom should one listen and give space in the interpretations and final research text? Everyone: those who are marginalized in many settings, those who are important (powerful), those who produce what one believes are insightful and revealing statements, those who convey problematic ideas (e.g. sexist) and whose beliefs should be critically scrutinized? Should the people one has interviewed (or observed in certain context) be represented as fairly integrated and holistic, or as expressing a variety of voices based on a multitude of fragmented identities? The more one tries to produce a rich picture of a set of varied subject positions and expressed concerns of individuals, the fewer people can be allowed space in the research project and the final text.

In many research projects, the interviewees (or observed individuals) produce statements with truth claims about other people and other groups. For Fine *et al.* (2000), studying people living on the margin of society, this issue was salient, as a lot of the interview accounts included strongly pejorative statements about other people and groups, sometimes of a racist or sexist nature. This provides the researcher with a double dilemma: should one present the interviewees' accounts in ways that might reinforce negative opinions about them, and should the 'victims' of this talk be 'defended' against the pejorative statements? Should they be approached and allowed to respond to the criticism? Should they be allowed to give their views on the subject matter without being placed in a defensive position? Should the researcher avoid giving the pejorative views any space in the research or should the potential negative effects be counteracted by more or less extensive comments by the researcher? This is not easy. The dilemma is not restricted to marginal groups that lack the politeness, sense of nuances and inclination to be politically correct that characterize the groups to which the reader of this book probably belongs. When studying well adapted people one frequently encounters statements in which various groups receive negative verdicts: stories with a negative orientation might concern senior management, a profession, males (or females) etc. Feminist and critical studies, for example, often emphasize voice: should those being criticized be listened to and represented in research or not? And if so, to what extent and in what way? Of course, how one deals with this is partly an ethical issue.

Dilemmas thus include how much emphasis should be put:

- on fieldwork versus textwork;
- on the group as the object (subject) of the research versus the researcher-author (whose subjectivity may be central in the process or for the product);
- on the author versus the reader.

Given an interest in the literal aspect of work, what about the 'author/reader ratio'? Is it the author and text production that is important, or should one, instead, hold the author back and in various ways try to activate the reader of the text? This would call for considerable consideration of the text production, but one should probably not emphasize one's authorly struggles and concerns explicitly at length in the text, instead taking a low-profile position as author. It is possible to pay careful attention to the process of authorship rather than the product of authorship.

There are, of course, no correct answers to these considerations of emphasis in representations and the ratios of fieldwork/textwork, researcher others being studied and author/reader. The careful researcher, eager to respond to the problems of voice, interpretation and authorship raised here, must develop her own way of dealing with the dilemmas. The specific research tasks addressed, of course, matter strongly – in some cases the representation of other people and institutions in interview talk never emerges as an issue. What also matter are, of course, the abilities, interests and creative moves of the researcher. There is little point in mechanically going through the themes raised here if one is not doing something interesting with them.

Note

1 It can be noted that the foreground figures of this preoccupation do not necessarily label their approach as postmodernism (e.g. Marcus 1992). Sometimes I get the impression that it is the less significant persons who are more eager to emphasize the pomo label. This makes sense: a person recognized for original and significant work may not bother about labelling the movement in a particular way.

8 Selectively applying pomo thinking: an illustration

In this chapter I illustrate how pomo ideas can be applied in empirical research. My own research field is organization studies. I have here typically worked with a combination of interpretive, critical theory and poststructuralist ideas. I have mainly concentrated my interpretations/readings on delimited empirical material, e.g. an interview or an observation of a social situation. A few years ago I wrote a book based on multiple interpretations of a two-hour 'information meeting' in a company in which an executive 'informed' subordinate managers about an organizational redesign (Alvesson 1996). I used a cultural (Geertzian), a Foucauldian and a Habermasian approach to the same empirical material. In two other studies I, together with colleagues, undertook poststructuralist and other readings of interview materials, showing how pomo ideas can encourage insights as well as questioning other kinds of interpretations (Alvesson and Deetz 2000: Chapter 6; Alvesson and Sköldberg 2000: Chapter 7). These three studies represent highly concentrated, dense, even narrow work – which is fairly common in postmodernist (poststructuralist) work on 'empirical' material (Linstead and Grafton-Small 1990; Martin 1990). The case illustration below summarizes a broader study, based on a number of interviews as well as some observations.

The study is not primarily postmodernistic – although it is not easy to establish once and for all what is pomo and what is not. It is not carefully selected in order to prove or show certain points made in this book. The methodological framework – or rather the way we work and think –

incorporates a moderate use of pomo thinking. To some extent the interpretations are also pomo-oriented. The text appears to be useful, partly to show how pomo themes can be used in empirical work, and partly to show how problems in texts and claims can be critically scrutinized based on postmodernist ideas. I also comment on and critically discuss the text, drawing upon pomo scepticism about naive claims of representation, over-bold interpretations and other kinds of insensitivities.

I start by presenting our case study text, based on research carried out simultanously with the writing of the present book. This is an edited excerpt from a research paper (based on Alvesson and Sveningsson 2001). I then take a number of pomo views on it. I then follow the structure of the previous chapters, looking at the case based on: the five key pomo themes reviewed in Chapter 3; one of the possible responses to the linguistic turn outlined in Chapter 4; the idea of unpacking key categories in Chapter 5; the pomo inspirations for interviewing and understanding interview material in Chapter 6; and the themes of voice, interpretation and writing in Chapter 7.

The case: leadership or non-leadership in a company?

Background

The paper is part of a larger study investigating organization, leadership, organizational culture, motivation, career issues and many other issues in knowledge-intensive companies, i.e. companies mainly employing professionals – people with a long education whose work calls for considerable discretion. The research programme includes in-depth studies of R&D companies, IT and management consultancies etc. The approach is fairly open and exactly what is studied in the various cases is to a large degree influenced by the experiences and ideas developed during the first stages of the process. That we studied leadership is partly a result of listening to people talking about the subject matter in surprising ways during initial interviews. This made us curious and therefore we pursued this line of inquiry in subsequent interviews.

This case investigates how managers position themselves and their work in terms of leadership in the large knowledge-intensive company 'Know-Much'. Contemporary discourses on leadership, practical aspects of managerial work and ambiguity as a central dimension of organization and leadership – particularly in knowledge-intensive settings – are highlighted.

Method

The modes of interpretation are vital in qualitative research. For a long time, data processing approaches like grounded theory have been very popular. They give privilege to data and give an impression of rationality by emphasizing procedures, rules and a clear route from empirical reality to theory (Glaser and Strauss 1967; Strauss and Corbin 1994). This paper draws upon a different approach, based on two interpretive principles. One is a hermeneutic reading, in which there is a circular move between part and whole and the pre-understanding that the researcher brings with herself into research is actively used, qualified, challenged and developed in the research process (Alvesson and Sköldberg 2000). Instead of the empirical material being codified in detail, it is looked upon as text, so that one tries to go beyond the 'surface' and look for something less obvious, or less easily revealed in a (quick) coding process. The text as a totality is borne carefully in mind, which means that variation and contradiction are taken seriously.

Another principle goes slightly against hermeneutics and is to some extent inspired by poststructuralism and discourse analysis: here empirical manifestations are understood not as revealing some underlying meaning, but as possible products of discourse in action. People's talk may, for example, be an affect of the discourse they are interpellated by, rather than an expression of their subjectivity or the cultural community they belong to (Potter and Wetherell 1987; Prior 1997). We do not favour a privileging of a strong constructivist approach, but try to work with a fairly broad interpretative repertoire, carefully considering the advantages and problems of different assumptions on how to understand and theorize empirical material.

In the present study we – my co-researcher and I – thought that the empirical material strongly pointed at interesting incoherencies, something that most of the literature on leadership does not prepare people for. The discrepancy between what one might expect and what one feels the empirical material to be saying is never a simple effect of openness to data leading one in the right direction (something which grounded theory and other empiricist versions of methodology imply). It is also an effect of particular kinds of readings. In our case the readings are inspired by ideas on ambiguity in organization literature (e.g. Martin and Meyerson 1988), as well as discourse analysis and poststructuralism (e.g. Foucault 1980; Potter and Wetherell 1987). As some of our previous and current work has critically reflected on these sources of inspiration, we have some hope that the theoretical and methodological inspiration has not put its imprint too strongly on the results. We thus work with the challenge of accomplishing a good tradeoff between theoretical inspiration and openness to empirical material, between reading into data a certain vocabulary and certain preferred results, and a naive empiricism in which theory-free data lead the researcher to the truth.

Theoretical context

Modern organizations are impregnated with fashionable ideas and concepts of what constitutes good, appropriate and effective managerial leadership. The leadership Discourse is constituted by repertoires of terms and commonsensical as well as more technical reasoning that informs how a manager should talk and act in order to practise modern leadership. The discourse does not determine or inform managerial actions but constitutes a useful and seemingly attractive resource to draw upon in exhibiting a modern managerial style. One element in this discourse, typically made critical in much leadership literature over a couple of decades, is that managers and their leadership matter, that leaders are central in determining direction and overall guidelines, setting strategy and creating visions without which any company, according to leadership scholars, would drift purposelessly in any direction and eventually lose its competitive edge. Frequently, leadership is viewed as different from management. Leaders and leadership are mainly about enthusiasm, commitment and voluntary following. Kotter (cited in Barker 2001), for example, says that leadership 'is the process of moving a group (or groups) of people through (mostly) noncoercive means'. Leaders affect minds and feelings, while managers affect behaviours (Nicholls 1987). Managers rely on their formal position and bureaucracy, while leaders draw upon persuasive capacities. There is, however, sometimes confusion on this point as leadership is often routinely connected with managers, e.g. when researchers send questionnaires to managers asking them to describe their 'leadership' style, behaviours or values. An essential idea of good leadership is being 'proactive', although in an indirect and presumably supporting manner. In a great deal of modern writing on leadership the metaphors of 'architect' and 'designer', among others, are used to denote a variety of positions with a positive image (Senge 1996). These positions refer to the importance of the leader as someone who is present, although in an indirect manner, someone who leads by means of visions, strategies and guidelines, rather than the traditional commands and/or work based on, and using the means of, bureaucracy.

The discursive material to a large extent emphasizes the visionary, strategic and sometimes heroic aspects of managerial work, predisposing managerial talk in the direction of those leading the masses, as Whittington (1993: 43) characterizes the (predominantly American) model of 'strategic leadership': there 'recently emerged a new model for top management, that of the heroic leader, whose inspired visions transcend the desiccated calculations of the humdrum professional'. A typical example from the popular literature is the catchy statement by Bennis and Nanus that 'managers are people who do things right and leaders are people who do the right things' (quoted by Barker 1997: 344). The leader is portrayed as superior to the manager, in terms of both cognitive orientations and moral value.

Having reviewed some of the methodological and theoretical ideas of the study we can move on to the empirical material.

Some empirical material

We interviewed people in middle and senior management about their jobs and asked them to describe their leadership. The responses typically circled around working with visions, strategies and providing guidelines. One manager, for example, put emphasis on deciding the vision as a way of establishing a common understanding and purpose:

> Well, I think it's important that we have a common understanding . . . a common vision really and a common purpose.
>
> (Doyle)

He also maintained that leadership is:

> putting people in the same direction, leadership, there's providing common vision . . . having to decide your vision, what are your values that your working to, what's the direction that the group is going in, you personally as a manager have to live that vision.
>
> (Doyle)

To lead is to direct, in line with the 'proactive' ideal implicit in much talk of 'strategic leadership' (Whittington 1993). Another manager drew on strategy when claiming that

> I now have a more strategic focus because you can't be operational with this type of work . . . you should be familiar with what is going on but [now] it's about doing strategic judgements.
>
> (Olsen)

The views put forward about how people exercise their leadership are quite coherent. When they were asked to specify and elaborate on how they accomplish the visionary, strategic and guidance work, the accounts became rather different. Managers fell back on rather traditional managerial issues, budgets, employee leave, work roles and other issues that demand fairly detailed administrative attention. The centrality of this kind of work creates problems for some of the managers, while others do not seem to view it as a source of frustration, worry or negativity. One manager, who earlier spoke of the importance of visions, said that

> the guys that now sit as product managers and have a more coordinating role, well they were local project leaders and that was a larger role compared to what they now have, and they want partly to continue to act in their old role by intervening in details out in the functions and that is a problem. My project leaders are researchers . . . and they also want to intervene a bit too much in details in certain cases.
>
> (Harkin)

Another, also claiming 'a strategic focus', when asked to be more specific emphasized 'directive ways of handling people':

> There are many different ways of working, but I mean . . . I think that as a manager here one has to implement significantly more directive ways of handling people, that is, that you say to people that 'you will for a month in fact occupy yourself with this development, I want you to learn about this' . . . I think that you have to have a much, much more directive way of handling people in these operations.
>
> (Olsen)

Olsen explained the need for more governing in areas such as education or job rotation to create more flexibility. This does not seem to align with the earlier talk of strategic focus.

A third manager, when asked to describe the relationship between himself and his subordinates, said: 'I suppose . . . it's more of a, as I say, a bigger picture, the strategic issue, rather than detail.' But then, when asked to be more specific, he said that the work is much more about having meetings dealing with budgets and people on educational leave: 'Sometimes operational matters rather than strategic matters . . . very frustrating that we discuss them as long as we do.'

Summary

Despite the 'discursive pressure' from contemporary knowledge on leadership, communicated by educators (such as ourselves), consultants, the business press etc., and supported by corporate management and the rooted idea of leadership as visionary and strategic, managers seem to be strongly inclined to (or forced to) focus on administrative and operative issues. This seemingly paradoxical and contradictory situation inspires us to draw attention to the ambiguity of leadership – as talk, behavioural style and philosophy. Understanding the specific corporate setting also calls for consideration of the highly ambiguous corporate context in which the managers investigated work.

The 'ideological' discursive demands, reinforced and strengthened by corporate talk, collide with the 'practical' organizational demands, also reinforced by corporate talk, creating some anxiety and frustration. The consistent and firm image of leaders as presumed visionaries and strategists thus disintegrates and dissolves. The corporate demands of administrative management in KnowMuch force managers into traditional managerial activities, without allowing them to talk easily and comfortably about their activities and work roles in such terms, since that does not follow the present discursive regime. The leadership role is positively framed in corporate rhetoric but not sustained in practical organizational arrangements. The managerial role is addressed negatively in the corporate rhetoric but sustained (or enforced) in practical organizational arrangements. Identity work might, then, be challenged and jeopardized by organizational demands on the managerial role, creating feelings of contradictions and a double bind. This leaves managers with an attractive leadership role which they cannot realize and a not so attractive managerial role which they are not 'ideologically' expected to realize, but in practice forced to do so.

Comments

The text is claimed to be to some extent inspired by poststructuralist (here synonomous with postmodernist) thinking. On the whole, it is structured and argued in accordance with conventional methodology and claims considerable empirical support for its result. It therefore deviates quite radically from many of the more excessive (novel, radical) pomo ideas.

I will comment upon the text in terms of the major points made in this book. As these to some extent overlap, some minor repetition cannot be avoided below. In the first sections I mainly point at ways in which the case study is affirmative of postmodernist concerns, at least as long as these are not put forward in any strict or narrow way, and then add some criticism when discussing the themes of Chapters 6 and 7.

Five key pomo themes

If we look at the five key themes of postmodernism identified in Chapter 3, I think we can see at least some consideration of all of them.

Centrality of discourse   The paper focuses relatively tightly on discourse, in the sense that language and language use is viewed as an important theme in organizations and leadership, and this deserves consideration on its own terms. The leadership discourse is viewed as a constituting power. At the same time, a discourse focus is not consistently pursued. Talk about managerial work is not seen primarily in terms of discourse, but is viewed as reflecting what people actually are doing, i.e. it stands in some kind of relationship to practice that pomo advocates would hesitate to claim.

Fragmentation of identities   The contradictions of the various claims of the interviewed managers are well in line with the postmodernist idea of the decentred, discourse-ridden self. The interviewees try to position themselves as leaders exercising leadership, but this position seems to be difficult to stick to. The case thus indicates 'process subjectivity' (Weedon 1987; Deetz 1992) in the sense that subjectivity moves with the discursive positioning that the subject is exposed to. The case indicates this despite the interview context only addressing the managers in terms of leadership. They were not asked to produce accounts based on positions as subordinates or professionals, on gender or anything like that. That people are constituted in different ways when called upon as woman, near retirement, chemist, senior manager or German is not surprising or interesting, but if more abstract talk of leadership and talk about specific, everyday managerial work go in different directions in terms of identity positioning, then this fits nicely into the pomo theme of fragmented identities.

Critique of representation   The paper is mixed in how it relates to the theme of representation. On the one hand it follows nicely the postmodernist emphasis on the problems or impossibilities of representation. Leadership is a discourse, it represents (!) a way of talking about and constituting the social world, and as a social manuscript currently in circulation it can be repeated, and is in certain kinds of situation, such as interview talk, seminars and other ceremonial situations. But the case suggests that this is the end of story, or at least that it is unclear whether this talk actually says something about what might go on 'out there'. Emphasizing the non-referential aspect of talk about leadership makes it possible to examine more functions and effects of this talk than its ability to reflect behaviour and 'substantive' consequences.

At the same time, the paper in vital respects comes close to a fairly conventional view on representation. It is indicated that the accounts of everyday work say something about how things 'really' are or at least how the interviewees view them. The paper probably avoids the stronger claims of such representation, but still deviates from pomo concerns in that in it vital respects deviates from a critique of representation. There are no claims about this and the possibility of representation is not explicitly addressed.

Illegitimacy of grand narratives   The paper does give some hints about a grand narrative of leadership putting its imprint on the academic and popular leadership literature, as well as the corporate world. It clearly goes against this narrative. Advocates of leadership take its universal presence and significance as given. There are widespread assumptions about a universally valid leadership approach (e.g. Fiedler 1996). The paper questions the notion of leadership and argues for a more distinct, local approach exploring what 'leadership' is about. There is, however, in the paper a (weak?) tendency to launch a kind of (counter-) grand narrative about the ideological or discursive nature of leadership as of significance for identity work rather than in practical matters about getting things done in cooperation with subordinates.

Power–knowledge connection   The paper makes references to Foucault, and Foucauldian thinking has an impact on the paper, even though strong and explicit power–knowledge claims are not made. Leadership is viewed as a discourse, backed up by a variety of institutionalized authorities, that imprints on the managerial subjects being studied. This discourse orders the world and sets up standards for how the manager should be, i.e. not a manager but a leader. The managers show how they have been normalized by distancing themselves from management control and instead describing themselves in terms of strategy and vision. Knowledge about leadership is thus not something that just neutrally and objectively reflects the world out there or gives inputs for right thinking. Instead, it creates managers with a particular set of orientations. The paper raises considerable doubt regarding the success of this normalization process, as people seem prepared to back off from it when administrative demands appear (more about this below).

One can talk about another power–knowledge connection, a managerial-bureaucratic Discourse – with an emphasis on administration, operational work and the significance of practical matters – governing managerial work. But the paper does not directly address this disourse, and the discussion of a power–knowledge connection focuses on the leadership discourse.

It must be added that the paper does not explicitly connect to these five themes very often and that a stronger case for postmodernist thinking could easily be made. In those respects where the paper *is* broadly in line with pomo thinking, sharper points using the postmodernist vocabulary could have been produced. The case lends itself nicely to the use of a number of postmodernist ideas. But more subtle points could be made, so as to avoid carrying the empirical material too far and to rely less on strong theoretical/philosophical claims.

Discursive pragmatism

The paper is fairly close to what in Chapter 4 was referred to as *discursive pragmatism*, i.e. the interpretive focus is relatively tightly on the significance of vocabularies and language used in social settings. The paper is hardly an example of discourse analysis in a strict sense. It addresses – speculates about – the consequences of the role of the leadership discourse as a source of worry and identity confusion, and it also assumes that descriptions of managerial administrative practice say something about 'practice'. In other words, leadership talk is seen as discourse, while administrative talk is not viewed in this way, but more as mirroring what people 'really do'. A rather pragmatic – even eclectic – view of language and language use is therefore expressed.

Unpacking

The notion of leadership is to some extent targeted for unpacking in the paper. It is not, however, the kind of analytic or research-driven unpacking that is suggested by deconstructionists. The talk of the 'natives' is what leads to a breaking down of the idea of leadership as a central, meaningful category through which organizational reality can be ordered. This indicates that careful interpretive work and the pomo problematic can go hand in hand, at least occasionally. It is possible that interpretive work needs to be backed up with some sensitivity to ideas of fragmentation, the fluidity of meaning etc. Otherwise, one might go around looking for the Meaning of leadership, being a manager etc., and then ultimately find or create one. A strong devotee of postmodernism would, however, hardly be satisfied with the rather cautious unpacking tendencies in the case, and prefer a stronger analytic deconstructivist move focusing on the term and various texts using it, and stronger conclusions tearing leadership into pieces.

In the case text, there are a lot of categories that are left intact as conventionally understood. Just consider the initial sentence: 'The paper is part of a larger study investigating organization, leadership, organizational culture, motivation, career issues and many other issues in knowledge-intensive companies, i.e. companies mainly employing professionals – people with a long education whose work calls for considerable discretion.' Here it is assumed that one can refer to and investigate 'organization', 'leadership', 'professionals', 'long education', 'discretion' etc. as if these signifiers can mirror, order and control the world. An ambitious pomo study would stop after this sentence and then take up an entire book playing around with these signifiers and any claim that they stand in any particular relationship to a neatly ordered set of phenomena outside discourse and possible to investigate as such. But such an ambitious pomo study, confining itself to language issues, is not really what most social scientists want to do. A moderate incorporation of pomo thinking could, however, reduce the use of too many categories in a seemingly straightforward, non-problematizing way. This would make possible a better balance between the unpacking of categories and their conventional use. The resulting text would be characterized by a fairly high degree of problematization of ordering categories, and show the fragmentations and undecidabilities of these, but still use many other categories as means for getting on with descriptions and analysis. Many postmodernistically oriented researchers would for a variety of reasons – the researcher's limited stamina, lack of imagination, space problems or anticipation of the reader's growing irritation – be inclined to try to unpack only a few of the categories that inform empirical studies. This would, however, imply a destabilization of other categories used, so one might not have to problematize all categories in order to encourage a general way of reading that is in line with pomo ideas.

Interviewing: gaze and exposure

This section connects to Chapter 6, but adds some further points.

The interviewing that preceded the published text was rather straightforward. When one is interviewing people in managerial positions, leadership is often considered to be part of what one talks about. General questions about leadership were followed up by encouragement being given to managers to develop how they exercise leadership in practice. This may seem to be innocent and credible as methodological practice. However, postmodernists remind us about the not-so-neutral and innocent nature of this kind of practice. A devotee of Foucault might point to the power element involved: the manager is the object of the researcher's knowledge-creating practice, based on the idea that the former is supposed to reveal his or her subjectivity and practice in a format accessible for the latter's analysis and assessment. The interview might on the surface be seen as innocent and positive, but can also be understood as an examination situation. When the researcher – with some authority and status in the area of management and leadership – asks a person about leadership the latter is assumed to be able to produce an appropriate response. The interviewee may feel the pressure to live up to the norms of (a) producing a response that is, or appears to be, honest and makes sense, and (b) providing an account of leadership that lives up to the current norms of good leadership. A sense of failure to do so may lead to self-doubt and embarrasment – and an urge to improve, e.g. by reading the literature or participating in leadership training activities.

In the paper the researchers carefully scrutinize the subjects' responses and reveal that their self-understanding appears to be contradictory and confused. They are exposed as victims of a popular leadership discourse which they try to identify with and embrace, but with limited success. Perhaps the researchers then implicitly use another norm for assessment: the (Western?) idea of the coherent subject, supposed to grasp her situation and not get caught in contradictory accounts and confusing situations. There is thus a scrutinization or examination that the interviewee gets located in. That the paper uses poststructuralist ideas and views identity fragmentation as 'normal' does not really help the situation of the people in the study: very few of the people we as social scientists study are well versed in pomo, but share a humanistic view of individuals in general and themselves in particular. Postmodernist thinking is easily used to expose the limitations of their own presented self-understandings.

I have here the feeling that I am perhaps too harsh in my self-critique. Foucauldian ideas and language encourage such inclinations: all knowledge projects and claims beg for self-scrutiny in rather pejorative terms: the researcher's gaze, normalization, discipline etc. One can feel disciplined enough to leave all the subjects in peace and direct one's investigative will to power to particular forms of (academic) knowledge, preferably historical, instead. But that would lead to a defeatist position, with an overemphasis on the negative compared to the positive, and must therefore be resisted.

Let us return more specifically to some of the points addressed in Chapter 6. The paper bears strong imprints of the Foucauldian idea of interpreting accounts not as mirroring reality out there, or the beliefs and meanings of the interviewees, but as outcomes of Big Discourse. This is at least the case with the accounts about leadership. One could perhaps also imagine a Big Discourse point about administrative details etc., but that would probably have been less interesting. That people say they are stuck in a lot of practical details and administrative routines does not offer grounds for a Foucauldian point as nicely as the leadership accounts – although of course a more detailed study of how administrative routines control people might be of interest.

In the context of the points made in Chapter 6, the paper misses the theme of the interview as local accomplishment. One could argue that people, when asked about leadership by an academic from a business school, respond by trying to produce an account in line with conventional ideas about the subject matter. The interview talk might only say something about the specifics and details of the interview as a social situation. This is what discourse analysis would emphasize. The paper could be criticized for not considering how 'leadership' is produced by the researcher asking questions about it, and for not considering the accounts as intimately contingent upon the social setting in which the talk is produced.

If pressed we – my co-author and I – could produce two lines of defence: one is that we have some observational material indicating the presence of similar talk outside interview situations; the other is that a local accomplishment focus would prevent us from making the somewhat wider and perhaps more socially relevant points that the paper tries to make.

Voice

As in the previous section, in the following sections I will to some extent emphasize critiques of the case that follow from pomo concerns.

As elaborated in the previous chapter, the idea of 'voice' typically points at a concern with subtle issues emerging from the field, rather than the perspective, research theme, analytic vocabulary or research community's conventions that might take the upper hand and dominate the research process and the product (text). To what extent has the researcher listened carefully to the variety of voices that the setting chosen for study may be said to harbour? Given the limited format of the paper extract there are, of course, strong constraints regarding the number of voices from the field that are represented and are allowed space. One can in this context note how the text is used: about 25 per cent of it claims to report interview material, either directly through short quotations or through brief summaries.

Voices typically seen as crucial are not strongly present in the text: different genders, subordinates, people with more nuanced (sceptical, resistant) voices on the leadership discourse, people with less fragmented or contradictory orientations in terms of the ideal and the practised. (In terms of gender, one of the cited persons is a woman/an XX-person, the others are men/XY-persons. In the interview material as a whole, there is no obvious gender difference in the accounts produced.) A perhaps more significant omission concerns the depth or nuances of the persons cited. In the text there are only short citations used to support the authors' claims. This may be motivated by the wish to make a point: a paper that is full of a variety of accounts and voices may just frustrate the reader and tell him or her little of interest. Still, the highly constrained voices, strongly edited by the authors, deserve mentioning. One can see the case study as yet another example of research-driven and structured research where the subjects under study definitively influence the study by forming a bulk of material for interpretation, but their voices are allowed little space and come through in a highly structured and orchestrated manner. The case can be justifiably criticized for paying insufficient attention to the voice problematic.

There is a clear dilemma here. Multiple voices and the avoidance of their repression by researchers sound good and it is far too easy to locate subjects in a single, seemingly uniform position – manager – and then only allow them one voice or possibly two voices that form a nice contradiction or paradox. On the other hand, the purpose of a research paper is to provide an illumination of a specific subject matter and to develop an idea and provide some kind of result – this calls for the omission of a lot that could be inserted. It is here important to think carefully about how much of the editing results from an anticipation of reader reactions and conformity to the established conventions of the academic community or a desire to produce a good story. The advantages of and problems with a severe taming of messy empirical material related to an equally messy social reality also offer much food for thought.

Interpretation

The theme of interpretation has been addressed in most of the previous sections and I will try to avoid repeating myself. The case is fairly strongly interpretive in the sense that it tries to point at three kinds of patterns or dimensions. One is the significance of leadership as Discourse, another is the absence of this leadership discourse at the level of practice and the third is the consequences of this apparent contradiction, including fragmented identities, and the superficial and fashionable character of leadership talk.

The interpretive project emphasizes the 'deeper' meaning behind surface manifestations. Postmodernism is interested in the 'surface', rejecting the idea of something behind it, to be revealed behind the manifested text, even though pomo is interested in what is absent (the repressed Other). As noted above, the text addressed here does not express a strong hermeneutic interest but explores meaning as fluid and discourse-connected. One can question claims about overall patterns (coherence) and contradictions as strongly tied to an idea that one can summarize empirical material by indicating one or a few underlying themes (patterns, dimensions). One can also question the assumption that the empirical material can be ordered and made sense of with some clever interpretations.

Postmodernism would encourage a much more cautious approach to interpretation, being more patient with ambiguities, fragmentations, undecidabilities etc. Here one could note the accounts provided, but let them stand for themselves, perhaps with comments or proposed readings fairly close to the manifest communication (talk). Take the first interview quote as an example: 'Well, I think it's important that we have a common understanding . . . a common vision really and a common purpose.' In the paper the signifier 'vision' seems to have triggered some reactions from the authors (i.e. myself and my co-author). As it also turns up in the other quote from this interviewee it seems to carry some meaning and signify something important. It is then interpreted as being a sign of 'visionary leadership', an idea that leadership is about developing inspiring ideals and goals and an overall sense of meaningful direction. But one could stop short of this and look at the ambiguities of the first sentence. The interviewee starts by referring to a common understanding, then goes on to the common vision and, in the next step, to a common purpose. How can we read this?

Perhaps 'vision' is picked as a word floating around in the corporate context and used to add something to common understanding. Perhaps 'common' is the key word – at least it is repeated three times – and understanding, vision and purpose should be seen as reinforcers of this more central signifier, which may tell us something about the interviewee's worries – perhaps her work group is characterized by diversity, conflict, language problems. Perhaps the concern is more an expression of an effort to stimulate good work relations than something else. That 'vision' is mentioned might not be that informative – it might only signal that the subject follows broadly shared norms that one should have a 'vision'. That 'vision' turns up in the next quote might appear to support the way the authors use the interview accounts, but the interviewee might have repeated it in the absence of more precise ways of illuminating matters, and the researchers' possible interest in this word might have subtly encouraged the interviewee to use it.

This kind of more detailed text reading would be in line with a postmodernist concern to avoid definitive interpretations and also to point at the undecidabilities of a text. A more strict discourse analysis of some chunks of text would be another option, not fully in line with pomo thinking but still less distant from it than the rather ambitious and far-reaching interpretations produced in the case paper.

Still another option is to propose several interpretations of the text, each perhaps going further than pointing at the undecidabilities of the various details of the empirical material. These interpretations could be similar to the line of interpretation in the case text, i.e. be fairly ambitious in their efforts to find a meaning in the empirical material. One could, for example, adopt a management or consultancy perspective and use the empirical material to point to managerial problems in the company: the managers seem to be incapable of exercising sufficiently strong and coherent leadership. The problems may be because of poor training, too much bureaucracy or a corporate culture preventing leaders from appearing as such and leading the troops as they should. Interpretations could also point to the ambiguities and uncertainties relating to 'leadership' in everyday settings.

The idea of multiple interpretations could, then, point to the ambiguities and undecidabilities of the empirical material and any single interpretation of it by offering several options, without trying to convince the reader (or oneself as an author) which is best. The varied interpretations to some extent challenge each other and introduce uncertainty, encouraging the reader to activate herself, assess the interpretations and, at best, come up with alternative ones.

Writing

In terms of text production a range of different aspects can be raised: structure, genre, rhetoric in order to appear credible, author's location (dislocation) etc. As the paper as it appears above is a brief summary of a longer text of above average length for academic articles (around 10,000 words), it is difficult for the reader of this book to grasp how the author makes the case and how the reader is passified into accepting the authors' authority or activated into taking a more independent, creative stance. I therefore make only a few points here, in particular drawing attention to some problematic aspects of the text.

The paper is structured in a way that is common in academic papers of a qualitative–interpretive character. Most of us tend to take the format for given: introduction, literature review, method sections, empirical study, discussion and conclusion sections. This logic also dominates the reporting of quantitative research, another example of the audience shaping the research.

The paper is clearly written to be persuasive. The text conveys the impression that the authors know what they are writing about and by reading this text the reader will know more about 'leadership' and the work situations and identity problems of (at least some) managers. At least this is what we hoped for. A variety of claims are made in the paper, explicitly or implicitly to convince the reader:

1 Factual claims about the leadership literature, about the research process, what the case study tells us.
2 That the authors have the right mindset (open).
3 Indications about others being 'caught' in a particular conviction, while the authors of this paper believe themselves to be more broadly intellectually oriented, capable of moving between interpretive and poststructural readings, open to empirical material but not naive about the option of data speaking directly to science.

The paper claims to be open but nevertheless makes a number of factual claims of a debatable nature: at the outset it establishes that 'Modern organizations are impregnated with fashionable ideas and concepts about what constitutes good, appropriate and effective managerial leadership.' This is presented as if it is a self-evident fact. It may well resemble the common sense and prejudices of the academic reader consuming texts like this, sometimes with a rather pejorative view of the intellectual level of managers.

The paper claims coherence in both how people present their leadership style and how they describe their actual work. The resulting contradictions become clear-cut. There are, the reader is led to believe, two lines of internally coherent accounts producing a contradiction-free contradiction, making it possible for the authors to present an elegant contradiction, revealing the 'emptiness' of leadership, at least in the studied company, and unmasking the powers of the leadership fashion to enrol the subjects being studied. Such coherence and the combination of the two sets of coherences, leading to a fundamental contradiction, is, of course, always constructed. It is an outcome of a reading and ordering of the material in a particular way. As discussed in the sections above, a careful, detailed interpretation of all the accounts in their specific local contexts might have led to a more varied picture, and made it impossible or at least more problematic to arrive at the broader claims of the paper.

Anti-PS point: against Foucault

A final comment concerns how the text can be mobilized against some postmodernist (Foucauldian) ideas. Above it was emphasized that the empirical material is broadly in line with pomo ideas of the fragmented subject, and the power–knowledge connection means that knowledge interpellates and subjugates the subjects. The managers seem to be caught by the leadership discourse developed and distributed by the leadership industry. The Foucauldian version of any deviation from it places the emphasis on resistance. Resistance means that subjects are not completely caught, constructing their selves within Discourse, but are slippery and ambiguous and strive to reduce the control. In the case it is difficult to see much resistance against the discourse, but the practice and experience of everyday life would appear to suggest the limitations of the leadership Discourse. Its identity-constituting effectiveness seems to be limited compared to the administrative and operational tasks of a large-scale bureaucracy. Massive anti-bureaucracy writing and talk, including a wealth of discourses and Discourses defining it as outdated and antithetical to R&D-oriented knowledge companies, do not seem sufficient to create a 'leadership'-based identity that has normalized the subject so strongly that this comes through in practice or even reported experiences of this practice.

Giving some space to empirical material not only confirming postmodernist ideas, but also ambiguously kicking back against them, would perhaps justify the viewpoint that this case shows the partiality and limitation of a Discourse approach to self-constitution and what structures social life. A Discourse enthusiast would, of course, here immediately counter and point at the Bureaucracy Discourse as the key element still dominating part of organizational life in this setting, and thus see the empirical material as fully compatible with a Discourse perspective. However, even though we have some sympathy with this reading and think that a Foucauldian point can productively be carried quite far, the Discourse concept is of most interest if it is not used to cover everything. The practical arrangements and administrative work that occupy managers – such as dealing with replacements for people on leave or deciding about new furniture or in which building different groups should be located – are not very elegantly illuminated through the notion of Big Discourse in the same way as the leadership talk addressed in the paper.

Summary

In this chapter I have provided an illustration of a number of the vital areas of postmodernist problematics in relationship to social research. The chapter to a certain degree provides a summary of large parts of the book, although there are some omissions contingent upon what it is relevant to address in the light of the case here presented and sceptically reviewed. (The merits and, in particular, problems with the term postmodernism, for example, received some attention at the beginning of this book, but are not reviewed here.) The set of themes covered in this book and to a large extent appearing in this chapter overlap to some extent but also point in slightly different directions. As I stressed in Chapter 2, postmodernism is not a coherent body of ideas and themes, but an assembly of various kinds of literatures and convictions.

The advantages of and problems with using a study conducted by oneself for the purpose of showing how postmodernist themes appear in the light of empirical research can be discussed. It is possible, indeed likely, that a person more committed to postmodernist themes than myself would give the case a more harsh treatment, being less positive on the various issues which I think the case handles well and even more critical on the many points in which the paper is not affirmative to pomo worries. The case is not, however, intended to be a strictly postmodernist piece. I still think it illustrates how some of the pomo encouragement to rethink basic issues, such as power–knowledge connections, the role of discourse or problems of representation, can be handled in a fairly conventional qualitative–interpretive work – perhaps in particular if the empirical material is productively in line with these pomo themes. I also think that pomo critiques can raise a lot of food for thought and inspire less conventional modes of writing and dealing with issues of voice and interpretation. Working through my own research example from the set of pomo points presented in this book is for me a valuable experience. One might consider research texts in which inspirations from postmodernism do not influence the research process or the major bulk of the product (text), as much as the final review of the work and text. The researcher can, for example, add sections presenting postmodernistic (or in other ways sceptical) comments on the text similar to those presented here. Typically, the text proportions would be different from those of this chapter, which devotes most space to pomo comments. In the 'normal' case, the study would be given most space, while postmodernist comments or re-readings (unpackings) of the main text would be less extensive and space-consuming.

9 Conclusions

In this final chapter I do three things. I start by addressing the criteria that we use in assessing social research. Occasionally, one reads remarks against 'criteriology'; the banning of efforts to establish rules for what is acceptable and not. But sometimes authors present all kinds of alternative versions of validity aimed at challenging and replacing conventional ideas on the subject. I do think we must carefully consider how to discuss what is good and not so good research. I then address a single overall guideline for doing social research that incorporates a significant element of pomo thinking in its philosophy, practice and text production. This guideline concerns trying to find and/or construct order and system as well as variation and fragmentation; going back and forth in research looking for patterns *and* for ambiguities. A third theme is the idea of reflexivity – which in my version refers less to the idea of self-scrutinization than to the use of alternative perspectives and vocabularies in interpreting work. Finally, I discuss how a strategy for the 'pomoization' of carefully selected parts of the research project may be a way of working reflexively. Pomo can thus be an aid rather than a full-scale framework for social research, to be used in thinking through what one is doing in carefully selected areas and moments of the research project.

Validity – or other criteria for deciding what is good

Some problems with dominant criteria

Postmodernism can be seen as representing (!) a broad stream of social science and philosophy (and other fields of academic thinking as well) that expresses doubt about traditional means of determining what is to count as valid or in other ways good knowledge. Conventional ideas about social research being in the business of serving the truth by producing authoritative knowledge based on the mirroring of, or testing of, hypotheses and ideas against reality revealed by data have been increasingly challenged: 'Ideas about empirical evidence, objectivity, reason, truth, coherence, validity, measurement, and fact no longer provide great comfort or direction' (van Maanen 1995: 15). The conventional criterion of good knowledge, that the theory fits the data, does not appear to be insightful or realistic, as empirical material is produced within discourse or – to use another expression – is impregnated with theory. Conventional understandings, such as the claim of grounded theorists that concept development should be checked out systematically with data (Strauss and Corbin 1994: 274), are increasingly viewed as naive and outdated, leading at least some of the proponents to try to develop a constructivist version of grounded theory (Charmaz 2000).

We can talk about a broad retreat from the notion of the search for truth as the ideal and viable option for social research (and perhaps for knowledge creation in general). More and more researchers accept that all observations and all data are theory-laden and in other ways depend on the view of the researcher – and his or her personal and social characteristics associated with preunderstandings and value commitments contingent upon paradigm, gender, class, political opinions etc. – and/or the languages used to construct. Smith and Deemer (2000: 878) state that 'relativism is nothing more or less than our condition in the world'. Postmodernism is only one way of summarizing some of these 'anti-truth' moves, although perhaps the most salient and extreme one. There is, however, a diversity of views on how far one should distance oneself from the objective truth standard for assessing knowledge. Those whom Rosenau (1992) refers to as sceptic postmodernists reject the idea of using specific criteria for separating the good from the bad, and suggest a 'non-judgemental' attitude. One can engage in quite a lot of questioning without necessarily rejecting all claims to be saying something that has strong support in empirical work. More or less 'soft' or 'alternative' claims of 'validity' or 'truth' may be proposed.

A partial acceptance of the impossibilities and limitations of strict truth criteria may be followed by a reluctance to go the entire way along a relativistic route that denies truth or the ability of empirical material to say yes or no to various ideas and claims.

Harding (1990: 100) argues that 'The postmodern critics of feminist science . . . appear to assume that if one gives up the goal of telling one true story about reality, one must also give up trying to tell less false stories' and suggests that one may aim 'to produce less partial and perverse representations'. The criterion for good knowledge would, then, be not the absolute truth or a perfect representation, but 'more true' stories, 'fairly total' and 'normal' representations. At least this seems to be the positive version of the avoidance of partial and perverse representations. Truth claims and efforts to accomplish representations would probably not differ that much from conventional criteria of validity, but the understanding of the project and the confidence in the claims made would be more moderate.

Harding's suggestions may seem uncontroversial. From a bold postmodernist view, their ambitions can, however, be challenged. The idea of true/false stories or even more or less true/false stories is not accepted by postmodernists. The ideals of less partial – i.e. more total – stories and non-perverse – normal – representations could be seen as examples of the totalizing and normalization impulse that postmodernists find problematic. They might lead to the ordering and control powers of 'modernist' knowledge. An emphasis on the partial and local in all stories and claims, and an appreciation of the surprising, shocking, unfamilar, perhaps even what to the advocate of the 'normal' might be seen as perverse, would offer alternative values for thinking about knowledge projects. Pomo 'unpacking' projects could include some of these 'partial' and 'perverse' qualities.

Nevertheless, I think that Harding has a point that a cautious approach to producing 'true stories' should not prevent us from being prepared to reject 'false' stories in our self-assessments and evaluations of others, realizing that perhaps most of what we study is too complex, ambiguous and interesting to be evaluated in terms of 'more or less false'. Even though the idea of avoiding the 'false' is one criterion that seems reasonable, it is often not very helpful. Many researchers inspired by pomo or other post-empiricist streams suggest other criteria instead. 'Constructions are not more or less "true", in any absolute sense, but simply more or less informed and/or sophisticated. Constructions are alterable, as are our associated "realities"' (Guba and Lincoln 1994: 111). Sometimes criteria such as trustworthiness (not dissimilar to validity) and plausibility have been suggested. Lincoln and Guba (2000) talk of validity as authenticity, and suggest various 'authenticity criteria', which the authors believe to be hallmarks of authentic, trustworthy, rigorous or 'valid' constructivist research. One such criterion is catalytic authenticity, which 'refers to the ability of a given inquiry to prompt . . . action on the part of the research participants' (p. 181). This criterion seems to overlap with what many refer to as pragmatism. Pragmatism is often used as an indicator of valuable knowledge. Knowledge is viewed as good if it is helpful for individuals and actors in coping with their circumstances: 'One story is truer than another to the extent to which it might more effectively guide human practice in that or a similar setting' (Watson 2000: 506).

Critical theories can be judged in a similar way; the crucial issue is the extent to which the inquiry 'acts to erode ignorance and misapprehensions, and the extent to which it provides a stimulus to action, that is, to the transformation of the existing structure' (Guba and Lincoln 1994: 114). The problem with this is that it is very difficult to evaluate these qualities. Does psychoanalysis – in general or a particular study informed by this theory – for example, 'effectively guide human practice'? Or does a particular feminist study 'provide a stimulus to action'? Perhaps, but different feminist studies may encourage radically different strategies, embracing contradictory objectives and directions (e.g. Martin 2002). Even if human practice or radical action is triggered and affected by a particular research product, how can we assess the outcomes? Presumably by reference to an empirical study – and thus we cannot avoid some kind of grounding in data. In addition, the value or 'truth' of the studies or theories become dependent on the reception and action of a group of practitioners – and their fortunes and misfortunes. As Hammersley (1992) points out, successful action may be based on false assumptions, and valid knowledge may be accompanied by unsuccessful action. In all but the most exceptional cases the researcher and the research results have only a limited impact. Marx can hardly be blamed for all the evil deeds of Stalin, Mao and Pol Pot. Under any circumstances, it is very difficult for people in an academic context to do more than speculate about how a particular piece of research might be helpful in informing practice or triggering social change, at least beyond their immediate social circle and their own well-being. To privilege pragmatic and political criteria for evaluating what is valuable knowledge might be quite unfair to social research that raises difficult questions with no straightforward answers, promises of technical fixes or rhetorical appeals about the bad and the good. So, although I am very positive about critical research and think these pragmatic and change-facilitating criteria are important for some types of research and definitely should be considered, I don't think they can work as the final criteria for assessing valuable knowledge, not even in critical studies guided by emancipatory ambitions.

Some broad post-empiricist criteria for evaluating empirical work

There are various suggestions for rethinking 'validity' and for more novel, productive notions of validity drawing upon postmodernist, feminist and other kinds of critique (Smith and Deemer 2000). I prefer to skip or at least downplay the notion of validity – its associations with objectivist thinking are too strong – and talk of ways of doing good social research instead.

Arguably, there are a few general criteria for social research that we can broadly apply, taking some of the post-empiricist arguments into consideration while still giving space for empirical material to be significant in social research. These criteria include the support of knowledge claims through empirical material based on: (a) care, awareness and insightful handling of the production/construction processes; and (b) care in the interpretation of it. This is quite different from the idea of validity being a fit of theory and observation. Through awareness of how language is central in work with empirical material, how any empirical material is constructed within a particular metaphor and discourse and how our interpretations can be based on broad consideration of alternative viewpoints and vocabularies, one can conduct good social research. One might not arrive at the truth with a big T, but perhaps produce an insightful and illuminating study of the phenomena one is addressing. Important here is the working back and forth between consideration of how theoretical frameworks, cultural assumptions, personal subjectivities and various uses of vocabularies and interpretive moves do construct empirical reality, but in qualified ways. Here the social reality and subjects being studied provide considerable inspiration and also exercise discipline on the researchers' imagination, preventing certain constructions or interpretations from being made.

One could propose the key themes covered in this book as criteria relevant for evaluating social research. Social research that deserves praise might, for example, be based on a skilful handling of the representation problem, of how the study of languages in social contexts can be handled with care and finess, of how the power–knowledge connection can be coped with, of how interview accounts can be understood in different ways. The result that the researcher produces is then grounded in how one simultanously – or in different steps – works with empirical material and all or a few of the mentioned themes involved in that work.

But in empirical studies these criteria must be balanced against the idea of using the empirical material for the illumination of a phenomenon. A deconstructive awareness, showing problems with all efforts to represent reality, is thus not sufficient. Simultaneous work with the deconstruction of problematic categories, ideas and rhetorical moves, and the construction of a 'positive' case that allows good understanding is then aspired to.

When one is evaluating research and saying that this is a good piece of research (worthy of research grants, being published, awarded a PhD) and this is a less good piece, it might be asking too much to demand a full consideration and highly detailed handling of all the pomo complications. However, it is reasonable to anticipate a general awareness and an avoidance of crudeness in claims to representation, naivety in the use of grand, totalizing frameworks, the treatment of interview statements as a simple mirror of what is on people's minds etc.

All the work done to pick apart or deconstruct texts, to illuminate their failures to make their points, reminds us of problems of representation and counters any naive faith in a simple and transparent social world, but gives no suggestions for better ways of doing social research. Even though many people now accept that the credibility of social research is contingent upon social, historical and institutional forces, and that there is no superior way of deciding what is good research, this does not change the basic situations for researchers trying to convince their audience. This is still accomplished 'through the hard work of presenting evidence, interpretations, elaborating analogies, invoking authorities, working through examples, marshalling the tropes and so on' (van Maanen 1995: 22).

The ways in which tricky issues in social research – addressed by post-modernists and others (critical theorists, constructionists outside 'hardcore pomo', interpretivists, feminists etc.) – are dealt with do not exclude the formulation and use of fairly conventional criteria, although these must be understood in ways that reflect post-empiricist insights. Credible empirical material and careful analysis, strong arguments for conclusions, good anchoring in the literature and an ability to establish a critical dialogue with other research texts are conventional criteria which one cannot escape. Taking pomo ideas into account involves a displacement rather than a replacement of the criteria for doing interpretive qualitative social research. Empirical material and support are important, but the uncertainties are so profound that one cannot privilege data as the road to results, but must add a number of additional considerations and criteria for the production of valuable knowledge.

Specific criteria: the example of multiple interpretation

The viewpoints just expressed are fairly general. More specific principles and criteria are needed to guide and assess specific kinds of work.

These more specific criteria are contingent upon which type of research one is doing and the particular strategy chosen for dealing with the problematic issues that seem relevant, given the research theme and response to, for example, the linguistic turn or the text production issue. One can work with a flexible list of criteria and guidelines modified to the specifics of a research task (Smith and Deemer 2000).

If, for example, one is doing discursive pragmatism work, then how one works with the theme of moving beyond language use, without jumping to problematic conclusions, becomes vital. The navigation between taking language use seriously and making cautious interpretations of chunks of social reality relatively close to language uses in different social contexts becomes an object for evaluation. One can also, as suggested by Richardson (2000), combine scientific and aesthetic criteria for evaluating research. Assessing aesthetic merit involves the extent to which 'the use of creative analytic practices opens up the text, invites interpretive responses' and the text is 'artistically shaped, satisfying, complex, and not boring' (p. 937). I will not, however, go more deeply into these particular issues here, nor treat all the other issues that might be relevant to specific projects. Instead, I will illustrate how one can develop guidelines and criteria for working with multiple interpretations. In the proposal below, the ideal of a good conversation between the various lines of interpretations is suggested, and some specifications for what this can look like are outlined.

One important criterion for assessing a study of this nature, in addition to the common post-empiricist ideals, such as novelty, conceptual appeal, empirical support for interpretations (plausibility rather than verification/falsification of hypotheses) and elegance (aesthetics), consists of how the different perspectives adopted function together in an intra-textual conversation. A good conversation involves a combination of consensus, variation in views and dissensus. Too much of any of these elements means that the conversation becomes uninteresting; it becomes repetitive, it comes to consist of monologues or turns into a quarrel. The voices involved should thus address similar problems and should, to a certain degree, have a shared vocabulary. They should indicate new (different) understandings in relation to interpretations made from the other perspectives involved, thus adding something to them. They should also be critical, challenging the assumptions and arguments of the other perspectives. This means that the mix of interpretations should facilitate reflection on the strengths and limitations of the perspectives and interpretations concerned, encouraging the researcher to self-critique. Not only should the conversation produced in a specific case be critically considered, but also the voices that are absent from it – bearing in mind that the presence of too many diverse voices obstructs a good conversation, which may degenerate into mere babble (Alvesson 1996).

Comments

As mentioned repeatedly, I have no intention to produce a text that strongly follows postmodernist authors or suggests anything that solves methodological issues associated with hardcore pomo. I do think that moderate responses to pomo problematics must think carefully about standards for good research. Different ideas about validity can be part of this, but there are other vocabularies and viewpoints that are perhaps of greater relevance.

In various manners, one can avoid the problems of postmodernist inspirations leading to a lack of standards, or the adoption of very fuzzy ideals. We must be careful about what criteria we are using and should have a broad-minded attitude here. We must also be very careful about avoiding sloppy work and an 'anything goes' attitude. In vital ways, I think inspiration from postmodernism can encourage more qualified work. But it calls for a lot of self-discipline and a push for standards. Even if one is, as sometimes is the case in pomo, celebrating 'playfulness, difference and undecidability', some idea is needed of what is meant by, for example, 'playfulness' and how we can encourage high standards in exercising playfulness. Devoting attention to criteria and insisting on having high standards does not mean, of course, that we can rely on fixed criteria or detailed, unambiguous norms that make it possible to check research and tick off whether it lives up to the evalution criteria, in a way corresponding to what quantitative people do by checking level of significance. Criteria are a matter of ongoing debate and dispute, and call for a lot of judgement and self-reflection. At the end of the day, any text will be evaluated for its pros and cons in a number of respects, and by a plurality of evaluators. Being explicit about the reasonable grounds for assessment, and meeting those one rejects with alternative ones, may facilitate communication and an increased level of mutual understanding – or at least a decreased level of hostility, ignorance and arbitrariness.

Navigating between patterns and ambiguity, between ordering and undecidability

Postmodernism is, for some, 'an assault on unity', as I quoted from one commentator (Power 1990) at the beginning of this text. Many definitions – to the extent one can talk about definitions here – of postmodernism emphasize things like undecidabilities, fragmentations, diversity and fluidity. The social world is complex and messy and any effort to find patterns will impose an arbitrary order through exclusion of what does not fit into a particular set of representations.

In the opposite camp we have all the traditional researchers interested in finding patterns. It is assumed that social reality is ordered and patterned. The researcher's task is to investigate and reveal how. Huberman and Miles (1994), for example, are convinced 'that social phenomena exist not only in the mind, but in the objective world as well and that there are some lawful, reasonably stable relationships to be found among them' (p. 429), and that 'the theories or constructs that we derive express these regularities as precisely as possible' (p. 431).

Postmodernism may be seen as a mega-project opening up the closure involved in various 'modernist' projects: from neo-positivist ones to hermeneutic efforts to locate some underlying meaning. Through the exploration of ambiguity, fragmentation, undecidabilities, variations, fluid pictures 'existing' in hyperreality, incoherences, a world in process and play etc., pattern, order and meaning vanish.

> Post-modernists rearrange the whole social science enterprise. Those of a modern conviction seek to isolate elements, specify relationships, and formulate a synthesis; post-modernists do the opposite. They offer indeterminacy rather than determinism, diversity rather than unity, difference rather than synthesis, complexity rather than simplification . . . social science becomes a more subjective and humble enterprise as truth gives way to tentativeness.
>
> (Rosenau 1992: 8)[1]

Pomo can be viewed as opening up a social world seemingly domesticated by the theories, methodologies, data, analysis and linear, rationally written research texts that turn messy reality into condensed knowledge products.

But is it necessarily so? All systems of thought include elements of totalization and closure. Postmodernism is no exception. It appears to insist on how we should understand and study the world once and for all. It comes close to postulating that the social world is discursively constituted, subjects are decentred, knowledge is dangerous, everything is undecidable etc. I reviewed the harsh critique of 'modernism' which is sometimes followed by an almost dogmatic postmodernist standpoint. Why give such a privilege to ambiguity over patterns, fluidity over stability, diversity over unity, indeterminacy over interpretation, discourse over meaning, complexity over partial knowledge? Strong postmodernist preferences may well lead to a new kind of closure – and result in researchers one-dimensionally governed by pomo convictions missing vital aspects.

One can here ironically turn pomo on pomo: a pomo critique of pomo would suggest that it tends to emphasize patterns of fragmentation, be determined about the indeterminacy, allow no ambiguity about ambiguity, not consider that there may be variation in terms of diversity (i.e. allow no space for the possibility that occasionally there may be less diversity/more unity) etc. As pomo is a philosophical style, a way of relating to the world, one cannot say that these are purely empirical questions – it is not a simple matter of going out there and finding out whether there are patterns and unities or fragmentations and diversities in, for example, a particular village. But one may be more or less hooked on this style.

I feel almost embarrassed to suggest more openness about looking for – considering interpretations and readings – patterns *and* ambiguity, trends *and* variation, order *and* fragmentation, regularities *and* disorder. This sounds watered down. But I think that there may be a point in exploring the qualities that promote the understanding of specific groups, settings and events in ways that are most fair and interesting in terms of the results produced. We don't have to commit ourselves *a priori* so strongly to a particular conviction and a language.

Of course, we can unpack the just mentioned dichotomies and try other entrances as well: instead of patterns and disorder we can investigate 'modes of ordering' (Law 1994), instead of systems and ambiguity we may be open to 'bounded ambiguities' (Alvesson 2002). The important thing is to be inspired by pomo thinking without this necessarily leading to a new kind of closure. A lot of social science – particularly in the qualitative traditions such as anthropology – has always taken the ambiguous, complex and fluid nature of social life seriously, but not emphasized it one-sidedly:

> Experience is messy . . . When human behaviour is the data, a tolerance
> for ambiguity, multiplicity, contradiction, and instability is essential . . .

As ethnographers, our job is not simply to pass on the disorderly complexity of culture, but also to try to hypothesize about apparent consistencies, to lay out our best guesses, without hiding the contradictions and the instability.

(Wolf 1992: 129)

Pomo writings offer strong encouragement to take the messy side of social life much more seriously and hesitate before finding, constructing or imposing tendencies and patterns on reality. But, as Falzon (1998: 17) points out, 'it is not possible to articulate the fragmentation thesis itself without continuing to employ some conception of unity'. Without the latter, fragmentation and multiplicity do not make sense. Going back and forth between assumptions and interpretive themes around patterns–order–dimensions–meanings, and ambiguity–diversity–multiplicity–fluidity, and being open about different ways of making sense of the empirical material might be a productive way forward.

Reflexivity

What is proposed here is what can be referred to as a reflexive pragmatist approach to social research (Alvesson and Sköldberg 2000). The increasingly popular term reflexivity is used in a variety of ways (Brewer 2000: 126–33). Perhaps the most common one emphasizes that the researcher is part of the social world that is studied, and this calls for exploration and self-examination. This typically leads to a preoccupation with the researcher-self and its significance in the research process. It can lead to forms of writing placing the researcher's personal experience in the centre (confessional tales: van Maanen 1988) or explorations of the various researcher-selves that are active in the process (Reinharz 1997).

I use the term reflexivity in a somewhat different way. It stands for conscious and systematic efforts to view the subject matter from different angles, and to avoid strongly privileging a favoured one. Rorty (1989) writes about irony, implying a constant awareness that there are always other vocabularies for addressing the line taken. One approach is to move between different lines of interpretation, varying and confronting an earlier used vocabulary with a line of interpretation that offers a different angle and a different vocabulary (Alvesson and Sköldberg 2000). This means challenging the chosen interpretation and the researcher confronting himself or herself and possibly the reader with alternative views, which may facilitate arriving at the 'strongest' or most interesting interpretation and/or offering alternative ones, in which the study may offer more than one type of result. One can, for example, conduct one's research and produce a preliminary text and then critically go through it from an postmodernist (or other challenging, e.g. feminist) angle. This can lead to more or less significant revisions of the text or the addition of sections including comments, reinterpretations, self-critique, deconstructions of the text etc. An example of how a pomo-inspired working through of the study and text can lead to added sections was provided in Chapter 8.

The ideal is to maintain an awareness that there is more than one good way of understanding something, and there is a great risk that the one chosen may hide more interesting understandings. *Pragmatism* here means a willingness to postpone some doubt and still use the material for what the researcher thinks is the best possible purpose. Pragmatism builds on an awareness that time, space and patience are not unlimited and a withholding of limitless reflexivity. It also means the bracketing of doubt and self-critique for the achievement of results. There is an adaption to constraints and a willingness to compromise between reflexive ideals and the idea of 'delivering knowledge'. Results are, however, informed by reflexive consideration of how the empirical material can be used – this should prevent highly speculative and naive uses of empirical material.

Reflexive pragmatism calls for epistemological awareness rather than philosophical rigour. Jumping between paradigms is a very difficult sport, but it is not impossible to widen and vary one's horizons, looking self-critically at favoured assumptions and lines of inquiry. In order to facilitate such a reflexive pragmatist approach, we need to have a fairly broad and multi-angled theoretical understanding of the research process and the almost endless spectrum of tricky issues involved – issues that cannot be resolved by conventional methodological means such as a rigorous design, a mass of data, subjected to data management procedures, confrontations between data and hypothesis/theory etc.

A reflexive approach means a meta-theoretical understanding – a framework involving a set of potential lines of thinking and theoretical ideas for how to understand a subject matter – rather than a definitive theoretical formulation and privileged vocabulary for grasping it. As noted, in most instances of social research it is easy to argue for the position that there is no definite meaning or truth. This calls for a preparedness to employ various 'seeing as' approaches. This does not mean, of course, that all angles are equally productive and worth developing in specific instances.

Summing up: selective pomoization

This entire book has been characterized by my strong ambivalence about many of the ideas of postmodernism. I am not fond of the label, but have still reluctantly chosen to use it in this book. Apart from in situations like this, where one is supposed to cover certain terrain and one has to communicate in a few words, as in book titles, what this is all about, I think people are wise to avoid using the label. In particular, in empirical work with ambitions to use fieldwork experiences and material as an important input to a text, I think one can signal or use pomo themes in subtle ways, without flagging them with pomo as a strong marker. In Chapter 2, I provided some cases where people taking strong pomo stands shot themselves in the foot when trying to make particular 'positive', empirical points about specific issues, such as the interests of women or how interviewees act in interview situations. Taking a strong ontological stance that prevents oneself from writing a lot of things that one cannot resist writing – and then mixing ontologies – is not a good idea. A less self-limiting positioning, perhaps a kind of postmodernistically aware interpretivist perspective, such as I have tried to express in this book, gives more space for making ambiguity-, fluidity- and uncertainty-affirming interpretations and pointing at the notorious uncertainty of all, or at least most, interpretations.

Postmodernism signals a preoccupation with themes that, if mastered reasonably well, can lead to creative and novel ways of studying social phenomena, and prevent the researcher from being naive and making mistakes in dealing with the traps and pitfalls of social research at a time of heightened scepticism and the rapid accumulation of a wealth of insights into complexities. Postmodernism may, however, also be a trap, in particular in the context of social research. Here the very idea is to take the extra-linguistic fairly seriously.

I think that care, caution and selectivity must be used when addressing the various problematics pushed by postmodernists with respect to empirical material. Much of it is incompatible with or destructive of the idea of social science developing knowledge based on empirical studies. Lincoln and Denzin (1994: 579), for example, argue that 'if there is a center to post-structuralist thought it lies in the recurring attempt to strip a text, any text, of its external claim to authority'. This external claim to some reality having been researched and possibly understood at some depth is the cornerstone of empirical work. If the *central* preoccupation is stripping the text of such claims, then pomo is of marginal interest for social science. One may, however, occasionally engage in such text-stripping work as part of (self-) critique and reflexivity. Unpacking key categories and stripping (pretentious) texts might then fulfil a destructive/constructive role. It is important to think through when and why such projects are appropriate.

There are also good reasons to avoid a strongly relativist, anti-truth stance. Postmodernists are afraid of the dangers of telling the truth because of the indeterminacy of social life and the power–knowledge connection. But relativism involves a perhaps even more dangerous association with powerful forces. 'Truth? What is truth? I don't know anyone in this business who talks about "truth".' The business referred to is not social science, but public relations (Jackall 1988: 184). This view reflects the mindset and marked relativism that public relations helps to shape for corporate managers:

This relativism has, at it happens, a close though largely unappreciated affinity with views currently propagated in literary and philosophical circles. Here truth is also either an irrelevant concept or one that is wholly kaleidoscopic . . . reality consists precisely of projected perspectives . . . Within such a framework, public relations specialists usually conclude very pragmatically that one might as well 'sing whatever song the client wants to hear'.

(Jackall 1988: 183)

Postmodernism might, as I pointed out in Chapter 2, have only a limited impact in large fields of social science, but is perhaps more successful in business. Perhaps those with a very strong urge to go totally pomo would feel more at home in public relations or advertising than in social science.

In a similar way, good judgement must be exercised when one is picking instances invoking pomo thinking, at least in its stronger versions. The problem of representation is, in a sense, fundamental, but that does not mean that one must make a big fuss about it all the time in the research process or every time one refers to something 'out there'. In most research there are a lot of issues which, for practical and political reasons, can or should be treated in a straightforward way. We can refer to these as *low-ambiguity* issues. They are typically characterized by a 'high level of intersubjectivity' – even among people with different intellectual backgrounds and preferences for languages – and can be seen in objective terms. Claims such as 'the Nazis murdered millions of Jews and other people', 'IBM is a large company', 'the use of condoms helps to prevent AIDS' and 'Derrida's work is not positivist' may count as true. All research deals to some extent with low-ambiguity issues. Discourse analysis and conversation analysis to some extent concentrate on data of this nature, as detailed transcripts of accounts and conversations rather well reflect the word use of subjects in studies. The reasons for invoking ambitious considerations of how the constructions of empirical material is central in social research may vary considerably: good research means doing so in the right moments. *High-ambiguity* issues are characterized by the profound indeterminacy of the phenomena and a loose or arbitrary relationship between something one aims to address and the language for doing so. Leadership may be one good example of this, as partly shown in Chapter 8. The distinction is, of course, fuzzy when it comes to practical matters, and its value is always context-dependent. Sometimes, what appear to be low-ambiguity issues may well be problematized and turn out to be less clear-cut and simple than they appear. In Chapter 5, I picked the example of 'woman' and tried to show how it might be unpacked, and how gender issues in many contexts of relevance to social science can be approached in less familiar and self-evident ways, e.g. in relationship to 'leadership'. However, there are instances where 'woman' stands for something of low ambiguity, e.g. in relationship to childbirth.

Postmodernism is in a sense caught by the dilemma of 'anything goes' and 'nothing goes'. One can see it as hyper-liberal, refusing the exercise of judgement, and allowing almost everything to be said. Lincoln and Guba (2000: 117), for example, write that, 'Unfettered from the pursuit of transcendental scientific truth, inquirers are now free to resituate themselves within texts, to reconstruct their relationships with research participants in less constricted fashions, and to create re-representations.' One can also view it as discouraging language as we normally think about it, as a sceptical approach to everything, parasitically waiting for something to be said and then tearing the claims into pieces (deconstruction) or showing the danger in saying anything about the world (the power–knowledge connection). The variation here reflects the great variation within what is labelled postmodernism, but it also tells us something about the contradictions of much pomo thinking. The major trend is probably in the direction of emphasizing caution in saying something about 'reality' and of stripping texts trying to do so. This is not very helpful for most social researchers. The trick is to be inspired by its questioning attitude but not to use it without discrimination. One can also be suspicious about the ideal of being suspicious. 'To be suspicious is good. To allow it to silence one is something else' (Wolf 1992: 122).

Qualitative social research is often confusing and messy. This might sometimes tell us something about the social worlds we are studying, but might also be an outcome of our cognitive and emotional problems in finding out what we are up to. Social research is not only or mainly about 'going out there and finding out what the natives think they are up to', it is also about the researcher trying to find out what he or she thinks he or she is up to. There is an overwhelming risk that a heavy inspiration from postmodernism might add more destructive confusion than constructive confusion leading to insight. This is not a minor reason for holding the postmodernist impulse back, at least for some researchers and at certain times.

Some people believe that the idea that social reality does not tell us how to produce representations and put together research texts might lead researchers-authors to take responsibility for the texts: 'moral responsibility is central because one must be morally responsible for what one constructs or makes' (Smith and Deemer 2000: 886). Conventionally, the researcher only partially, or to a very limited extent, does so. The active researcher-author is absent; instead the research process and results is described as if earlier research + methodological rules + design + data + analysis = text and result. The social world is there, it is something targeted for 'discovery' or 'findings'.

Postmodernists like fluidity. They claim that texts do not have fixed meanings and that readers do not produce stable interpretations. I think that one should not necessarily privilege this idea in social research, but consider it carefully and bear it in mind as an interpretive option: social phenomena may sometimes be productively interpreted as fluid. As a metaphor fluidity gives us some hints on how to think about various pomo themes. Pomo thinking in social studies can productively fluctuate between being present and absent. But taking full responsibility for the text and not allowing social reality to give any direction or put any restrictions on what the researcher can do means that the researcher might not be responsible in relationship to the behaviours, the talk, the events etc. that make up social reality. An ambitious and competently conducted empirical study does, in a sense, mean that authorly discretion is reduced: observations of events and accounts of those being studied make a significant input to the research process and the text. The social researcher is neither an author responsible solely for the text nor someone equipped with methodology, skills and high ambitions, capable of simply 'collecting' and 'reporting' the insights, meanings and experiences of those being studied. The trick for pomo-aware qualitative research is to navigate between awareness of how perspectives, research language and text composition make all empirical material a construction, and how something going on 'out there' makes certain constructions superior and better grounded in that 'out there' than others.

It is possible to work with a structure of separation and connection of the various elements in research: protect research from pomo at certain stages of the research process; confront empirical work, analysis and writing with pomo ideas at particular times. How much, which version and theme of postmodernism and when it is invoked is then a matter of judgement and political and ethical considerations.

In sum, postmodernism should not, in my humble opinion, replace earlier ways of doing social research with an interpretive bent, but a partial and moderate incorporation of pomo ideas might encourage more interesting social studies. The stronger formulations of pomo can perhaps best be seen as a provocation, and as such a potentially valuable one. Pomo offers a challenge and an inspiration to revise and make qualitative research more sophisticated and creative. This is not bad, and a strong reason for taking it seriously. But not too seriously.

Note

1 Like many other authors Rosenau refers to 'the subjective'. Given pomo's rejection of the centrality of the subject, this can be seen as a lapse.

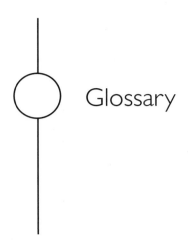

Glossary

To produce a glossary runs against the very idea of postmodernism, which rejects the idea of words having specific, stable, broadly agreed upon meanings. With considerable doubt, I have produced a brief glossary. The terms are addressed within a postmodernist context. The reader is advised against taking them too literarally, realizing that there are different and conflicting views on how to use the terms. Nevertheless, they give some indications of how the terms can be understood and are sometimes used.

Discourse: As with many popular words, this is used in a variety of ways by different people. One version refers to all spoken and written language in a social context. Discourse in this sense means paying attention to language use as action, as expressing something that can be understood in terms of its possible effect and function. Another version, associated with Foucault, views discourse as a line of thinking about and the making of truth claims about certain segments of the world, thus constituting it. Discourse in this sense is related to historically grounded language use and lines of reasoning that are anchored in social institutions, and thus intervene in and regulate social reality. It combines power and knowledge. In this book I refer to discourse in this Foucauldian sense as Big Discourse.

Constructionism (sometimes also labelled constructivism): A theoretical orientation emphasizing that we do not have any direct access to an objective, independent reality, but by trying to describe it we create a particular version of it. 'Reality' is always filtered through the perspective taken and the language used.

Deconstruction: A postmodern approach to analysis, which aims to show the fragility of all positive statements. Deconstruction points at the contradictions and cracks in any text and the assumptions it builds upon.

Ethnography: The study of cultures in which the researcher has 'been there' for some time and done participant observation. Postmodernists emphasize the difficulties or impossibilities of letting fieldwork determine results. They emphasize textual strategies for writing the ethnography as a key element in research.

Fiction: The invented, creative element in the production of texts. For postmodernism, fiction is always central to all efforts to say something about 'reality'. Social researchers are not very different from writers of fiction. Some pomos do, however, allow elements of facts or reality to exist as an element in fictional texts, but it is seen as difficult to separate out facts and fictions – one views 'fiction woven around facts'.

Hyperreality: Reality as a robust social structure has collapsed and is replaced by images and mass media representations that make up society.

Indeterminacy: Social reality is ambiguous and impossible to determine once and for all. Slipperiness and uncertainty should be acknowledged.

Knowledge: For postmodernists, knowledge is not an outcome of research that makes the understanding and control of reality possible. Knowledge is made up of claims to knowledge, which mask its relationship to power and control.

Meaning: The perception and orientation that characterize people's relationship to a phenomenon. While most non-pomos assume the stability and accessibility of meaning, pomos tend to emphasize its fluidity. It does not exist continuously as much as it is produced temporarily.

Modernism: An orientation towards knowledge and social institutions that emphasizes rationality, reason and progress.

Narrative: The framing and story-like character of any line of reasoning and development of knowledge. Postmodernists disapprove of – and/or emphasize diminishing belief in – 'master narratives', universal theories and political projects. Micro-narratives and local knowledge are, on the other hand, celebrated.

Ordering: While most people would emphasize the patterned, law-like character of social worlds, postmodernists emphasize that the search for patterns is a matter of creating particular orders, thus creating rather than revealing the world.

Postmodernism: An assault on the belief in rationality and reason, as well as on the stability of meaning.

Poststructuralism: A term overlapping postmodernism and often used as a synonym to it. Poststructuralism is, however, often used with a strong emphasis on epistemology and method, while the term postmodernism sometimes also refers to cultural and social changes. Postmodernism (postmodernity) is then sometimes used to refer to a societal period.

Power: Conventionally power is seen as an attribute of subjects (invididuals, groups or social institutions). For pomo, power is tightly coupled with language use and knowledge. When reality and the normal are defined in a particular way, reality is shaped and regulated. Knowledge includes power and creates the world, rather than revealing it.

Reader: A central role in all knowledge projects and the workings of a text is taken by the reader. The idea is that texts are not seen as communicating any definitive meaning, but depend on the meaning ascribed by the reader.

Reflexivity: An effort to reflect upon how the researcher is located in a particular social, political, cultural and linguistic context.

Rhetoric: The artful presentation of ideas in a persuasive manner. Rhetoric is not viewed as being the opposite to 'truth' or 'substantive' content of texts, including scientific writings, but integral to this.

Representation: While modernists believe that representation, in the sense of one object standing for another, is possible, postmodernism views this logic as false or at least problematic. Representation is difficult, or even impossible, in particular when language is used to portray something else. In relationship to conventional scientific texts, novel forms of writing and new media – literary techniques, poetry, paintings – must be considered and experimented with. Representation is problematic. Every effort to describe a phenomenon means an arbitrary choice of a particular vocabulary. The language used constructs a particular version of what one is referring to.

Subject: A pomo term for the individual. The subject is an outcome of subjectification, in which discourse creates the individual in a particular way. Pomos want to remove the subject from the centre stage of life and reject the humanistic understanding of the individual as integrated and a source of meaning and intention.

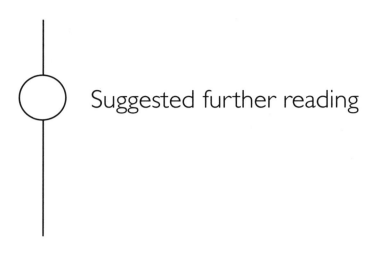

Suggested further reading

The literature list includes texts on a variety of topics that either directly emphasize postmodernism or have a strong relevance for a postmodernist understanding of social research. The suggested readings on the state of affairs in qualitative method, interviews and ethnography all take pomo issues seriously.

General introductions to postmodernism

Rosenau, P. M. (1992) *Post-modernism and the Social Sciences: Insights, Inroads and Intrusions*. Princeton, NJ: Princeton University Press.
Sarup, M. (1988) *An Introductory Guide to Post-structuralism and Post-modernism*. Hemel Hempstead: Harvester Wheatsheaf.
Theory, Culture and Society (1988) no. 2/3 (special issue on postmodernism).

Development, perspectives and state of affairs in qualitative method

Alvesson, M. and Sköldberg, K. (2000) *Reflexive Methodology*. London: Sage.
Denzin, N. and Lincoln, Y. (eds) (2000) *Handbook of Qualitative Research*, 2nd edn. Thousand Oaks, CA: Sage.
Crotty, M. (1998) *The Foundations of Social Research*. London: Sage.

Postmodernism and critical research

Agger, B. (1991) Critical theory, poststructuralism, postmodernism: their socio-logical relevance, *Annual Review of Sociology*, 17: 105–31.
Alvesson, M. and Deetz, S. (2000) *Doing Critical Management Research*. London: Sage.

The textual turn in ethnography

Clifford, J. and Marcus, G. (eds) (1986) *Writing Culture: The Poetics and Politics of Ethnography*. Berkeley: University of California Press.
Geertz, C. (1988) *Work and Lives: The Anthropologist as Author*. Cambridge: Polity Press.
Sangren, S. (1992) Rhetoric and the authority of ethnography, *Current Anthropology*, 33 (supplement): 277–96.
van Maanen, J. (ed.) (1995) *Representation in Ethnography*. Thousand Oaks, CA: Sage.

Feminism and postmodernism

Nicholson, L. (ed.) (1990) *Feminism/Postmodernism*. New York: Routledge.
Skeggs, B. (1997) *Formations of Class and Gender*. London: Sage.
Weedon, C. (1987) *Feminist Practice and Poststructuralist Theory*. Oxford: Basil Blackwell.

Discourse analysis

Alvesson, M. and Kärreman, D. (2000) Varieties of discourse: on the study of organizations through discourse analysis, *Human Relations*, 53(9): 1125–49.
Potter, J. and Wetherell, M. (1987) *Discourse and Social Psychology: Beyond Attitudes and Behaviour*. London: Sage.

Constructionism

Steier, F. (ed.) (1991) *Research and Reflexivity*. London: Sage.

Power/knowledge

Foucault, M. (1977) *Discipline and Punish: The Birth of the Prison*. New York: Random House.
Foucault, M. (1980) *Power/Knowledge*. New York: Pantheon.

Reflexivity

Alvesson, M. and Sköldberg, K. (2000) *Reflexive Methodology*. London: Sage.
Hertz, R. (ed.) (1997) *Reflexivity and Voice*. Thousand Oaks, CA: Sage.

Interviews in a postmodernist perspective

Scheurich, J. (1997) *Research Method in the Postmodern*. London: Falmer.

Writing and representation

Fine, M., Wise, L., Weseen, S. and Wong, L. (2000) For whom? Qualitative research, representations and social responsibilities, in N. Denzin and Y. Lincoln (eds) *Handbook of Qualitative Research*, 2nd edn. Thousand Oaks, CA: Sage.
Richardson, L. (2000) Writing: a method of inquiry, in N. Denzin and Y. Lincoln (eds) *Handbook of Qualitative Research*, 2nd edn. Thousand Oaks, CA: Sage.

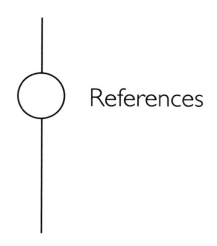

References

Acker, J. (1989) Making gender visible, in R. A. Wallace (ed.) *Feminism and Sociological Theory*. Newbury Park, CA: Sage.

Agar, M. H. (1995) Literary journalism as ethnography: exploring the excluded middle, in J. van Maanen (ed.) *Representation in Ethnography*. Thousand Oaks, CA: Sage.

Agger, B. (1991) Critical theory, poststructuralism, postmodernism: their sociological relevance, *Annual Review of Sociology*, 17: 105–31.

Albert, S. and Whetten, D. (1985) Organizational identity, in L. L. Cummings and B. M. Staw (eds) *Research in Organizational Behaviour, Volume 7*. Greenwich: JAI Press.

Alvesson, M. (1990) Organizations: from substance to image?, *Organization Studies*, 11: 373–94.

Alvesson, M. (1994) Talking in organizations. Managing identity and impressions in an advertising agency, *Organization Studies*, 15(4): 535–63.

Alvesson, M. (1995) *Management of Knowledge-intensive Companies*. Berlin/New York: de Gruyter.

Alvesson, M. (1996) *Communication, Power and Organization*. Berlin/New York: de Gruyter.

Alvesson, M. (2001) Beyond neo-positivists, romanticists and localists. Working paper. Dept. of Business Administration, Lund University.

Alvesson, M. (2002) *Understanding Organizational Culture*. London: Sage.

Alvesson, M. and Billing, Y. D. (1997) *Understanding Gender and Organization*. London: Sage.

Alvesson, M. and Deetz, S. (2000) *Doing Critical Management Research*. London: Sage.

Alvesson, M. and Kärreman, D. (2000) Varieties of discourse: on the study of organizations through discourse analysis, *Human Relations*, 53(9): 1125–49.

Alvesson, M. and Köping, A.-S. (1993) *Med känslan som ledstjärna. En studie av reklamarbete och reklambyråer (Guided by the Feeling. A Study of Advertising Work and Agencies)*. Lund: Studentlitteratur.

Alvesson, M. and Sköldberg, K. (2000) *Reflexive Methodology*. London: Sage.

Alvesson, M. and Sveningsson, S. (2001) The good visions, the bad micro-management and the ugly ambiguity: contradictions of (non-)leadership in a knowledge-intensive company. Paper presented at the Third Oxford Workshop on Knowledge-intensive Firms, Oxford University, September.

Andersen, J. (2000) Leadership and leadership research, in S. B. Dahiya (ed.) *The Current State of Business Disciplines, Volume 5*. New Delhi: Spellbound Publishing.

Anthony, P. (1994) *Managing Organizational Culture*. Buckingham: Open University Press.

Asplund, J. (1970) *Om undran inför samhället*. Lund: Argos.

Astley, G. (1985) Administrative science as socially constructed truth, *Administrative Science Quarterly*, 30: 497–513.

Baker, S. (1990) Reflection, doubt and the place of rhetoric in postmodern social theory, *Sociological Theory*, 8: 232–45.

Baker, C. (1997) Membership categorizations and interview accounts, in D. Silverman (ed.) *Qualitative Research*. London: Sage.

Barker, R. (1993) Tightening the iron cage: concertive control in self-managing teams, *Administrative Science Quarterly*, 38: 408–37.

Barker, R. (1997) How can we train leaders if we don't know what leadership is?, *Human Relations*, 50: 343–62.

Barker, R. (2001) The nature of leadership, *Human Relations*, 54: 469–93.

Bärmark, J. (1984) Vetenskapens subjektiva sida, in J. Bärmark (ed.) *Forskning om forskning*. Stockholm: Natur och Kultur.

Baudrillard, J. (1975) *The Mirror of Production*. St Louis, MO: Telos Press.

Baudrillard, J. (1983a) The ecstacy of communication, in H. Foster (ed.) *Postmodern Culture*. London: Pluto Press.

Baudrillard, J. (1983b) *Simulations*. New York: Semiotext(e).

Baudrillard, J. (1984) År 2000 kommer inte att äga rum (The year 2000 will never occur), *Res Publica*, 1: 23–37.

Bauman, Z. (1988) Is there a postmodern sociology?, *Theory, Culture & Society*, 5: 217–37.

Berg, P.-O. (1989) Postmodern management? From fact to fiction in theory and practice, *Scandinavian Journal of Management*, 5: 201–17.

Berman, M. (1992) Why modernism still matters, in S. Lash and J. Friedman (eds) *Modernity and Identity*. Oxford: Basil Blackwell.

Bernstein, R. (1983) *Beyond Objectivism and Relativism*. Oxford: Basil Blackwell.

Beronius, M. (1991) *Genealogi och sociologi*. Stehag: Symposion.

Billig, M. and Simons, H. (1994) Introduction, in H. Simons and M. Billig (eds) *After Postmodernism*. London: Sage.

Boje, D. (1991) The story-telling organization: a study of story performance in an office-supply firm, *Administrative Science Quarterly*, 36: 106–26.

Boje, D. (1995) Stories of the story-telling organization: a postmodern analysis of Disney as 'Tamara-land', *Academy of Management Journal*, 38(4): 997–1035.

Boorstin, D. (1961) *The Image*. New York: Atheneum.

Bordo, S. (1990) Feminism, postmodernism and gender-scepticism, in L. Nicholson (ed.) *Feminism/Postmodernism*. New York: Routledge.

Bourdieu, P. (1979) *Outline of a Theory of Practice*. Cambridge: Cambridge University Press.

Brewer, J. (2000) *Ethnography*. Buckingham: Open University Press.

Brown, R. H. (1976) Social theory as metaphor, *Theory and Society*, 3: 169–97.

Brown, R. H. (1977) *A Poetic for Sociology*. Chicago: University of Chicago Press.

Brown, R. H. (1990) Rhetoric, textuality and the postmodern turn in sociological theory, *Sociological Theory*, 8: 188–97.

Bryman, A., Bresnen, M., Beardsworth, A. and Keil, T. (1988) Qualitative research and the study of leadership, *Human Relations*, 41(1): 13–30.

Burrell, G. (1988) Modernism, postmodernism and organizational analysis 2: the contribution of Michel Foucault, *Organization Studies*, 9(2): 221–35.

Burrell, G. (1994) Modernism, postmodernism and organizational analysis: the contribution of Jürgen Habermas, *Organization Studies*, 15: 1–19.

Calás, M. and Smircich, L. (1987) Post-culture: is the organization culture literature dominant but dead? Paper presented at the SCOS International Conference on the Symbolics of Corporate Artifacts, Milan.

Calás, M. and Smircich, L. (1988) Reading leadership as a form of cultural analysis, in J. G. Hunt *et al.* (eds) *Emerging Leadership Vistas*. Lexington, MA: Lexington Books.

Calás, M. and Smircich, L. (1991) Voicing seduction to silence leadership, *Organization Studies*, 12: 567–602.

Calás, M. and Smircich, L. (1999) Past postmodernism? Reflections and tentative directions, *Academy of Management Review*, 24(4): 649–71.

Calhoun, C. (1992) Culture, history and the problem of specificity in social theory, in S. Seidman and D. Wagner (eds) *Postmodernism and Social Theory*. Oxford: Blackwell.

Castoriadis, C. (1992) Power, politics, autonomy, in A. Honneth, T. McCarthy, C. Offe and A. Wellmer (eds) *Cultural–Political Interventions in the Unfinished Project of Enlightenment*. Cambridge, MA: MIT Press.

Charmaz, K. (2000) Grounded theory: objectivist and constructivist methods, in N. Denzin and Y. Lincoln (eds) *Handbook of Qualitative Research*, 2nd edn. Thousand Oaks, CA: Sage.

Chodorow, N. (1978) *The Reproduction of Mothering: Psychoanalysis and the Sociology of Gender*. Berkeley: University of California Press.

Cicourel, A. (1964) *Method and Measurement in Sociology*. New York: Free Press.

Clegg, S. (1990) *Modern Organization. Organization Studies in the Postmodern World*. London: Sage.

Clegg, S. (1994) Weber and Foucault: social theory for the study of organizations, *Organization*, 1: 149–78.

Clifford, J. (1986) Introduction: partial truths, in J. Clifford and G. Marcus (eds) *Writing Culture*. Berkeley: University of California Press.

Clifford, J. and Marcus, G. E. (eds) (1986) *Writing Culture: The Poetics and Politics of Ethnography*. Berkeley: University of California Press.

Cockburn, C. (1991) *In the Way of Women*. London: Macmillan.

Collins, R. (1992) The confusions of the modes of sociology, in S. Seidman and D. Wagner (eds) *Postmodernism and Social Theory*. Oxford: Blackwell.

Cooper, R. (1989) Modernism, postmodernism and organizational analysis 3: the contribution of Jacques Derrida, *Organization Studies*, 10: 479–502.

Cooper, R. and Burrell, G. (1988) Modernism, postmodernism and organizational analysis: an introduction, *Organization Studies*, 9: 91–112.

Coser, R. L. (1989) Reflections on feminist theory, in R.A. Wallace (ed.) *Feminism and Sociological Theory*. Newbury Park, CA: Sage.

Covaleski, M., Dirsmith, M., Heian, J. and Samuel, S. (1998) The calculated and the avowed: techniques of discipline and struggles over identity in big six public accounting firms, *Administrative Science Quarterly*, 43: 293–327.

Crotty, M. (1998) *The Foundations of Social Research*. London: Sage.

Daudi, P. (1990) Con-versing in management's public place, *Scandinavian Journal of Management*, 6: 285–307.

Deetz, S. (1992) *Democracy in an Age of Corporate Colonization: Developments in Communication and the Politics of Everyday Life*. Albany: State University of New York Press.

Deetz, S. (1995) *Transforming Communication, Transforming Business: Building Responsible and Responsive Workplaces*. Cresskill, NJ: Hampton Press.

Denzin, S. (1994) The art and politics of interpretation, in N. Denzin and Y. Lincoln (eds) *Handbook of Qualitative Research*. Thousand Oaks, CA: Sage.

Denzin, S. (1997) *Interpretive Ethnography*. Thousand Oaks, CA: Sage.

Denzin, S. and Lincoln, Y. (1994) Introduction: entering the field of qualitative research, in N. Denzin and Y. Lincoln (eds) *Handbook of Qualitative Research*. Thousand Oaks, CA: Sage.

Denzin, S. and Lincoln, Y. (2000) Introduction: the discipline and practice of qualitative research, in N. Denzin and Y. Lincoln (eds) *Handbook of Qualitative Research*, 2nd edn. Thousand Oaks, CA: Sage.

Di Stefano, C. (1990) Dilemmas of difference: feminism, modernity and postmodernism, in L. Nicholson (ed.) *Feminism/Postmodernism*. New York: Routledge.

Easterby-Smith, M., Thorpe, R. and Lowe, A. (1991) *Management Research: An Introduction*. London: Sage.

Ehn, B., Haferkamp, H. and Löfgren, O. (1982) *Kulturanalys*. Lund: Liber.

Eisenhardt, K. (1989) Building theories from case study research, *Academy of Management Review*, 14: 532–50.

Ellis, C., Kiesinger, C. and Tillman-Healy, L. (1997) Interactive interviewing, in R. Hertz (ed.) *Reflexivity and Voice*. Thousand Oaks, CA: Sage.

Eriksson, E. H. (1968) *Identity. Youth and Crises*. New York: Norton.

Fagenson, E. and Jackson, J. (1993) Final commentary, in E. Fagenson (ed.) *Women in Management. Trends, Issues, and Challenges in Managerial Diversity*. Thousand Oaks, CA: Sage.

Falzon, C. (1998) *Foucault and Social Dialogue*. New York: Routledge.

Featherstone, M. (1988) *Postmodernism*. Newbury Park, CA: Sage.

Featherstone, M. (1989) Toward a sociology of postmodern culture, in H. Haferkamp (ed.) *Social Structure and Culture*. Berlin and New York: de Gruyter.

Feyerabend, P. K. (1975) *Beyond Method*. London: New Left Books.

Fiedler, F. (1996) Research on leadership selection and training: one view of the future, *Administrative Science Quarterly*, 41: 241–50.

Fine, M., Wise, L., Weseen, S. and Wong, L. (2000) For whom? Qualitative research, representations and social responsibilities, in N. Denzin and Y. Lincoln (eds) *Handbook of Qualitative Research*, 2nd edn. Thousand Oaks, CA: Sage.

Firat, F. and Venkatesh, A. (1992) The making of postmodern consumption, in R. Belk and N. Dholakia (eds) *Consumption and Marketing: Macro Dimensions*. Boston: PWS-Kent.

Flax, J. (1990) *Thinking Fragments: Psychoanalysis, Feminism and Postmodernism in the Contemporary West*. Berkeley: University of California Press.

Fontana, A. and Frey, J. (1994) Interviewing: the art of science, in N. Denzin and Y. Lincoln (eds) *Handbook of Qualitative Research*. Thousand Oaks, CA: Sage.

Fontana, A. and Frey, J. (2000) The interview: from structured questions to negotiated text, in N. Denzin and Y. Lincoln (eds) *Handbook of Qualitative Research*, 2nd edn. Thousand Oaks, CA: Sage.

Foster, H. (1983) *Postmodern Culture*. London: Pluto.

Foucault, M. (1976) *The History of Sexuality*. New York: Random House.

Foucault, M. (1977) *Discipline and Punish: The Birth of the Prison*. New York: Random House.

Foucault, M. (1980) *Power/Knowledge*. New York: Pantheon.

Foucault, M. (1983) Structuralism and post-structuralism: an interview with Michel Foucault, by G. Raulet, *Telos*, 55: 195–211.

Foucault, M. (1984) The ethic of care for the self as a practice of freedom: an interview with Michel Foucault, in J. Bernauer and D. Rasmussen (eds) *The Final Foucault*. Cambridge, MA: MIT Press.

Fraser, N. and Nicholson, L. (1988) Social criticism without philosophy: an encounter between feminism and postmodernism, *Theory Culture and Society*, 5: 373–94.

Geertz, C. (1973) *The Interpretation of Cultures*. New York: Basic Books.

Geertz, C. (1983) *Local Knowledge*. New York: Basic Books.

Geertz, C. (1988) *Work and Lives: The Anthropologist as Author*. Cambridge: Polity Press.

Gergen, K. (1978) Toward generative theory, *Journal of Personality and Social Psychology*, 31: 1344–60.

Gergen, K. (1989) Warranting voice and the elaboration of the self, in J. Shotter and K. Gergen (eds) *Texts of Identity*. London: Sage.

Gergen, K. (1992) Organization theory in the postmodern era, in M. Reed and M. Hughes (eds) *Rethinking Organizations*. London: Sage.

Gergen, K. and Gergen, M. (1991) Toward reflexive methodologies, in F. Steier (ed.) *Research and Reflexivity*. London: Sage.

Giddens, A. (1991) *Modernity and Self-identity*. Cambridge: Polity Press.

Giesen, B. and Schmid, M. (1989) Symbolic, institutional, and social-structural differentiation: a selection-theoretical perspective, in H. Haferkamp (ed.) *Social Structure and Culture*. Berlin and New York: de Gruyter.

Glaser, B. and Strauss, A. (1967) *The Discovery of Grounded Theory: Strategies for Qualitative Research*. Chicago: Aldine.

Grant, J. (1988) Women as managers: what can they offer to organizations?, *Organizational Dynamics*, 16(1): 56–63.

Gregory, K. L. (1983) Native-view paradigms. Multiple cultures and culture conflicts in organizations, *Administrative Science Quarterly*, 28: 359–76.

Gronn, P. C. (1983) Talk as the work: the accomplishment of school administration, *Administrative Science Quarterly*, 28: 1–21.

Guba, E. and Lincoln, Y. (1994) Competing paradigms in qualitative research, in N. Denzin and Y. Lincoln (eds) *Handbook of Qualitative Research*. Thousand Oaks, CA: Sage.

Gubrium, J. and Holstein, J. (2001) Introduction. Trying times, troubled selves, in J. Gubrium and J. Holstein (eds) *Institutional Selves*. Oxford: Oxford University Press.

Habermas, J. (1972) *Knowledge and Human Interests*. London: Heinemann.

Habermas, J. (1975) *Legitimation Crisis*. Boston: Beacon Press.

Habermas, J. (1984) *The Theory of Communicative Action, Volume 1*. Boston: Beacon Press.

Habermas, J. (1987) The critique of reason as an unmasking of the human sciences: Michel Foucault, in M. Kelly (ed.) *Critique and Power*. Cambridge; MA: MIT Press.

Hall, E. (1993) Smiling, deferring and flirting. Doing gender by giving 'good service', *Work and Occupations*, 20(4): 452–71.

Hammersley, M. (1992) On feminist methodology, *Sociology*, 26(2): 187–206.

Hammersley, M. (1993) The rhetorical turn in ethnography, *Social Science Information*, 32(1): 23–37.

Harding, S. (1990) Feminism, science, and the anti-enlightenment critiques, in L. Nicholson (ed.) *Feminism/Postmodernism*. New York: Routledge.

Hartsock, N. (1987) The feminist standpoint: developing the ground for a specifically feminist historical materialism, in S. Harding (ed.) *Feminism and Methodology*. Milton Keynes: Open University Press.

Hern, J. and Parkin, W. (1993) Organizations, multiple oppressions and postmodernism, in J. Hassard and M. Parker (eds) *Postmodernism and Organizations*. London: Sage.

Hertz, R. (1997) Introduction: reflexivity and voice, in R. Hertz (ed.) *Reflexivity and Voice*. Thousand Oaks, CA: Sage.

Hollway, W. (1984) Fitting work: psychological assessment in organizations, in J. Henriques, W. Hallway, C. Urwin, C. Venn and V. Walkerdine (eds) *Changing the Subject*. New York: Methuen.

Hollway, W. (1989) *Subjectivity and Method in Psychology*. London: Sage.

Hollway, W. (1991) *Work Psychology and Organizational Behavior*. London: Sage.

Hollway, W. and Jefferson, T. (2000) *Doing Qualitative Research Differently*. London: Sage.

Holstein, J. A. and Gubrium, J. (1997) Active interviewing, in D. Silverman (ed.) *Qualitative Research*. London: Sage.

Hoy, D. (ed.) (1986) *Foucault: A Critical Reader*. Oxford: Basil Blackwell.

Huberman, M. and Miles, M. (1994) Data management and analysis methods, in N. Denzin and Y. Lincoln (eds) *Handbook of Qualitative Research*, 2nd edn. Thousand Oaks, CA: Sage.

Jackall, R. (1988) *Moral Mazes*. New York: Oxford University Press.

Jackson, J. (1995) 'Déjà entendu': the liminal qualities of anthropological field-notes, in J. Van Maanen (ed.) *Representation in Ethnography*. Thousand Oaks, CA: Sage.

Jaggar, A. M. (1989) Love and knowledge, *Inquiry*, 32: 51–176.

Jameson, F. (1983) Postmodernism and consumer society, in H. Foster (ed.) *Postmodern Culture*. London: Pluto Press.

Jameson, F. (1984) Postmodernism, or the cultural logic of late capitalism, *New Left Review*, 146: 53–93.

Jeffcutt, P. (1993) From interpretation to representation, in J. Hassard and M. Parker (eds) *Postmodernism and Organization*. London: Sage.

Jorgenson, J. (1991) Co-constructing the interviewer/co-constructing 'family', in F. Steier (ed.) *Research and Reflexivity*. London: Sage.

Kanter, R. M. (1977) *Men and Women of the Corporation*. New York: Basic Books.

Kaplan, G. and Rogers, L. (1990) The definition of male and female: biological reductionism and the sanctions of normality, in S. Gunew (ed.) *Feminist Knowledge: Critique and Construct*. London: Routledge.

Kellner, D. (1988) Postmodernism as social theory: some challenges and problems, *Theory, Culture and Society*, 5(2/3): 239–69.

Kelly, M. (1995) Introduction, in M. Kelly (ed.) *Critique and Power*. Cambridge, MA: MIT Press.

Kilduff, M. and Mehra, A. (1997) Postmodernism and organizational research, *Academy of Management Review*, 22: 453–81.

Kincheloe, J. and McLaren, P. (1994) Rethinking critical theory and qualitative research, in N. Denzin and Y. Lincoln (eds) *Handbook of Qualitative Research*. Thousand Oaks, CA: Sage.

Knights, D. (1992) Changing spaces: the disruptive impact of a new epistemological location for the study of management, *Academy of Management Review*, 17: 514–36.

Knights, D. and Willmott, H. (1992) Conceptualizing leadership processes: a study of senior managers in a financial services company, *Journal of Management Studies*, 29: 761–82.

Kuhn, T. S. (1970) *The Structure of Scientific Revolution*. Chicago: University of Chicago Press.

Kuhn, T. S. (1977) *The Essential Tension: Selected Studies in Scientific Tradition and Change*. Chicago: University of Chicago Press.

Kunda, G. (1992) *Engineering Culture. Control and Commitment in a High-tech Corporation*. Philadelphia: Temple University Press.

Kvale, S. (1996) *Inter-viewing*. London: Sage.

Lasch, C. (1978) *The Culture of Narcissism*. New York: Norton.

Lash, S. (1988) Discourse or figure? Postmodernism as a 'regime of signification', *Theory, Culture and Society*, 5: 311–36.

Lash, S. and Urry, J. (1987) *The End of Organized Capitalism*. Cambridge: Polity Press.

Law, J. (1994) *Organizing Modernity*. Oxford: Blackwell.

Leach, E. (1982) *Social Anthropology*. Glasgow: Fontana.

Lee, N. and Hassard, J. (1999) Organization unbound: actor–network theory, research strategy and institutional flexibility, *Organization*, 6(3): 391–404.

Lincoln, J. and Kalleberg, A. (1985) Work organization and workforce commitment: a study of plants and employees in the US and Japan, *American Sociological Review*, 50: 738–60.

Lincoln, Y. and Denzin, N. (1994) The fifth moment, in N. Denzin and Y. Lincoln (eds) *Handbook of Qualitative Research*. Thousand Oaks, CA: Sage.

Lincoln, Y. and Guba, E. (2000) Paradigmatic controversies, contradictions, and emerging confluences, in N. Denzin and Y. Lincoln (eds) *Handbook of Qualitative Research*, 2nd edn. Thousand Oaks, CA: Sage.

Linstead, S. and Grafton-Small, R. (1990) Theory as artifact: artifact as theory, in P. Gagliardi (ed.) *Symbols and Artifacts: Views of the Corporate Landscape*. Berlin and New York: de Gruyter.

Linstead, S. and Grafton-Small, R. (1992) On reading organizational culture, *Organization Studies*, 13: 331–55.

Lyotard, J.-F. (1984) *The Postmodern Condition: A Report on Knowledge*. Minneapolis, MN: University of Minnesota Press.

Madison, G. B. (1991) The politics of postmodernity, *Critical Review*, Winter, 53–79.

Marcus, G. (1992) Past, present and emergent identities: requirements for ethnographies of late twentieth-century modernity worldwide, in S. Lash and J. Friedman (eds) *Modernity and Identity*. Oxford: Blackwell.

Marcus, G. and Fisher, M. (1986) *Anthropology as Cultural Critique*. Chicago: University of Chicago Press.

Margolis, S. (1989) Postscript on modernism and postmodernism: both, *Theory, Culture and Society*, 6: 5–30.

Marshak, R. (1998) A discourse on discourse. Redeeming the meaning of talk, in D. Grant and C. Oswick (eds) *Discourse and Organization*. London: Sage.

Martin, J. (1990) Deconstructing organizational taboos: the suppression of gender in conflict in organizations, *Organization Science*, 11: 339–59.

Martin, J. (1992) *The Culture of Organizations: Three Perspectives*. New York: Oxford University Press.

Martin, J. (1994) Methodological essentialism, false difference and other dangerous traps, *Signs*, 19: 630–57.

Martin, J. (2002) Feminist theory and critical theory: unexplored synergies, in M. Alvesson and H. Willmott (eds) *Advances in Critical Management Studies*. London: Sage.

Martin, J. and Meyerson, D. (1988) Organizational cultures and the denial, channeling and acknowledgement of ambiquity, in L. R. Pondy, R. J. Boland and H. Thomas (eds) *Managing Ambiguity and Change*. New York: Wiley.

Martin, J., Feldman, M. S., Hatch, M. J. and Sitkin, S. B. (1983) The uniqueness paradox in organizational stories, *Administrative Science Quarterly*, 28: 438–53.

Martin, J., Knopoff, K. and Beckman, C. (1998) An alternative to bureaucratic impersonality and emotional labour: bounded emotionality at the Body Shop, *Administrative Science Quarterly*, 43: 429–69.

Melia, K. (1997) Producing 'plausible stories': interviewing student nurses, in G. Miller and R. Dingwall (eds) *Context and Method in Qualitative Research*. London: Sage.

Miller, J. and Glassner, B. (1997) The 'inside' and the 'outside': finding realities in interviews, in D. Silverman (ed.) *Qualitative Research*. London: Sage.

Mills, C. W. (1940) Situated actions and vocabularies of motives, *American Sociological Review*, 5: 904–13.

Morgan, G. (1980) Paradigms, metaphors, and puzzle solving in organization theory, *Administrative Science Quarterly*, 25: 605–22.

Morgan, G. (ed.) (1983a) *Beyond Method: Strategies for Social Research*. Beverley Hills, CA: Sage.

Morgan, G. (1983b) More on metaphor: why we cannot control tropes in administrative science, *Administrative Science Quarterly*, 28: 601–8.

Morgan, G. (1997) *Images of Organization*. Thousand Oaks, CA: Sage.

Morgan, G., Frost, P. and Pondy, L. (1983) Organizational symbolism, in L. Pondy, P. Frost, G. Morgan, T. Dandridge (eds) *Monographs in Organizational Behaviour and Industrial Relations: Organizational Symbolism: Vol 1*. Greenwich, CT: JAI Press.

Morrow, R. (1994) *Critical Theory and Methodology*. Thousand Oaks, CA: Sage.

Mumby, D. and Putnam, L. (1992) The politics of emotion: a feminist reading of bounded rationality, *Academy of Management Review*, 17: 465–86.

Newton, T. (1998) Theorizing subjectivity in organizations: the failure of Foucauldian studies, *Organization Studies*, 19(3): 415–47.

Nicholls, J. (1987) Leadership in organisations: meta, macro and micro, *European Journal of Management*, 6: 16–25.

Parker, M. (1992) Post-modern organizations or postmodern organization theory?, *Organization Studies*, 13: 1–17.

Parker, M. (1993) Life after Jean-François, in J. Hassard and M. Parker (eds) *Postmodernism and Organizations*. London: Sage.

Parker, M. (2000) *Organizational Culture and Identity*. London: Sage.

Peters, T. J. and Waterman, R. H. (1982) *In Search of Excellence*. New York: Harper and Row.

Pinder, C. C. and Bourgeois, V. (1982) Controlling tropes in administrative science, *Administrative Science Quarterly*, 27: 641–52.

Popper, K. (1976) On the logic of the social sciences, in T. W. Adorno, H. Albert, R. Dahrendorf *et al.* (eds) *The Positivist Dispute in German Sociology*. London: Heinemann.

Potter, J. (1997) Discourse analysis as a way of analysing naturally occurring talk, in D. Silverman (ed.) *Qualitative Research Quarterly*. London: Sage.

Potter, J. and Wetherell, M. (1987) *Discourse and Social Psychology: Beyond Attitudes and Behaviour*. London: Sage.

Power, M. (1990) Modernism, postmodernism and organisation, in J. Hassard and D. Pym (eds) *The Theory and Philosophy of Organisations*. London: Routledge.

Prior, L. (1997) Following in Foucault's footsteps: text and context in qualitative research, in D. Silverman (ed.) *Qualitative Research*. London: Sage.

Reed, M. (1993) Organisations and modernity: continuity and discontinuity in organization theory, in J. Hassard and M. Parker (eds) *Postmodernism and Organizations*. London: Sage.

Reinharz, S. (1997) Who am I? The need for a variety of selves in fieldwork, in R. Hertz (ed.) *Reflexivity and Voice*. Thousand Oaks, CA: Sage.

Reskin, B. and Padavic, I. (1994) *Women and Men at Work*. Thousand Oaks, CA: Pine Forge Press.

Richardson, L. (1994) Writing: a method of inquiry, in N. Denzin and Y. Lincoln (eds) *Handbook of Qualitative Research*. Thousand Oaks, CA: Sage.

Richardson, L. (1995) Narrative and sociology, in J. van Maanen (ed.) *Representation in Ethnography*. Thousand Oaks, CA: Sage.

Richardson, L. (2000) Writing: a method of inquiry, in N. Denzin and Y. Lincoln (eds) *Handbook of Qualitative Research*, 2nd edn. Thousand Oaks, CA: Sage.

Rorty, R. (1989) *Contingency, Irony and Solidarity*. Cambridge: Cambridge University Press.

Rorty, R. (1992) Cosmopolitanism without emancipation: a response to Lyotard, in S. Lash and J. Friedman (eds) *Modernity and Identity*. Oxford: Blackwell.

Rose, D. (1990) *Living the Ethnographic Life*. Newbury Park, CA: Sage.

Rosenau, P. M. (1992) *Post-modernism and the Social Sciences. Insights, Inroads and Intrusions*. Princeton, NJ: Princeton University Press.

Ruigrok, W., Pettigrew, A., Peck, S. and Whittington, R. (1999) Corporate restructuring and new forms of organizing: evidence from Europe, *Management International Review*, 39(2): 41–64.

Sampson, E. (1989) The deconstruction of the self, in J. Shotter and K. Gergen (eds) *Texts of Identity*. London: Sage.

Sangren, S. (1992) Rhetoric and the authority of ethnography, *Current Anthropology*, 33 (supplement): 277–96.

Sarup, M. (1988) *An Introductory Guide to Post-structuralism and Post-modernism*. Hemel Hempstead: Harvester Wheatsheaf.

Scheurich, J. (1997) *Research Method in the Postmodern*. London: Falmer.

Schneider, B. (2000) Managers as evaluators: invoking objectivity to achieve objectives, *Journal of Applied Behavioural Science*, 36: 159–73.

Scott, J. (1991) Deconstructing equality-versus-difference: or, the uses of poststructuralist theory for feminism, in M. Hirsch and E. F. Keller (eds) *Conflicts in Feminism*. New York: Routledge.

Senge, P. (1996) The leader's new work: building learning organizations, in K. Starkey (ed.) *How Organizations Learn*. London: Thomson Business Press.

Shotter, J. (1993) *Conversational Realities: The Construction of Life through Language*. Newbury Park, CA: Sage.

Shotter, J. and Gergen, K. (eds) (1989) *The Text of Identity*. London: Sage.

Shotter, J. and Gergen, K. (1994) Social construction: knowledge, self, others and continuing the conversation, in S. Deetz (ed.) *Communication Yearbook 17*. Newbury Park, CA: Sage.

Silverman, D. (1970) *The Theory of Organizations*. London: Heinemann.

Silverman, D. (1985) *Qualitative Methodology and Sociology*. Aldershot: Gower.

Silverman, D. (1993) *Interpreting Qualitative Data*. London: Sage.

Silverman, D. (1997) The logics of qualitative research, in G. Miller and R. Dingwall (eds) *Methods and Context in Qualitative Research*. London: Sage.

Simons, H. (ed.) (1989) *Rhetoric in the Human Sciences*. London: Sage.

Skeggs, B. (1994) Situating the production of feminist ethnography, in M. Maynard and J. Purvis (eds) *Researching Women's Lives from a Feminist Perspective*. London: Taylor & Francis.

Skeggs, B. (1997) *Formations of Class and Gender*. London: Sage.

Smart, B. (2000) Postmodern social theory, in B. Turner (ed.) *The Blackwell Companion to Social Theory*. Oxford: Blackwell.

Smircich, L. and Calás, M. (1987) Organizational culture: a critical assessment, in F. Jablin (eds) *Handbook of Organizational Communication*. Beverly Hills, CA: Sage.

Smith, J. and Deemer, D. (2000) The problem of criteria in an age of relativism, in N. Denzin and Y. Lincoln (eds) *Handbook of Qualitative Research*, 2nd edn. Thousand Oaks, CA: Sage.

Steier, F. (1991) Reflexivity and methodology: an ecological constructionism, in F. Steier (ed.) *Research and Reflexivity*. London: Sage.

Strauss, A. and Corbin, J. (1994) Grounded theory, in N. Denzin and Y. Lincoln (eds) *Handbook of Qualitative Research*. Thousand Oaks, CA: Sage.

Thompson, P. (1993) Post-modernism: fatal distraction, in J. Hassard and M. Parker (eds) *Postmodernism and Organizations*. London: Sage.

Thompson, P. and Warhurst, C. (1998) Hands, hearts and minds: changing work and workers at the end of the century, in P. Thompson and C. Warhurst (eds) *Workplaces of the Future*. London: Macmillan.

Tsoukas, H. (1991) The missing link: a transformational view of metaphors in organizational science, *Academy of Management Review*, 16: 566–85.

van Maanen, J. (1988) *Tales of the Field: On Writing Ethnography*. Chicago: University of Chicago Press.

van Maanen, J. (1995) An end to innocence: the ethnography of ethnography, in J. van Maanen (ed.) *Representation in Ethnography*. Thousand Oaks, CA: Sage.

Walzer, M. (1986) The politics of Foucault, in D. Hoy (ed.) *Foucault: A Reader*. Oxford: Basil Blackwell.

Watson, T. (1994) *In Search of Management*. London: Routledge.

Watson, T. (2000) Ethnographic fiction science. *Organization*, 7: 489–510.

Weedon, C. (1987) *Feminist Practice and Poststructuralist Theory*. Oxford: Basil Blackwell.

Whittington, R. (1993) *What Is Strategy – and Does It Matter?* London: Routledge.

Whyte, W. F. (1960) Interviewing in field research, in R. Burgess (ed.) *Field Research*. London: Routledge.

Willmott, H. (1992) Postmodernism and excellence: the de-differentiation of economy and culture, *Journal of Organizational Change Management*, 5(3): 58–68.

Willmott, H. (1994) Bringing agency (back) into organizational analysis: responding to the crises of (post)modernity, in J. Hassard and M. Parker (eds) *Towards a New Theory of Organizations*. London: Routledge.

Wolf, M. (1992) *A Thrice-told Tale: Feminism, Postmodernism, and Ethnographic Responsibility*. Stanford: Stanford University Press.

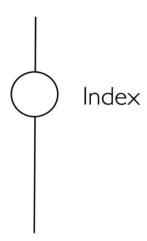

Index

Note: Page numbers in **bold type** refer to glossary entries

SURVEYING THE SOCIAL WORLD
PRINCIPLES AND PRACTICE IN SURVEY RESEARCH

Alan Aldridge and Ken Levine

- What are the strengths and limitations of social surveys?
- How can the principles of surveying be put into practice?
- How are findings analysed and results presented?

The survey has become a widely used technique for gathering information and opinions from individuals, organizations, and other groups. In *Surveying the Social World*, Aldridge and Levine begin by examining the contemporary state of surveys within society and social science methodology, explaining the potential of the survey method and the ways it can be used effectively when resources are limited. They then take the reader systematically through the process of conducting survey research, covering in turn: the role of theory; the planning and design of projects; pilot work; access to informants; ethical issues; sampling methods; the preparation of questionnaires; interviewing; the use of computer packages; processing responses; statistical methods of data analysis; and the presentation of findings.

Unlike some rival texts that stress complications and difficulties of conducting social surveys, this book adopts a consciously 'can-do' approach, emphasizing strategies and practical tips. Written in a direct style with a clear structure, each chapter begins with a list of key elements and concludes with summary points, points for reflection and suggestions for further reading. As well as examples of techniques and good practice from a variety of surveys, the authors use their own Travel Survey throughout the book to illustrate the decisions that need to be taken at each stage of the survey process. For the technical topics, there is a glossary containing over 130 technical terms that are highlighted in the text. The result is an essential guide to conducting social surveys for students in the social sciences, and for others who need to carry out a community of organizational survey but who may have no previous training in social research methods or experience of survey work.

Contents
Why survey? – Theory into practice – Planning your project – Selecting samples – Collecting your data – Designing the questions: what, when, where, why, how much and how often? – Processing responses – Strategies for analysis – Presenting your findings – Glossary – Appendix 1: The Travel Survey questionnaires – Appendix 2: Websites of professional associations – References – Index.

208pp   0 335 20240 3 (Paperback)   0 335 20241 1 (Hardback)

BIOGRAPHICAL RESEARCH

Brian Roberts

- What is biographical research?
- Why has it attracted so much interest?
- How can biographical research be carred out?

Biographical Research reflects a rapid expansion of interest in the study of lives taking place within the social sciences. Life story, oral history, narrative, autobiography, biography and other approaches are being used more and more to explore how individuals interpret experiences and social relationships. This book examines the methodological and theoretical developments associated with research on lives in sociology, oral history, ethnography, biography, and narrative analysis. The author includes numerous examples of biographical research from his own work and other studies, and addresses important areas such as the collection and interpretation of materials, uses of biographical research, oral and written accounts, the interview relationship, the construction of the story, memory, audience, and the researcher's own biography. In conclusion it draws out common themes and emerging concerns. *Biographical Research* is a comprehensive guide to major issues in the study of lives for students and researchers in the social sciences and related fields.

Contents

224pp   0 335 20286 1 (Paperback)   0 335 20287 X (Hardback)

QUALITATIVE DATA ANALYSIS
Explorations with NVivo

Graham R. Gibbs

> . . . a very detailed, clearly expressed and structured text which will be of immense help to anyone wanting to use NVivo for a research project.
> Professor Colin Robson, author of *Real World Research*

- How can qualitative analysis of textural data be undertaken?
- How can the core procedures of qualitative analysis be followed using computer sortware such as NVivo?
- How can the extra tools NVivo offers the analyst be used to support and improve qualitative analysis?

Qualitative Data Analysis introduces readers to key approaches in qualitative analysis, demonstrating in each case how to carry them out using NVivo. NVivo is a new, powerful computer package from QSR, the developers of NUD*IST. It provides the researcher with an extensive range of tools and the book shows clearly how each can be used to support standard qualitative analysis techniques such as coding, theory building, theory testing, cross-sectional analysis, modelling and writing. The book demonstrates how different styles of analysis, such as grounded theory and narrative, rhetorical and structured approaches, can be undertaken using NVivo. In most cases, the analysis is illustrated using documents from a single data set. There are copious figures, tables, guides and hints for good practice. The result is an invaluable text for undergraduates and an essential reference for post-graduates and researchers needing to learn both qualitative analysis techniques and the use of software such as NVivo.

Contents
Introduction – What is qualitative analysis? – Getting started with NVivo – Data preparation – Coding – Memos and attributes – Searching for text – Developing an analytic scheme – Three analytic styles – Visualizing the data – Communicating – Glossary – References – Index.

272pp   0 335 20084 2 (Paperback)   0 335 20085 0 (Hardback)

ETHNOGRAPHY

John D. Brewer

- What is ethnography?
- To what use can ethnographic data be put?
- Who are its fiercest critics?
- Does ethnography have a future?

Ethnography is one of the principal methods of qualitative research with a long-established tradition of use in the social sciences. However, the literature on ethnography has become a battleground as ethnography is attacked from within and without the qualitative tradition. Post-modern critics effectively deny the possibility of any objective research, whilst globalization challenges the relevance of the local and the small scale.

In this book you will be presented with a robust defence of ethnography and its continued relevance in the social sciences. The author sets out the competing methodological bases of ethnography and details its different uses as a research method. You will find guidelines for good practice in the research process, as well as advice on the analysis, interpretation and presentation of ethnographic data.

Ethnography is written as a textbook with many features to help the learning process. However, its contents are research led, informed by the author's own extensive experience of undertaking ethnographic research in dangerous and sensitive locations in Northern Ireland and elsewhere. It is a lively and engaging read on an essential topic.

Contents
Introduction – What is ethnography? – Ethnography as method and methodology – The research process in ethnography – The analysis, interpretation and presentation of ethnographic data – Uses of ethnography – Conclusion: whither ethnography? – Glossary – Bibliography – Index.

224pp   0 335 20268 3 (Paperback)   0 335 20269 1 (Hardback)

UNOBTRUSIVE METHODS IN SOCIAL RESEARCH

Raymond M. Lee

How do you obtain data about the way people live without asking them directly? One answer is to observe the traces which they leave behind them as they move through their physical and social environments. For example, you could measure the wear on the floor tiles in a museum to get an impression of visitor flows around certain exhibits; or you could compare the sizes of items of clothing from Tudor times to the present day and deduce that the average height of human beings has been gradually increasing over the centuries. These are unobtrusive methods of research.

Social researchers often collect 'self-report' data based on interviews and surveys. There are major problems associated with data obtained by these methods. For example, people are not always honest when asked to supply information on 'sensitive' issues. In this book you will discover how data can be 'found' in the world, captured from different forms of observation and retrieved from data banks of various kinds. There is a particular focus on use of the Internet, which promises to be a major source of unobtrusive data. You will learn how to generate unobtrusive measures, and also look at some of the wider ethical issues raised by the use of unobtrusive data.

Unobtrusive Methods in Social Research is up to date, comprehensive and clearly written. If you are an undergraduate it will help you to expand your understanding of this popular research methods topic; if you are a postgraduate student or a professional researcher this book will encourage you to make more use of unobtrusive methods in your research.

Contents
Introduction to unobtrusive methods – Found data – Captured data – Retrieved data: running records – Retrieved data: personal and episodic records – Unobtrusive methods and the Internet – Conclusion – Glossary – References – Index.

192pp   0 335 20051 6 (Paperback)   0 335 20052 4 (Hardback)